ACT, DECLARATION, & TESTIMONY FOR THE WHOLE OF OUR COVENANTED REFORMATION, AS ATTAINED TO, AND ESTABLISHED IN BRITAIN AND IRELAND; PARTICULARLY BETWIXT THE YEARS 1638 AND 1649, INCLUSIVE.

ACT, DECLARATION, & TESTIMONY FOR THE WHOLE OF OUR COVENANTED REFORMATION, AS ATTAINED TO, AND ESTABLISHED IN BRITAIN AND IRELAND; PARTICULARLY BETWIXT THE YEARS 1638 AND 1649, INCLUSIVE.

REFORMED PRESBYTERY OF NORTH AMERICA

ISBN: 978-93-88396-31-8

First Published: 1850

LECTOR HOUSE LLP
E-MAIL: lectorpublishing@gmail.com

ACT, DECLARATION,

AND

TESTIMONY,

FOR THE

WHOLE OF OUR COVENANTED REFORMATION, AS ATTAINED TO, AND ESTABLISHED IN BRITAIN AND IRELAND; PARTICULARLY BETWIXT THE YEARS 1638 AND 1649, INCLUSIVE.

AS, ALSO,

AGAINST ALL THE STEPS OF DEFECTION FROM SAID REFORMATION, WHETHER IN FORMER OR LATER TIMES, SINCE THE OVERTHROW OF THAT GLORIOUS WORK, DOWN TO THIS PRESENT DAY:

BY

THE REFORMED PRESBYTERY.

PSALM IX, 4.—Thou hast given a banner to them that fear thee: that it may be displayed because of the truth.

ISAIAH VIII, 16.—Bind up the testimony, seal the law among my disciples.

JUDE, verse 3.—That ye should earnestly contend for the faith which was once delivered to the saints.

REVELATION III, 11.—Behold, I come quickly: hold that fast which thou hast, that no man take thy crown.

TO WHICH IS NOW ADDED,
A HISTORICAL AND DECLARATORY SUPPLEMENT.

1850.

CONTENTS

INTRODUCTION.

The Presbytery, soon after their erection, being convinced of the expediency and necessity of emitting a judicial testimony, to discover to the world the principles upon which, as a judicatory of the Lord Jesus Christ, they stood, in opposition to the different, so called, judicatories in the land; together with the agreeableness of these principles to the Word of God, the only rule of faith and practice, and to the covenanted constitution of the church of Scotland in her purest periods; did therefore, after a proposal for said effect, agree in appointing one of their number to prepare a draft of this kind to be laid before them, who, after sundry delays, to their grief of mind, at once cut off their hopes of all assistance from him, in that or any other particular, by laying himself obnoxious to the censures of the church; which the presbytery, in duty both to him, to God, and to his people, were obliged to put in execution against him, while he, in contempt of that ordinance, and other means used for his conviction and recovery, obstinately persists in his impenitency and defection. And although the presbytery, few in number, were thus diminished, yet, being still resolved to prosecute their former design, they renewed their appointment upon another brother, who, in consequence of his undertaking, was allowed a cessation from his other public work, in order to expedite the proposed draft: and now, when nothing was expected that should retard the finishing of such a necessary work, the lamentable fire of division, that had long been smothered, unhappily broke forth into a violent flame, whereby the presbytery was rent asunder, and that brother, on whom the appointment was formerly laid, happening to be of the separating party, a second stop was not only put to the publication of this testimony, but the presbytery, from the absence of a brother removed to a distant part of the world, together with the paucity of their number, were almost wholly discouraged from attempting again what they had been oftener than once disappointed in.

But notwithstanding of the above, with many other difficulties which we shall not at present take notice of, the presbytery, still considering, that, even in their present circumstances, when their number is few and despicable, their adversaries many, and such as are in repute in the world, whereby the opposition made to them, and the conspiracy formed against the covenanted testimony of the church of Scotland maintained by them, must needs be strong; there is yet a gracious door of opportunity left open for them to attempt, in their judicative capacity, the prosecution and accomplishment of the necessary work formerly proposed; and which they could not but judge the Lord still called them unto, while after all the above-mentioned breaches made upon them, he still continued to give them a nail in his holy place, and a wall in Judah and Jerusalem, *Ezra* ix, 8, 9, they therefore again laid their appointments upon some others to prepare a draft of *An Act, Declaration, and Testimony,* &c., and which, under the favor of Divine Providence, has at length been finished and laid before the presbytery. We only need to observe further with reference to this, that the long delay of what is now agreed upon did not proceed from any design in the presbytery, of depriving either the people of their particular inspection, or the generation, of any benefit that might be obtained by a work of this nature, but partly from the fewness of their number, and great extent of their charge, and partly from the great distance of members' residence from each other, whereby they can seldom have access to meet all together, for expediting this or any other work of public concern they have in hand.

It is, therefore, with an eye to the Wonderful Counselor (when Zion's faithful counselors are so few) for light and direction in the management of this great and important work, that the presbytery have resolved upon the publication hereof at this time, for the reasons which follow:

1. Because this duty of bearing witness for truth, and declaring against all error, and defection from it, and transmitting the same uncorrupted to posterity, is expressly enjoined on the church by the Spirit of God in the Scriptures of truth. *Psal.* lxxviii, 5: "For he hath established a testimony in Jacob, and appointed a law in Israel, which he commanded our fathers that they should make them known to their children." *Isaiah* xliii, 10: "Ye are my witnesses, saith the Lord." *Matth.* x, 32: "Whosoever, therefore, shall confess me before men, him will I also confess before my Father who is in heaven." *John* xv. 27: "Ye also shall bear witness." *Acts* i, 8: "And ye shall be witnesses unto me."

2. Because, in agreeableness to the above scripture warrant, it has been the constant practice of the church in all ages, when in such capacity, judicially to assert, and declare their approbation of the truths of the everlasting gospel, and attainments of the church, joined with the condemnation of all contrary error, as appears from their harmonious confessions: and particularly, this has been the honorable practice of the once famous church of Scotland, witness her excellent confessions, covenants, &c., whose posterity we are, and, therefore, in duty bound to homologate, and approve her scriptural form and order, by a judicial asserting of her attainments, as saith the apostle, *Philip.* iii, 16: "Nevertheless whereunto we have already attained, let us walk by the same rule, let us mind the same thing." *Rev.* iii, 3: "Remember, therefore, how thou has received, and heard, and hold fast, and repent."

3. That, notwithstanding many, both ministers and private Christians, have been honored faithfully to publish their testimonies and declarations, and to seal them with their blood, in opposition to the growing defections in the land, being through the tyranny of the times prevented from acting in any other capacity: yet never, since the national overthrow of the glorious structure of reformation, has any church judicatory; constituted purely on the footing of our covenanted establishment, appeared in a judicial vindication of our Redeemer's interest and

injured rights.

4. The unspeakable loss sustained by the present generation, through the want of a full and faithful declaration of the covenanted principles of the church of Scotland, which they in the loins of their ancestors were so solemnly engaged to maintain; whereby, as ignorance must be increased, so prejudices are also gradually begotten in their winds against the truth in the purity thereof. And this, through the many mistaken notions at present prevailing among the different contending parties of professors in these nations, concerning the distinct ordinances of divine institution, viz., the ministry and magistracy, or ecclesiastical and civil government; and, more especially, the presbytery reckon themselves, and all professing their allegiance unto Christ and his cause, obliged to maintain the testimony of our ancestors for the divine institution and right constitution of civil government, according to the law of God, as what they found to be, and still is, indispensably necessary for the outward defense and preservation of righteousness and true religion; and because the very foundation and ends of this ordinance have been doctrinally subverted, and the generation taught the most licentious principles concerning it, by a body of professed witnesses among ourselves: and this they design to do, without (as they are slanderously reported of by some) laying aside themselves, or withdrawing others, from the study of internal and habitual or practical holiness.

5. To wipe off the reproach of that odium cast upon the presbytery and community belonging thereto, by some who invidiously call them a headless mob, whose principles cannot be known, anti-government men, men of bloody principles, &c., than which nothing can be more unjust: seeing, as a body distinct from all others, they have still stood upon the footing of the covenanted establishment, as has been frequently declared to the world, and as the constitution of the presbytery bears; so that they can no more be said ever to have wanted a proper testimony exhibiting their principles to the world, than the reformed church of Scotland, whereof they are a part.

6. The present broken and divided situation of the members of CHRIST'S mystical body, together with the abounding of error, seems necessarily to require it as a proper mean, under the divine blessing, for gathering again the scattered flock of Christ, the chief shepherd, to the one sheepfold, and putting a stop to the current of prevailing apostasy and defection.

For these reasons (with more that might be adduced) the presbytery find themselves in duty bound, to God, the present and succeeding generations, to throw in their small mite of a testimony, against the manifold avowed backslidings and defections of all degrees of men, both in the former and present times, from the precious truths of Christ, and purity of his ordinances; unto the maintenance whereof, not only they, but all in these lands, are solemnly bound by covenant engagements.

And, to conclude, let none mistake the presbytery's aim and intention, in the whole or any part of the following testimony, as if they minded nothing else but magistracy, &c., and that to have civil government, and governors established, according to the rule of God's word, was all the religion they intended, without regarding or opposing any other of the prevailing evils and iniquities of the present time. So some are pleased to allege, as has been hinted above; but such might do well to consider, that, as the sovereign and distinguishing goodness of God is clearly evidenced in giving his statutes and judgments unto his Israel, in all ages, while he has not dealt so with the other nations of the world, wherein his will is manifestly revealed, determining his people's duty in all their regulations; so his glory is equally concerned, that they receive, observe, keep pure and entire, all the ordinances he hath appointed in his word. The sinful prostitution of any of these, or breaking over the boundaries which Jehovah hath set is an evident contempt of his sovereign authority, and violation of the moral law. God requires of his people an universal respect to all his ordinances and commandments. Hence what is designed by them in this undertaking, is equally to testify their adherence unto, and approbation of the doctrine, worship, discipline and government of the house of God; and to signify their opposition to, and dissatisfaction with, all the apostatizing, backsliding courses in principle and practice, from that reformation purity, both in church and state (which, as the attainment of the nations of Britain and Ireland, was by them accounted their chief ornament and glory), that have taken place, especially in this kingdom, since our woful decline commenced: whereby the witnesses for Scotland's covenanted reformation, have been deprived of any legal benefit, as well, since as before the late revolution; in which the reformation, neither in civil nor ecclesiastical constitutions, was adopted. The intent, therefore, of this work is of very great importance; no less being proposed, than the right stating of the testimony for the covenanted interest of Christ in these lands, and judicial vindication of all the heads thereof, after such a long and universal apostasy therefrom: a work that must needs be attended with great difficulties, and labor under manifold disadvantages, as in other respects, so particularly from the consideration of the temper of this age, wherein nothing almost is pleasing, but what is adapted to the taste, not of the best, but of the greatest: and naked truth without the varnish of flattery, and painting of carnal policy, is generally treated with contempt, and exposed to ridicule. And therefore, to remove as much as possible the prejudice of a critical age, who are ready to reject every thing as new, which is in some respects singular, and not suited to their favorite sentiments; the presbytery have endeavored, in this work, to conform, as much as possible, to the faithful contendings of former honest contenders for the truths and testimony of JESUS, and that, both as to matter and manner: and as the grounds of this testimony are not any needless scrupulosities, or strange novelties, but precious and weighty truths, of the greatest value and importance, and of nearest affinity unto the continued series and succession of the testimonies of the church of Scotland, in former and more ancient periods; so it is the presbytery's ambition, that nothing, as to the subject matter of what is here contained, be looked upon as theirs, but may be regarded as an ancient plea, wherein is nothing but what has been maintained and confirmed by authors of the greatest fame and reputation in the church; has been asserted by the greatest confessors, and sealed by the best blood of the honored and faithful martyrs of Jesus: so that it may appear, the cause and truths here judicially stated and vindicated, are not of yesterday's date, but the same old paths and good way, that we are commanded to ask for, and walk in, though paths that are not now much trodden, a way that is not much paved by the multitude of professors walking therein.

ACT, DECLARATION, AND TESTIMONY.

PART I.

Containing a brief historical narration of the several periods of the Testimony of the Church of Scotland, and of the faithful contendings of the witnesses for Christ, particularly from the commencement of the Reformation in these lands, down to the late Revolution; with the Presbytery's approbation thereof.

PLOUGHLANDHEAD, JUNE 6, 1761.

The which day and place, the Reformed Presbytery being met, and taking into their most serious consideration, the deplorable situation of the interest of Christ and religion at present, in these sinning lands wherein so few are asking for the old path, saying, Where is the good way, that we may walk therein? but, on the contrary, an avowed apostasy and backsliding from the right ways of the Lord, is by the generality carried on, with a secret undermining of reformation interests, by some, under more specious pretenses; and, further, considering the general deluge of error and heresy, that has overrun these lands, and the swarm of erroneous heretics that has overspread the same, making very impious attacks upon the most part of revealed religion, who, notwithstanding, have found such shelter under the wings of a Laodicean church, and almost boundless state toleration, that they walk on without fear in the foresaid broad way of sin and error. And, moreover, all kinds of sin and wickedness so universally abound and pass, without any suitable check, that he who departs from iniquity maketh himself a prey; together with the woful insensibility, and deep security of all, under our spiritual plagues and impending temporal strokes. And yet, while the land so evidently groans under its inhabitants, very few either acknowledge themselves guilty, or turn from the evil of their ways, saying, What have we done? Also, considering the horrid breach and contempt of sacred vows unto the Most High, the great effusion of the saints' blood, shed in our late persecution under prelacy (which is yet to be found in our skirts), and the faithful testimony they therewith sealed, remains buried under the gravestones, both of ecclesiastical and civil deeds of constitution, unto this day. So that we may rather admire, that the Lord hath not made such inquisition for blood, as to make our land an aceldama, than that we are yet under a dispensation of divine forbearance. All which is followed with a deep oblivion of most or all of the memorable instances of the Lord's goodness, mercy and power, manifested unto his church, in these lands; the remembrance whereof ought still to be retained, and the same acknowledged with thankfulness, by all the children of Zion, unto the latest ages.

Wherefore the presbytery, amidst their many difficulties, partly noticed in the introduction, as a court of the true Presbyterian Covenanted Church of CHRIST in Scotland, constituted in the name of the LORD JESUS CHRIST, the alone KING and HEAD of his church, judicially to commemorate: Likeas, they did, and hereby do acknowledge, with the utmost gratitude, the great goodness and tender mercy of our God unto our church and land; who, in consequence of that early new covenant grant, made by JEHOVAH to his eternal SON, to give him the heathen for his inheritance and the uttermost parts of the earth for his possession, caused the day spring from on high to visit us. Our glorious Redeemer, that bright and morning Star, having, by his almighty power, shaken oft the fetters of death, wherewith it was impossible that he could be held, and, as a victorious conqueror, leading captivity captive, ascended into the highest heavens, and there sat down on the right hand of God, did very soon discover his cordial acceptance of, and superlative delight in, possessing his Father's extensive grant, by stretching forth the lines of his large and great dominion unto the distant nations of the world, involved in the thickest darkness of stupidity and idolatry; and, in a particular manner, did, as the glorious sun of righteousness, graciously illuminate this remote and barbarous isle, causing the refulgent beams of gospel light to dissipate the gross darkness that, covered the people, which prevailed so far (according to very authentic historical accounts), that, about the beginning of the third century, those of the highest dignity in the nation, voluntarily enlisted themselves under the displayed banner of CHRIST, the captain of salvation, and became nursing fathers and nursing mothers to his church, employing their power to root out Pagan idolatry, and bring their subjects under the peaceful scepter of the SON of GOD. This plant of Christianity having once taken root, did, under all the vicissitudes of divine providence, grow up unto a spreading vine, which filled the land, and continued to flourish, without being pressed down with the intolerable burden of prelatical or popish superstition: the truths and institutions of the gospel being faithfully propagated and maintained in their native purity and simplicity by the Culdees some hundreds of years before ever that man of sin and son of perdition, by the door of prelacy, stepped into the temple of God in Scotland. Those early witnesses for CHRIST, having no other ambition but that of advancing piety and the doctrines which were according to godliness, were therefore called *Culdees*, that is, *Cultores Dei*, or worshipers of God. The doctrine, worship, discipline, and government of the house of GOD being thus established, continued for many years, taught and exorcised, according to divine institution. But, in process of time, the Church of CHRIST in this land came to be assaulted with the corruptions of the see of Rome, by means of Palladius, the Pope's missionary to the Britons, who made the first attempt to bring our fathers' necks under the anti-christian yoke, which gradually increasing by little and little, clouded the sunshine of prosperity the church then enjoyed, till about the eleventh century, when the Romish fraternity fully established themselves, by usurping a diocesan supremacy over the house of God; after which a midnight darkness of popish error and idolatry overwhelmed the nation, for near the space of five hundred years. Yet, even in this very dark period, the LORD left not himself altogether without some to bear witness for him, whose steadfastness in defense of the truth, even unto death, vanquished the inhuman cruelty of their savage enemies. The honor of the church's exalted Head being still engaged to maintain the right of conquest he had obtained over this remote isle, and raise up his work out of the ruins, under which it had lain so long buried; he, about the beginning of the 15th century, animated some valiant champions (Messrs. Hamilton, Wishart, and others) with a spirit of truth and heroic courage, to contend against the abominations of the Babylonish whore, whose labors, by the blessing of Heaven, were rendered successful, to open the eyes of some to see, and engage many others to inquire after, and espouse the truth as it is in JESUS. These, not regarding the fear of man, nor the cruelty of their enemies, but as good soldiers of JESUS CHRIST, enduring hardness, chose, rather than desert their Master's cause, to offer their bodies to be devoured by the tormenting flames, no more merciless than their hellish persecutors; while in that fiery chariot, through the serial regions, their souls ascended to the celestial country. And herein, also, did GOD frustrate the expectation of that monster of iniquity, Cardinal Beaton (whose memory let it for ever perish), and his wicked accomplices, and turned their counsel into foolishness, who, by the death of a few zealous contenders for the faith, intended the total suppression of CHRIST'S truth for ever; but GOD having purposed the contrary, made the effusion of their blood the occasion of rousing many from the deep sleep of gross ignorance, by putting them to search into the truth of those doctrines, which these martyrs sealed with their blood; so that JESUS CHRIST, the only true light in the orb of the gospel, began again to shine forth within this realm.

Upon this begun revival of reformation, the glory of the LORD went remarkably before his people, and the GOD of Israel was their reward, uniting the hearts, and strengthening the hands, both of noble and ignoble, to a vigorous and active espousing of his gospel, and concerns of his glory, in opposition to the tyranny of the lordly bishops, persecuting rage, and masked treachery of the two bloody Marys, the mother and daughter, who then successively governed, or rather tyrannized, in Scotland. Their number, as well as their zealous spirit, still increasing, they, for the more effectual management of this noble enterprise, entered into covenants to advance that begun work of reformation, and to defend the same and one another in the maintenance thereof, against all opposition whatsoever. Several such covenants our early reformers solemnly entered into at Edinburgh, Perth and Leith, in the years 1557, '59, '60 and '62. In 1560, *the Confession of the Faith, and doctrine believed and professed by the Protestants within, the realm of Scotland*, was compiled and civilly ratified, or allowed of, in free and open parliament, afterward sworn to in the National Covenant *annis* 1580, 1581 and 1590. At the same time, some other acts were passed, in favor of reformation; one against the mass and abuse of the sacraments; another, abolishing the Pope's jurisdiction and authority with this realm, &c. In the above mentioned year 1560, the first book of policy and discipline, containing the form and order of presbyterial church government, was composed, approven and subscribed by the ministry, and a great part of the nobility. Thus, by the wisdom and power of GOD, who takes the wise in their own craftiness, by means, especially, of the indefatigable labors of the renowned Mr. KNOX (whose memory is still savory in the churches), was this surprising work of reformation advanced, until it obtained the authority of a law; whereby, was not only the presbyterian protestant interest ratified, but anti-christian supremacy and superstition abolished.

The church, gradually increasing in beauty and perfection, did, with much painfulness and faithful diligence, labor after a more full establishment of the house of GOD, in all its privileges, until, by perfecting the second book of discipline, they completed the exact model of presbytery, which, though they had enjoyed national assemblies for a considerable time, yet was not brought to such an entire conformity to the divine pattern, nor so generally acquiesced in until now, that it was unanimously approven by the assembly 1590, and particularly enjoined to be subscribed by all who did bear office in the church; and, at last, they prevailed to get it publicly voted and approven in parliament, June, 1592; and also at the same time, obtained by act of parliament, the ratification of all the privileges and liberties of the church, in her assemblies, synods, presbyteries, &c.

And here we may observe, that while this church and nation contended for the obtaining of a legal establishment of the ecclesiastical polity, they were no less concerned to have that other distinct ordinance of GOD, civil magistracy, unalterably settled, in agreeableness to the rule of GOD'S word. This appears, not only by their earnest contendings against the abuse of that ordinance among them; but also, by the public acts of parliament, obliging prince and people to be of one perfect religion, and wholly incapacitating all persons, for bearing any office, supreme or subordinate, who refused, by their solemn oath, to approve of, and, to the utmost of their power, engage to defend the true religion, as contained in the word of GOD, and confession of faith founded thereon, then believed, and publicly professed within the realm, ratified and generally sworn to in the National Covenant, during the whole course of their lives, in all their civil administrations. See *Acts Parl. 1st*, James VI, 1567.

Thus the hand of GOD was remarkably seen, and his powerful arm evidently revealed, in delivering this nation both from Pagan darkness and Popish idolatry, the memory whereof ought not to be lost, but thankfully acknowledged, to the honor of GOD'S great name, by all such as favor the dust of Zion, for her sake, and long to see her breaches, now wide as the sea, repaired.

But to proceed: The church's grand foe envying her growing prosperity, did soon disturb her peace, by insinuating himself upon those of superior dignity, who were intrusted with the administration of civil affairs, both supreme and subordinate, blowing up into a flame that inbred and rooted enmity, which they still retained, at the simplicity, strictness and scriptural purity of the reformation in Scotland. The then supreme civil ruler, king James VI, formed a scheme for ruining the church of Scotland, and stripping her of those comely and beautiful ornaments of reformation purity, in doctrine, worship, discipline and government, which she had now put on, by introducing episcopacy, and establishing bishops. "This he did for no other reason (says one), but because he believed them to be useful and pliable instruments for turning a limited monarchy into absolute dominion, and subjects into slaves; that which of all other things he affected most:" and for this purpose (after several subtle and cunningly devised steps, previously taken, with design to do by degrees what could not be done at once) he makes an open attack upon the general assembly, robbing them of their power and liberty to meet, judge and determine, in all ecclesiastical concerns (well knowing, that so long as assemblies might convene in freedom, he would never get the estate of bishops established in Scotland), and imprisoning and banishing many faithful ministers, members of the general assembly, who opposed him, testified and protested against his wicked invasion, and sacrilegious robbery of the church's rights and privileges. And, having at last obtained the supremacy and headship over the church, which was granted him by an impious act of a pretended parliament, of his own stamp, called by him for that purpose, proceeded with his design, until he had again established Prelacy, and razed Presbytery almost to the very foundations, notwithstanding all the opposition made to it by the faithful in the land, both ministers and people.

Thus, after several former attempts to this effect, was Episcopacy again established, and prelates lording over GOD'S heritage advanced, imposing their popish ceremonies, which in that pretended assembly convened at Perth, anno 1618, were enacted, and afterward ratified in a subsequent parliament in the year 1621. And as the father had thus violated his solemn professions, declarations and engagements, to maintain the covenanted interest; so likewise, upon the accession of the son to the throne, there was no amendment nor redress had: but he followed the same iniquitous course, walking in the way of his father, and in the sin wherewith he made Israel to sin. And further, obtruded upon the church a service book, a book of popish and prelatical canons, which was followed with a violent prosecution of the faithful contenders for the former laudable constitutions of the church, carried on by that monstrous Erastian high-commission court, patched up of statesmen and clergymen: and hereby was the church again brought under the yoke of anti-christian prelacy, and tyrannical supremacy; which lese-majesty to Zion's King was also ratified with the sanction of civil authority. To this yoke, oppressing CHRIST'S loyal subjects, many of his professed servants submitted their necks, and, Issachar-like, became servants to tribute for a considerable time.

But when the LORD'S set time to favor Zion came, he made the long despised dust thereof again to be more pleasant and precious than ever unto his servants and people, and the long night season and thick clouds of adversity under which his church labored, amid some day-sky, and sun-blinks of prosperity, she at times enjoyed, to issue in the dawning of a day of clearer light wherein the glorious SUN of Righteousness shone in his meridian splendor, with greater brightness both in this and the neighboring nations, than at his first arising therein, in a gospel dispensation; whose benign influences caused the small grain of good seed, sown by the skill of the Great Husbandman, to grow up to a fruitful plant, the tender twig to spread itself into a noble vine, and the little cloud, like a man's hand, to cover the whole hemisphere of the visible church of Scotland, which long ago, as a church and nation, had enlisted themselves under the LORD JESUS CHRIST, as their Royal Prince; whose peaceful and righteous scepter being now also extended to England and Ireland, they soon submitted themselves thereto, in a religious association and union with Scotland in covenant engagements, for reformation from prelacy, as well as Popery, which they had never hitherto yielded to.

Upon this gracious return of divine favor, and discovery of Almighty power manifested against the mighty agents for prelatical superstition, both in church and state, when, from the paucity of those who appeared in favor of truth, in the year 1637, small opposition unto its enemies could be expected; yet their magnanimity in witness-bearing was so followed by manifestations of the divine countenance and favor, that both their number and courage daily increased. The National Covenant was again, after mature deliberation, anent both the lawfulness, expediency and seasonableness thereof, with great solemnity renewed in *March*, 1638, with the general concurrence of the ministry, noblemen, gentlemen, and others, humbling themselves before the LORD for their former defections and breach of covenant; though, at the same time, the court faction, and many temporising ministers, continued in their opposition, but which was indeed too weak to make resistance unto the cause of GOD, and force of truth carried home with suitable conviction upon the conscience.

The covenant being first renewed at Edinburgh, they provided next, that it should also be renewed through the kingdom; and for this purpose, copies thereof were sent with all convenient speed to the several presbyteries, together with suitable exhortations, and instructions for renewing of the same in every parish of their bounds; and by this means it came to pass, through the good hand of their GOD upon them, that in a little time almost every parish through Scotland did, with much solemnity, cheerfulness and alacrity, renew the same, and publicly with uplifted hand avouch the LORD to be their GOD. And as this solemn action was everywhere accompanied with remarkable evidences of divine power and presence in a plentiful effusion of a spirit of grace and supplication; so the joy of the LORD herein became their strength, and greatly increased the faith and hopes of all the church's real friends, that as the LORD had begun, so he would also make an end, and carry on his work to perfection, amid the terrible threatenings both of king and court; his majesty being highly displeased that his authority was contemned, and no concurrence of his royal pleasure sought in the renovation of the Covenant: but their righteousness in this particular was brought forth as the light, when the legality of this and their other proceedings was afterward attested to the king by the ablest lawyers in the kingdom.

The zealous contenders for the church's liberties, by supplications, reasonings, and proposed articles, for enjoying what they much longed for, at last obtained, before the foresaid year 1638 expired, a lawful and free General Assembly (constituted in the name of the LORD JESUS CHRIST, the alone King and Head of his church), consisting of able members, both ministers and elders, who would not suffer an infringement upon their regular manner of procedure, or right to act as unlimited members of a free court of CHRIST, notwithstanding the constant attacks made upon their freedom by the king's commissioner, and protestations by him taken against their regular procedure, which issued in his Erastian declaration of the king's prerogative, as supreme judge in all causes, ecclesiastical as well as civil, and renewing all his former protestations in his royal master's name; further protesting in his own name, and in the name of the lords of the clergy, that no act passed by them should imply his consent, or be accounted lawful, or of force to bind any of the subjects; and, then in his majesty's name dissolving the assembly, discharging their proceeding any further, and so went off. But the assembly judging it better to obey GOD than man; and to incur the displeasure of an earthly king, to be of far less consequence than to offend the Prince of the kings of the earth, entered a protestation against the lord commissioner's departure without any just cause, and in behalf of the intrinsic power and liberty of the church; also assigning the reasons why they could not dissolve the assembly until such time as they had gone through that work depending upon them. This was given in to the clerk by Lord Rothes, and part of it read before his grace left the house, and instruments taken thereupon. Then, after several moving and pathetic speeches delivered on that occasion, for the encouragement of the brethren to abide by their duty, by the moderator, Mr. Alexander Henderson, and others, ministers and elders, exhorting them to show themselves as zealous for CHRIST their LORD and Master, in his interests, as he had shewed himself zealous for his master; they unanimously agreed that they should continue and abide by their work until they had concluded all things needful, and that on all hazards. And so they proceeded to the examination of that complaint against the bishops, who, on account of their, tyranny, superstition, and teaching of Popish, Arminian, and Pelagian errors, were all laid under the sentence of deposition; and many of them, for their personal profaneness, wickedness and debauchery proven against them, together with their contumacy, were also excommunicated with the greater excommunication, for the destruction of the flesh, that the spirit might be saved in the day of the LORD JESUS. They gave their approbation of the National Covenant; and Prelacy, with the five articles of Perth, were found and declared to be abjured by it, together with the civil places and power of kirkmen, their sitting on the bench as justices of the peace, sitting in council, and voting in parliament. Subscription of the Confession of faith, or covenant, was also enjoined, presbyterian church government justified and approven, and an act made for holding yearly General Assemblies; with many other acts and constitutions tending to the advancement of that begun reformation, and purging the church of CHRIST of those sinful innovations, crept into it, which may be seen more at large in the printed acts of that assembly. The lawful and just freedom which the church now claimed and stood upon, so highly incensed the court, because their Erastian encroachments were not yielded to, that all warlike preparations were speedily made for having them again reduced, by force of arms, to their former slavery. Yet, what evil seemed intended against the church by the king, with his popish and prelatical accomplices, was by her exalted King and Head happily prevented, and they obliged, at least, to feign subjection, and yield to a pacification. In which it was concluded, that an assembly be holden at Edinburgh, *August 6th*, 1639, and the parliament the 20th of the same month, that same year, for healing the wide breaches, and redressing the grievances both of church and state; that what was determined by the assembly, might be ratified by the parliament. In this assembly, the covenant was ratified and subscribed by the commissioner, and an injunction laid upon the body of the kingdom for subscribing the same, with an explication, wherein the five articles of Perth, government of bishops, the civil places and power of kirkmen were expressly condemned. Hereby the hopes of the Prelates again being in a great measure lost, and they receiving fresh assistance from the king (who seemed to have little conscience in making laws, and found small difficulty in breaking them), recruited themselves the year following, and took the field, but with no better success than formerly, which obliged them to yield to another pacification, wherein both religious and civil liberties were ratified; and in 1641, these were further confirmed by the oaths, promises, laws, and subscriptions of both king and parliament, whereat the king was personally present, and gave the royal assent to all acts made for the security of the same; while at the same time he was concurring in the bloody tragedy acted upon the Protestants in the kingdom of Ireland.

The gracious countenance and abundant evidence of divine approbation wherewith the LORD vouchsafed to bless his contending, reforming and covenanting church in Scotland, in a plentiful effusion of his Holy Spirit on the judicatories and worshiping assemblies of his people, proved a happy means to excite and provoke their neighbors in England and Ireland, to go and do likewise. For in the year 1643, when the beginning of a bloody war between the king and parliament of England threatened the nation with a series of calamity and trouble; the parliament having convocated an assembly of divines to sit at Westminster for consulting about a reformation of religion in that kingdom, sent commissioners, consisting of members of both houses and assembly, to treat with the assembly of the church of Scotland, and convention of estates about these things. In the month of *August*, they presented their proposals to the convention of estates and assembly, desiring, that because the popish prelatical faction is still pursuing their design of corrupting and altering the religion through the whole island, the two nations might be strictly united for their mutual defense against them and their adherents, and not to lay down arms until those, their implacable enemies, were disarmed, &c. Commissioners were deputed from the estates, and assembly, to convene with those from England, in order to consider their proposals. And, at the first conferences, it was agreed that the best and speediest means for accomplishing the union and assistance desired, was for both nations to enter into a mutual league and covenant for reformation and defense of religion and liberty against its enemies. Which being drawn up, and affectionately embraced, was unanimously approved by the general assembly and sent up to England by the hands of the ministers and elders, sent commissioners from the church of Scotland to the synod at Westminster, where (being proposed by the parliament to the consideration of the synod), after the interpolation of an explanatory note in the second article, it was approven, and with public humiliation, and all other religious and answerable solemnity, taken and subscribed by them (the synod), and by both honorable houses of parliament and by their authority taken and subscribed by all ranks in England and Ireland that same year, ratified by act of the parliament of Scotland, *anno* 1644, and afterward renewed in Scotland, with an acknowledgment of sins, and engagement to duties by all ranks in the year 1648, and by the parliament, 1649.

Thus, to the rejoicing of all true lovers of the prosperity and beauty of the church, who longed for CHRIST the salvation of Israel, his coming forth out of Zion, these three churches and nations combined and embarked together in the same honorable and glorious cause of reformation, and solemnly bound themselves by the oath of GOD, to maintain and defend the same against all its enemies and opposers whatever; thereby publicly professing their subjection to Christ, and their preferring of pure and undefiled religion, the advancement of the interest, kingdom and glory of JESUS CHRIST, to their nearest and dearest interests in this world. And the Lord was with us while we were with him, and steadfast in his covenant; but when we forsook him, and broke his covenant, he also forsook us, and delivered his strength into captivity, and his glory into the enemies' hand.

In the next place, the assembly at Westminster, with the assistance of commissioners from the general assembly of the church of Scotland, proceeded to conclude on what was needful for furthering and completing this intended and covenanted uniformity in religion, that the Lord might be one, and his name one in the three lands. And for this purpose, a confession of faith was composed, and agreed upon by that venerable assembly, together with catechisms larger and shorter, propositions concerning church government, ordination of ministers, and directory for worship; all which were received and approved by the General Assembly, and convention of estates in Scotland.

The Lord thus prospering his work in the hands of his servants employed in ecclesiastical affairs, gave no less countenance unto the parliament of England, with the assistance they received from Scotland, in defeating all the wicked attempts of the popish, prelatical and malignant party in England, overthrowing their tyranny, and reducing the supporters thereof. A like victory was at length obtained over Montrose in Scotland, who commanded the royalist, or malignant party there, and had for some time carried all before him. And so the King being worsted at all hands, and despairing of overtaking his designs, his army having been almost all cut to pieces, and himself obliged to fly, resigned himself over to the Scots army at Newark, in the year 1646, and marched along with them to Newcastle; and they, upon the frequent solicitations of the English parliament, and their engaging for the King's honorable treatment, delivered him over to them. Afterward, he falling into the hands of Cromwell and the English army, a number in this nation violated the oath of GOD, which they had lately come under, by engaging in an unlawful war with England, commonly called the Duke's engagement, in order to rescue the King from his captivity (notwithstanding that he still persisted in his opposition to the just claims, both of the church and nation, and after all that was come upon him, could not be reconciled to the covenants and work of reformation); where they were in *July* 1648, totally routed by Oliver Cromwell; and Duke Hamilton, their general, being made prisoner, was incarcerated, and afterward beheaded. This engagement was remonstrated against, and judicially condemned by the General Assembly of the church of Scotland; and the sinfulness of it was publicly acknowledged as a breach of the covenant-union between the two nations, by all ranks in Scotland that same year, at the renovation of the Solemn League and Covenant therein. At last the king being seized upon by Cromwell and his sectarian army, was, notwithstanding all the remonstrances both of church and state, removed by a violent death. Upon which the parliament of Scotland, on the *5th* of *February*, 1649, caused proclaim his son Charles II, king of Great Britain, France, and Ireland (which title he had assumed himself at the Hague, as soon as the report of his father's death came to his ears), promising their fidelity and defence of his person and authority, according to the National Covenant, and the Solemn League and Covenant. And at the same time declaring, that before he be admitted to the exercise of the royal power, he shall give security for the preservation and maintenance of the true reformed religion, and unity of the kingdoms, now established, by laws both civil and ecclesiastical, according to the covenants: which security for religion and liberty, at the first proposed treaty at the Hague, he deferred to grant, and afterward postponed the signing of the treaty at Breda, when everything was agreed upon, from the great hopes he entertained of accomplishing his design, without acquiescing with their demand from Montrose's expedition, whom he had sent into Scotland with an army, in order to prepare his way into that kingdom, by devastation with fire and sword. But this intrigue not succeeding, he found himself obliged to comply with all their proposals, and signed the treaty. This treaty the king did in effect break, before he left Breda, by communicating after the episcopal manner, contrary to the express warning and remonstrance of the commissioners from the church of Scotland, who went to him, and showed him his sin in so doing, and how inconsistent it was with his own concessions in the present treaty; and an evidence that he had no intention to perform what he had agreed to, but dissembled with GOD and man; and he, on the other hand, put them off with sham excuses and professions; and so, from their too much credulity to his fraudulent professions and promises all along, they brought him over to Scotland, and before his landing in this kingdom, he takes the covenant at Spey, on the *23rd* of *June*, 1649, by his oath subjoined in allowance and approbation of the Covenants National, and Solemn League, obliging himself faithfully to prosecute the ends thereof in his station and calling; and for himself and successors, he shall agree to all acts of parliament enjoining the same, and establishing presbyterial church government the directory for worship, confession of faith and catechisms, in the kingdom of Scotland, as approven by the General Assemblies of this kirk, and parliament of this kingdom. And for their further satisfaction, according to the act of the West Kirk, Edinburgh, *August 13th*, 1650, approven the same day by the committee of estates, he emitted a declaration at Dunfermline, by profession, fully and heartily acquiescing with all their demands, all which afterward served for nothing but as a lasting monument of his horrid perjury, wicked dissimulation, and mockery of God and man. And even then, when this declaration was published, he had formed a design for bringing in the enemies of the covenant, and work of reformation, both into the army and judicatories, and for dividing the Presbyterians among themselves. And this he effectually managed for both foresaid ends, by the public resolutions, on the 14th of *December*, that same year 1650. This woful and prime step of defection, so contrary to the word, and injurious to the work of God, was faithfully testified against by many, both ministers, and whole presbyteries, who were sensible of the present sinfulness and evil of it, and foresaw the bitter and dismal consequences that followed upon it.

In the meantime, notwithstanding this, and other shrewd evidences, the king gave of his double dealing and hypocrisy, he was crowned at Scoon, on the first of *January*, 1651, and had the Covenants National and Solemn League again administered unto him, by the reverend Mr. Douglas, after a sermon from 2 *Kings* xi, 12, 17, which he, in a most solemn manner renewed, before the three estates of parliament, the commissioners of the General Assembly, and a numerous congregation, in the words of his former oath at Spey; with the coronation oath, as contained in the 8th *Act, Parl.* 1st, James VI, to all which he engaged before his coronation; and on these terms, and no other, were the oaths of fidelity to him, as the lawful supreme magistrate, taken, at his receipt of the royal authority. And consequently, these covenant engagements became fundamental constitutions, both in church and state, and the door of access into office-bearing in either, and formal ground of the people's subjection. Then was the church's appearance "Beautiful as Tirzah, comely as Jerusalem, and terrible as an army with banners."

From what is noticed above, the presbytery cannot but declare their hearty approbation of the zeal, courage, and faithfulness of our honored ancestors, in their valiant contendings for the valuable liberties and privileges of the spiritual kingdom of the MESSIAH, until they got the same established, and the nations brought under the most solemn, sacred, and inviolable engagements, to maintain every branch of this glorious reformation; a reformation, not only from the more gross errors, and idolatries of Popery, but from the more refined superstition of Prelacy, and all that Antichristian and Erastian supremacy, that in former times had been exercised on the heritage of the LORD; a reformation of both the divine ordinances of ministry and magistracy, from all the abuses and corruptions thereof, by the inventions of men, joined with the above mentioned establishment of them, in some measure of agreeableness unto their scriptural institution.

Likeas, the presbytery did, and hereby do declare their approbation of, and adherence unto foresaid reformation, in all the different parts and branches thereof, attained from 1638 to 1650 inclusive, and sworn to in the National and Solemn League and Covenant, not exclusive of such parts of reformation as were attained unto prior to this, but as a further advance on this foundation, and as being much more pure and agreeable to the infallible standard of scripture, than any formerly arrived at in these nations.

The daughter of Zion, thus going forth in the perfection of her beauty, when all ranks and degrees voluntarily subjected themselves unto the royal scepter of the SON of GOD, was most comely in the eyes of her Beloved; But oh! how is the gold become dim, and the most fine gold changed; the stones of the sanctuary are poured out on the top of every street, so that the house that was called of all people the house of prayer, is now become a den of thieves, being no less infamously despicable for deformation, than formerly, for purity of reformation, highly admired. This, at first, began with the public resolutions of the commission of the General Assembly 1650, above noticed, for taking into places of power and trust, in judicatories and armies, such persons as were known malignants, and in heart disaffected to the work, and people of GOD, putting it in their power to destroy and pull down the LORD'S work at their pleasure; a practice manifestly inconsistent with their covenant engagements, and the word of GOD, *Deut.* xxiii, 9, 2 *Chron.* xix, 2. Those that were then called protestors (from their opposing and protesting against these resolutions), continued steadfastly to witness against the same, as the first remarkable step, to make way for that bloody catastrophe, that afterward befell the church. The Lord, then, in his righteous displeasure and controversy with the nation, for betraying of his cause and interest into the hands of his enemies, sold them into the hand of that conquering usurper, Oliver Cromwell, who, having stript them of their civil liberties, as the most effectual method to rob the church of her spiritual privileges, and nullify the forcible obligation of the sacred covenants (which, when preserved, serve as a strong barrier against all such usurpations), framed a hellish and almost unbounded toleration in Scotland, of heretical and sectarian errors, for gratification of the abettors thereof, which was followed with a deluge of irreligion and impiety, drowning the nation in a still deeper apostasy.

In this hour of temptation, the witnesses for CHRIST, endeavoring to keep the word of his patience, testified against these evils, as contrary to the word and oath of God, and destructive of the church's former glory. And Charles II, who had lately, by all the confirmations of word, writ, and solemn oath, obliged himself for the maintenance and defense of religion and liberty, having cast off the thing that was good, the enemy did pursue him so, that he, instead of being able to stand as a head of defense to the nations, narrowly escaped with life from the enemies' hands, being obliged to abscond and fly before the sectaries into France; where, and in other parts, he remained an exile for the space of ten years, and there discovered, he had no regard to the principles he had lately professed and sworn to maintain: but breaking his professed wedlock with CHRIST, is said, at that juncture, to have joined hands with the Romish whore, laying aside his cloak of professed godliness, and again taking up with the mystery of iniquity.

During the ten years' usurpation of Cromwell, those who endeavored faithfulness, had a fight of affliction to keep their ground; yet, after this came to a period, they had a far more fierce encounter, and of longer duration, to engage in, in the cruel and bloody tragedy acted upon them, for the space of 28 years.

As, by the public resolutions, and foresaid unbounded toleration, the bounds fixed by JEHOVAH, and homologated and sworn to, in our national attainments and constitution, were greatly altered, so the parliament of England prepared the tools, whereby the carved work of the sanctuary (as far as human craft and cruelty could invent), was broken down, in restoring Charles II, without any conditions required, or express limitations set. And Sharp being sent from the church of Scotland, to stand up for her rights and privileges, fraudulently sold her into the hands of her enemies; upon which, many of the professed disciples of CHRIST, who followed him in the sunshine of prosperity and reformation, forsook him, and fled into the enemies' camp. Thus our decline began; but, oh! to what a dreadful height Erastianism, tyranny, and bloodshed arrived, before the Lord, in his providence, put a stop to it.

Although the Presbytery cannot be supposed, in a consistency with their present design, to reckon up all, yet they would endeavor to take notice of some of the most remarkable instances of backsliding, treachery and oppression, bloodshed, &c, acted in those nations during the late persecuting period, together with the faithful contendings, and patient sufferings unto death of the saints and servants of CHRIST, in this hot furnace of affliction into which they were cast. As, 1, The unhappy restoration of Charles II, in manner before mentioned commencing. The faithful declarations and testimonies given in favor of the covenanted reformation and uniformity, were all on a sudden given up with; the viper received into our bosom, and again advanced unto the regal dignity, who soon discovered himself to be of the serpentine seed, and by his wicked agency imped the dragon his master, by casting out of his mouth a flood of persecution after the church, that he might cause her to be destroyed therewith. To this effect the anti-christian yoke of abjured Prelacy, with all its tyrannical laws, and canonical train of observances, service book, ceremonies, &c., was speedily wreathed about England's neck, and Scotland soon felt part of its weight. For, in the month of *August*, 1660, when some of her most zealous and faithful ministers met upon this emergency, in order to send an address to the king, reminding him of his duty, and solemn obligations to perform the same; the committee appointed by the parliament, *anno* 1651, for exercise of government, until another parliament should meet, who then showed themselves zealous for the reformation, yet now acted a counter-part, by incarcerating the foresaid ministers, and emitting a proclamation, prohibiting all such meetings without the king's authority, and all petitions and remonstrances, under pretense that they were seditious. This was the first beginning of those sorrows and calamities that ensued in the many sanguinary laws afterward made and executed upon the true friends of Zion.

2. When the ministry, by means of the foresaid prohibitions, were much dispirited from their duty, dreading such usage as they had lately met with, the parliament which met in Scotland in *December*, 1661, falls upon breaking down the carved work of the sanctuary effectually, and robbing our church of that depositum committed unto her by her glorious Head. Thus did they wickedly combine and gather themselves together to plot against the Lord, and against his Anointed, that they might break his bands, and cast his cords from them. For which in-

tent, after besmearing the consciences of most of the members with the guilt of that abominable and wicked oath of allegiance and supremacy, that they might be secured to the court and king's interest, and ready to swallow down whatever might be afterward proposed, they passed an act rescissory, declaring all the parliaments, and acts of parliament made in favor of reformation, from the year 1640 to 1651, null and void. The king's supremacy over all persons, and in all causes, is asserted. All meetings, assemblies, leagues, and covenants, without the king's authority, are declared unlawful and unwarrantable. The renewing of the solemn league and covenant, or any other covenants or public oaths, without the king's special warrant and approbation, is discharged. Besides these, another heinous act was framed by the same parliament, for observing every 29th of *May* as an anniversary thanksgiving, in commemoration of the unhappy restoration of this ruiner of religion and reformation.

3. In the second session of the pretended parliament, *anno* 1662 diocesan Erastian Prelacy is established, and the king solemnly invested with the church's headship, by act of parliament; wherein it is blasphemously declared, "That the ordering and disposal of the external government and policy of the church, doth properly belong unto his majesty as an inherent right of the crown, by virtue of his royal prerogative and supremacy in all causes ecclesiastical." All such acts of parliament or council are rescinded, which might be interpreted (as their acts bear) to give any church power, jurisdiction, or government, to the office-bearers of the church, other than that which acknowledges a dependence upon, and subordination to, the sovereign power of the king as supreme. And although the lordly prelates were hereby promoted to all the privileges and dignities they possessed before the year 1638, yet must they be all accountable to the king, in all their administrations, and in subordination to him, as universal bishop of all England, Scotland, and Ireland. By which the fountain of church power and authority is lodged in the king's person, and CHRIST is exauctorated and dethroned as King and Head in Zion. And further, by the second act of that perfidious parliament, the covenanted reformation, and all that was done in favor thereof, from 1638 to 1650, was declared treasonable, and rebellious. Alike treasonable it was reckoned for subjects, on pretense of reformation, or any other pretense whatsoever, to enter into any federal association, or take up arms against the king. They also declared, that the National Covenant, as sworn in the year 1638, and the Solemn League and Covenant, were, and are in themselves unlawful oaths, and that they were imposed upon, and taken by the subjects of this kingdom, contrary to the fundamental laws and liberties thereof. And to complete all, they repealed all acts, ecclesiastical and civil, approving the covenants, particularly the acts of the venerable assembly at Glasgow 1638, declaring it an unlawful and seditious meeting. And thereafter, by a wicked act of the council of Glasgow, more than three hundred ministers were illegally thrust from their charges, for their non-conformity, in discountenancing a diocesan meeting, or synod, appointed by the archbishop of Glasgow, and not observing the anniversary thanksgiving, *May* 29th, enjoined by the parliament. The rest were violently ejected from the lawful exercise of their ministry in their several parishes, and were afterward commanded by act of par-

liament to remove themselves and their families twenty miles distant from their respective flocks, and not to reside within six miles of any of their (so called) Cathedrals, or three miles of a Burgh. By these means, many of those poor persecuted ministers, with their families, were brought into great hardships and wants, being so far removed from their beloved and affectionate flocks, that they were deprived of that help from them, that doubtless they would cheerfully have ministered, for relieving them in their necessities and straits. All this was done at the instigation of the prelates, who could not endure to have a godly presbyterian minister near them, and were resolved to make them as miserable as possible.

As the observation of that anniversary holy day, *May* 29th, was again enjoined by this parliament 1662, with certification, the non-observance of which was one main cause of the sufferings of the ministers above noticed, we cannot pass over without mentioning that most abhorred and heaven-daring ignominy and contempt put upon our solemn and sacred covenants, and upon GOD the great Party in them, at Linlithgow on that day, by a theatrical exposing, and presumptuous committing them to the flames, together with *The causes of GOD'S wrath, Lex Rex,* acts of parliament, acts of committees of estates, and acts of assemblies made, during what they called the twenty-two years' rebellion, that is, from 1638 to 1660, done by the authority of the pretended magistrates there; one of which, and the minister Ramsay, were formerly zealous and active covenanters, and consequently now publicly avowed and proclaimed their perjury in the face of the sun, and left an indelible stain upon their memory.

Hitherto, although many, both ministers, gentlemen and others, had endured unexpressible hardships and severities, yet few or none suffered to the death, save that noble peer, the Marquis of *Argyle,* who was condemned by the parliament 1661, and beheaded *May* 27th; and the Reverend Mr. *James Guthrie,* who suffered five days thereafter. These two were singled out—the one in the state, the other in the church—to fall a victim to the resentment and fury of the enemies of that covenanted work of reformation, which they had both, in an eminent manner, been honored of GOD to support and advance; and also as a specimen of what was afterward to be the fate of all that should adhere to the same glorious cause, and stand up for God against these workers of iniquity. And, as the foundation of that anti-christian and wicked hierarchy in the church, and of arbitrary power and absolute tyranny in the state, was laid in the blood of these two proto-martyrs for the covenant and cause of GOD, so they now (*July,* 1663,) proceeded to build it up with the blood of another noble and worthy patriot, the eminently religious and learned Lord *Warriston.* He having before, in 1660, when *Argyle* was apprehended, been ordered, together with several others, to be secured and committed to prison, fled beyond sea, to escape the fury of his enemies, and even there did their crafty malice reach him; for, having sent out one of their blood-thirsty emissaries in quest of him, he was apprehended by him at Roan, in France, brought over to London, and sent thence to Edinburgh, where he was executed on a former unjust sentence of forfeiture and death, passed upon him in his absence. Thus they built up Zion with blood, and Jerusalem with iniquity. But all this was nothing to the cruelty that followed, and the righteous blood afterward shed in that quarrel.

4. Although the faithful servants of CHRIST gave too silent submission for a time to these encroachments made upon their sacred functions, yet, as they received not their mission from men, so they resolved not to become the servants of men, but to hazard the loss of every thing that was dear to them in this world, that they might show themselves faithful unto their Lord and Master, and valiant for his truth upon the earth, in going forth without the camp, bearing his reproach. When they could no longer, with a safe conscience, enjoy their benefices and churches, and the Lord so expressly called for their service, in feeding the starving souls of his people, they betook themselves to the open fields, setting their faces to all the storms to which they were exposed by that high commission court that was erected; wherein the bishops were chief agents, being made therein necessary members for putting the former, with what subsequent wicked laws were made against the servants of CHRIST, in execution. And, by this time, that deceiving, cruel, perjured, apostate bishop, *Sharp*, had obtained the presidency in this and all other public courts in the kingdom. The proceedings of this court were very unjust, cruel and arbitrary, similar to its preposterous and illegal constitution. Persons were, without any accusation, information, witness or accuser, arraigned before them, to answer *super inquirendis* to whatever interrogatories they were pleased to propose, without license to make any lawful defense, or, upon their offering so to do, were required to take the oath of supremacy, their refusal of which was accounted cause sufficient for proceeding against them. And although taking order with papists was first in their commission, yet last, or rather not at all, in execution; while their infernal rage was principally set on Presbyterians, in fining, confining and imprisoning them, for the non-conformity of ministers, and their disregarding their pretended sentences of deposition, and the people's refusing to countenance the authority and ministry of these prelatic wolves, who came in to scatter and tear the flock of CHRIST, but endeavoring to cleave to their lawful pastors, have equal friends and foes with them, and hear CHRIST'S law of kindness from their mouth. The idol of jealousy was thus set up in the house of GOD, and our LORD JESUS CHRIST sacreligiously robbed of his incommunicable supremacy and headship over his church by the state; whereby the Pope's supremacy was well nigh claimed, and Spanish inquisition cruelty almost acted, by this abominable court; and all at the instigation and for the gratification of these monsters of iniquity, the prelates, who still agitated the court to exercise more cruelty than even of themselves they were inclined to.

5. Upon the decline of this rigorous court, new measures were again fallen upon for the oppression, suppression and extirpation, of the true reformed religion, and the professors of it. The council being very diligent and careful to deprive the LORD'S people of every thing which might contribute to their establishment and confirmation in the righteousness and equity of the cause and covenant of God for which they suffered, and which tended to expose their tyranny and treason against GOD, ordered the famous Mr. Brown's *Apologetical Relation* to be burnt in the high street of Edinburgh, on February 14th, 1666, by the hand of the

common hangman; and all persons who had copies of said book were required to give them up, and such as concealed them to be fined 2000 £. *Scots*, if discovered. Such was their hellish enmity and spite against our covenanted reformation, and every thing written in defense thereof, and in vindication of those that suffered for their adherence to it. About the same time, *Sharp*, for the more effectual accomplishment of his wicked designs (the high commission being now dissolved, and his guilty conscience, it seems, suggesting fears of an insurrection of the oppressed, to relieve themselves from their cruel oppressors), obtains an order from the king for raising an additional number of forces, for the security and establishment of himself and his associates in their thrones of iniquity, by destroying all the faithful in the land, oppressing and wearing out the saints of the Most High, and burning up and dispersing all the synagogues of GOD in the nation. In consequence of this, about three thousand foot, and eight troops of dragoons were got together, and the command of them given to *Dalziel* of *Binns*, a wicked, fierce, cruel man. These were the instruments of that unprecedented barbarity, cruelty and oppression, committed in the West, after the defeat of Colonel Wallace and his little army of covenanters, at Pentland Hills, *November* 28th, 1666. The occasion and cause of which rising was, in short, this: Sir *James Turner* had been sent the year before into the south-west shires of Dumfries and Kirkcudbright, in order to suppress conventicles (so they called the assemblies of God's people for public worship and other religious exercises), levy the fines appointed by the parliament, and oblige the people to conform and submit to the bishops and curates by force of arms. Turner, in pursuance of these cruel orders, committed great severities, dreadfully oppressed, robbed and spoiled the country. In the parish of Dalry, in Galloway, three or four of his blackguard crew, seizing upon a poor countryman, carried him to his own house, and were going to torture him in a cruel manner, by setting him naked on a red-hot gridiron; which four of the persecuted party hearing of, they repaired to the house, disarmed the soldiers (upon their refusing to be entreated in behalf of the poor man), and delivered their fellow sufferer. And lest the rest of the soldiers quartered in the parish (to force people to keep their parish church), should fall upon them, being joined with seven or eight more of their friends, they attacked them early next morning, being about twelve in number, and disarmed them, killing one that made resistance. Whereupon, the country being alarmed, and being apprehensive, from sad experience, of the revenge Sir James would take upon the whole country for this affront, without distinction of age or sex, they determined to stand in their own defense. And, getting together a good number of horse and foot, they march to Dumfries, surprise Turner himself, take him prisoner, and disarm his soldiers, without any further violence. Being thus by Providence engaged, without any hope of retreat, and being joined by many more of their brethren in the same condition with themselves, some ministers, and Colonel Wallace (afterward chosen general), they come to Lanerk, where they renew the covenant, *November* 26th, 1666, and thence to Pentland Hills, where, being attacked by Dalziel and his blood-hounds, they were, notwithstanding their bravery in repulsing the enemy twice, at last totally routed, many killed and taken prisoners, most of the prisoners treacherously executed (notwithstanding they were taken upon solemn promise to have their lives spared), of whom the Lord was graciously pleased, not only to accept of a testimony, by sufferings, but also countenanced them, even to admiration, in sealing the same with their blood. After this, there were severe edicts issued out against all who had any hand in this appearance for GOD'S cause and covenant (called by them rebellion, a horrible conspiracy, and what not); all the subjects were strictly charged not to harbor, reset, supply, or in any manner of way correspond with any that were concerned in this engagement, but that they pursue and deliver them up to justice, or otherwise be esteemed and punished as favorers of it. This appearance for religion and liberty became, for a time, the principal crime of which those were indicted who were prosecuted by this wicked council, and other merciless enemies, to whom they committed the management of their affairs.

6. Although the cruelty of the court had hitherto been very great, yet they had not wholly effectuated their wicked design of exterminating and destroying true religion, and the professors thereof, both ministers and people; but, like Israel under Pharaoh's yoke, the more they oppressed them, and suppressed their meetings, the more numerous and frequent they grew, so that their enemies were obliged to alter their course a little from cruelty into craft. This appeared in the first indulgence, granted *anno* 1669, with design to divide Presbyterians among themselves, that they might the more easily destroy them. Hereby a pretended liberty was given to several ministers ejected by the act of Glasgow, 1662 (especially public resolutioners, who had formerly served the court interest in that matter), under certain restrictions, destructive of their ministerial freedom and faithfulness, to preach and exercise the other functions of the ministry in vacant churches. In this fraudulent snare many were taken; and even such of them as did accept of the indulgence, but did not keep by the instructions given them by the council, and observe the wicked anniversary, &c, were afterward prosecuted, fined, and some turned out. And those who refused compliance therewith, and testified against it, as flowing from that blasphemous supremacy and absolute power, which the king had assumed, were most severely handled, and their assemblies for public worship interdicted under the highest pains. A second indulgence was framed in the year 1672, in which net they expected to inclose such as the first had not caught. By this, liberty was granted to a number of non-conformed ministers, named by the council, not yet indulged, to exercise their ministry in such places as the council thought fit to ordain and appoint them, conforming themselves to the rules given by the council to those that were formerly indulged, besides other restrictions, wherewith this new liberty was clogged. And, as one special design of the court, in granting both the first and this second indulgence, was to put an effectual stop to the meetings of the LORD'S people, ludicrously called by them field conventicles, so they took occasion, on account of their contempt of this their indulgence and liberty, to prosecute all such as kept, or attended on, these meetings, in a more merciless and furious manner. This indulgence was accepted by many ministers; and part thereof, by others, represented as a grievance, and redress required. But although nothing of this kind was obtained, yet it was fallen in with and accepted by most of those who subscribed the remonstrance against it; and those few who rejected it, and continued faithfully to discharge their official trust in the

open fields, without coming under any of these sinful restrictions, became, more especially, the butt of their enemies' malice and tyranny, were more vigorously prosecuted, and such as were suspected or convicted of attending on their field meetings, were fined in an exorbitant manner, and ministers imprisoned, when they could be apprehended. And because these field meetings, the great eye-sore of the prelates, still increased, they prevailed with the council 1674, to take more special notice of the preachers at said meetings, who appointed a committee for that effect, and ordered their chancelor to send out parties to apprehend certain of them, according to their direction. And the same year, a bond was imposed, binding and obliging tenants, that if they, their wives, or any of their children, cottars or servants, should keep or be present at any conventicles, either in houses or fields, that every tenant laboring land be fined for each house conventicle in 25£. *Scots*; each cottar in 12_£. Scots_; each servant man in a fourth part of his year's fee, and husbands the half of these fines for such of their wives and children as shall be at house conventicles; and the double of these respective fines for each of the said persons who shall be at any field conventicles, &c. And upon refusal of said bond, they were to be put to the horn, and their escheat or forfeiture given to their masters. They likewise, at the same time, issued forth another proclamation, for apprehending the holders of, and repairers to, field meetings, by them designed rebels, and whoever should seize such should have the fines, so unjustly imposed, for their reward; with a particular sum offered for apprehending any of the conventicle preachers, and this sum doubled for some that were more eminent among them, and diligent in working the work of him that sent them, against whom their malice was more especially turned. These rigorous measures they continued to prosecute; and in the year 1675, letters of intercommuning were given out against several ministers and private Christians, by name, both denouncing them rebels, and secluding them from all society in the kingdom of Scotland; further requiring, that no accommodation should be given, or communication any manner of way held with them, under the pain of being (according to them) accounted *socii crimi-nis*, and pursued as guilty, with them, of the same crimes. These inhuman and un-precedented methods reduced the sufferers to many wanderings and great hard-ships. It is impossible to recite the miseries these faithful confessors underwent—wandering about in deserts, in mountains, in dens, and in caves of the earth, des-titute, afflicted, tormented; besides the other severe impositions upon the country in general, the bonds imposed, and rage of the *Highland* host then raised, which, together with the soldiers, greatly spoiled and robbed the west country especially, by which means, poor people were brought to very low circumstances.

7. Notwithstanding of all the tyranny and treachery hitherto exercised, the word of GOD grew, and converts unto CHRIST, and the obedience of the gospel, were daily multiplied; ministers being forward and willing to preach, and the peo-ple willing to hear and receive the law from their mouth, on all hazards. And the LORD JESUS, following his word and ordinances with his blessing, showed him-self as mighty and powerful in the open fields, whither they were driven, as ever he had done in their churches, from whence they were driven, and which were now shut against them, and filled with time-servers, and antichrist's vassals. But

against CHRIST'S standard and banner thus displayed, the tyrant Charles II erected his opposite standard for the utter destruction of CHRIST'S true servants and subjects. And having declared their lawful meetings for the worship of GOD, according to his word, execrable rendezvouses of rebellion; a convention of estates, *anno* 1678, was called and met, by which a large cess was imposed to maintain an additional army, for the suppression of the true religion and liberty, and securing tyranny and arbitrary government. On account of the imposition of this cess, and the rigorous exaction of it, together with the cruelties and ravages of this new army maintained by it (the soldiers having commission to dismiss and disperse their meetings, disarm, imprison and kill preachers and people, in case of resistance; and a price being put upon the heads of several faithful ministers if brought to the council dead or alive), both ministers and people were laid under the necessity of carrying arms for their own defense when dispensing and attending upon gospel ordinances. And it was no wonder that, finding themselves thus appointed as sheep for the slaughter, they looked upon this as their duty, and accordingly provided themselves with arms for their necessary defense against the wicked violence of those who thirsted after their blood, and (which was to them much more dear and precious) the ruin and destruction of the cause, interest, and gospel of CHRIST in the land. Unto these severe and hellish measures fallen upon at this time, for the more effectual suppression and extirpation of the gospel of CHRIST, and professors of it, the managers were principally instigated by that arch-apostate *Sharp*; though a bad preparative for his exit out of this world, which soon came to pass, *anno* 1679, in the dispensation of adorable providence and righteous judgment of God, executed upon such a notorious traitor, who, having first betrayed the church, and all along deeply imbrued his hands in the blood of GOD'S saints and servants; had blood given him to drink because he was worthy.

8. That the land might be more deeply soaked with blood, and made more heavily to groan under the inhabitants thereof, "Who had transgressed the laws, changed the ordinances, and broken the everlasting covenant;" that the scene of cruel suffering might be more widely opened, and the bloody tragedy more effectually acted; the primate's death must now be added to the other pretended crimes of the sufferers. Many were terribly harrassed on that account, who were no ways concerned in the action; and some were cruelly tortured and butchered by them for the same cause, though innocent thereof (for none of the actors did ever fall into their hands). These enemies were hereby rendered more rude, barbarous and hard-hearted to all the sufferers who afterward fell into their hands, and breathed out threatenings and slaughter against the whole body of the persecuted Presbyterians through the nation. All this, however, did not dispirit these zealous witnesses, or discourage them from attending to their work and duty; for we find them on the 29th of *May*, 1679, publishing their testimony at *Rutherglen*, against the wicked anniversary, on the same day appointed by the court for its celebration, and against all that had been done publicly by these enemies of CHRIST for the overthrow of his work and interest in the lands. They likewise committed their acts rescissory, supremacy, act restoring abjured Prelacy, act of *Glasgow*, 1662, the presumptuous act for appointing *May* 29th for an unholy anniversary, indulgenc-

es, &c., all to the flames, their just desert, in retaliation of the impious treatment given unto our solemn and sacred covenants, and other good and laudable acts and laws for reformation, by their sacrilegious enemies in sundry cities of these covenanted kingdoms. And so, after extinguishing the bonfires, a part of the unholy solemnity of the enemies' anniversary day, and concluding what they had done with prayer and praise, as they had begun (Mr. *Douglas*, one of their ministers being along with them), they withdrew. This Christian valor was followed with the LORD'S appearance for them, in a remarkable manner, on the following *Sabbath* at *Drumclog* near *Lowdonhill*, where being attacked by *Claverhouse*, when attending on public worship, they completely routed him and his troops, rescued Mr. *John King*, and a number of other prisoners, whom *Claverhouse* had seized that morning, from their hands. Afterward they declared the grounds and causes of their present defensive posture, in that short manifesto, or declaration, published at *Glasgow, June 6th*, 1679. But when their numbers multiplied, their divisions increased, and lawful means for honestly defending the cause were by the majority refused. Mr. *Welsh* and that Erastian party with him, being by this time come up, did in their declaration at *Hamilton*, take in the tyrant's interest; against which, those who were honest and faithful to the interest of Zion's king contended, and protested, that in conscience they could not take in the interest of one into the state of the quarrel who had manifestly stated himself in opposition to the interest of CHRIST; that it was inconsistent with the covenant, which could not bind them to espouse the interest of its destroyers, and the destroyers of all that adhered to it; and also contrary to their testimony and declaration for the covenants and work of reformation at *Rutherglen, Glasgow, &c.*, and against all defection from the same.

Thus, when the most part in a great measure forsook the LORD, he was justly provoked to forsake them, and their great divisions landing them in such confusion, they became an easy prey to the enemy, by whom they were totally routed at *Bothwell, June. 22d*, 1679, where they felt the dismal fruits and consequences of joining at all with that Erastian faction, after they had openly declared and discovered what they were. This was so far from proving any defense to them, notwithstanding the numbers of that party, that it proved their destruction. And those whose hearts were upright and honest in the cause of GOD, by their means, in holy sovereignty, were made to fall a sacrifice to their enemies' wrath. The slain on that day were many, and the after-cruelty to prisoners great; they being carried into and kept for a long time in the *Gray-friars* church yard of *Edinburgh*, exposed, defenseless, night and day, to tempests of all kinds. By this inhuman usage (with design to wear out the saints of the Most High), together with the insinuations and persuasions of some of the indulgence favorers, their faith failing them in this hour of temptation, and fear prevailing, a number of these prisoners were persuaded to take the insnaring bond of peace, whereby they were engaged to own their rising at *Bothwell* to be rebellion, and to oblige themselves never to rise in arms against the king, and to live peaceably, &c., while others of them were tortured, not accepting deliverance.

9. Although this defeat and dispersion of the espousers of the truth and cause

of CHRIST, in opposition both to its avowed enemies and secret betrayers, brought the remnant that were left into very melancholy circumstances, their enemies having in a great measure extinguished the light of the gospel, by apprehending and shedding the blood of their faithful pastors, who used to hold forth the word of life unto them, as a light whereby they might discern between sin and duty; and others who had formerly been helpful unto them, in strengthening their hands, and encouraging their hearts, in the way of their duty, were overtaken and overborne with fainting and discouragement; so that, in respect of public guides, they wore at this time as sheep without a shepherd. Yet, in this disconsolate and scattered state and condition, CHRIST, the chief shepherd, had compassion on them, and raised up those two faithful ministers and zealous contenders for the faith once delivered to the saints, Messrs. *Richard Cameron* and *Donald Cargill*, to come forth for the help of the LORD against the mighty, and to jeopard their lives along with his people in the high places of the field, in bearing faithful testimony for his noble truths and cause, and against all the sins and defections of the time. The first of these, soon after he had showed his activity and zeal in that banner displayed against the church's enemies, in the declaration published at *Sanquhar, June 22d,* 1080, did honorably and bravely finish his course, among many others of Zion's true friends, in the defeat they again sustained at *Airsmoss,* where, in imitation of his princely Master, he valiantly fought his way to the incorruptible crown. The latter afterward narrowly escaped his enemies' hands (by means of Mr. *Henry Hall,* of *Haughhead,* that honest sufferer for truth, who, to save his minister's life, lost his own; on whom the *Queensferry* paper, a draft of a covenant engagement unto certain duties, was found), and was, by the power and providence of GOD, preserved, until he accomplished that signal piece of generation work in drawing forth the sword of excommunication against the tyrant *Charles* II, and some others of the chief actors in that bloody tragedy. And that, because of their bloodshed, perjury, heaven-daring profaneness, debauchery, inhuman and savage cruelty acted upon the people of GOD. The which sentence stuck fast in the hearts of these enemies of Zion's king unto the day of their death, and, by some of their own acknowledgments, would through eternity. Shortly after this, that faithful minister crowned his work with martyrdom, and entered into his Master's joy.

This murdering period spared neither pastor nor people, age nor sex; while gross transgressors, and deluded enthusiasts, as *Gib* and his faction, were screened from condign punishment, though some of them had arrived at that prodigious length in wickedness as to commit the Holy Scriptures and Confession of Faith to the flames.

10. So many of these once living and lively witnesses for CHRIST being, now slain, and what was yet surviving of the scattered flock deprived of their painful shepherds, and not being able to drink of the sanctuary waters, so muddied by their former pastors, who had defiled the same by sinful compliance with the time's defections, they resolved, under divine direction, to gather themselves together into a general meeting, for advising and informing one another anent their duty, in such critical times of common danger, that so whatever concerned the

whole, might be done with due deliberation and common consent. The which general meetings afterward afforded them both good comfort amidst their discouragements, and also good counsel amidst their perplexities and doubts, and proved an excellent expedient for preserving the remnant from the destruction and contagion of the times, propagation of the testimony, and keeping alive the public spirit of zeal and concern for the cause and interest of CHRIST; and for these ends they have been kept up ever since.

In the meantime, that evil instrument, *James*, duke of *York*, receiving commission from his perjured brother to preside in the whole administration of *Scots'* affairs, upon his arrival for this effect, held a parliament, which began *July* 28th, 1681; wherein, besides other of his wicked acts, that detestable, blasphemous, and self-contradictory test was framed, which, in the first part thereof, contains the swearer's solemn declaration, by oath, of his sincere profession of the true Protestant religion, contained in the first confession of faith, ratified by *Parl. 1st, James VI*, 1567 (which confession asserts, in the strongest terms, CHRIST'S alone headship and supremacy as lawgiver and king in his church, without copartner or competitor), and that he shall adhere thereunto all the days of his life, and renounce all doctrines, principles, or practices contrary thereto, and inconsistent therewith; while, in manifest contradiction thereto, the blasphemous supremacy, in the utmost extent thereof, is asserted — the Covenants National and Solemn League, the chief barriers against Popery, Erastianism, and arbitrary power, are renounced, and unlimited allegiance unto the occupant is enjoined and sworn to, and the prelatical government of the church confirmed.

This oath was at first administered to those in public trust only, and thereby all were turned out of their places who had any principles of common honesty remaining in them; but afterward it was imposed on all persons of all ranks. Against which sinful encroachments on religion and liberty, the witnessing persecuted remnant accounted themselves bound in duty to emit their testimony, which they published at *Lanerk, January* 12th, 1682, adhering to, and confirming their former at *Sanquhar*, and giving reasons at length for their disowning the unlawful authority of *Charles II.* Upon intelligence hereof, this declaration, with those at *Rutherglen* and *Sanquhar*, were, by order of the council, with great solemnity, burnt at the cross of *Edinburgh*, by the magistrates in their robes, together with the Solemn League and Covenant, which had been burnt formerly: but now they would give new demonstrations of their rage against it, in conjunction with these declarations, which they saw and acknowledged were evidently conformed to, and founded upon it. After the publication of this testimony, the sufferings of that poor people that owned it were sadder and sharper than ever before, by hunting, pursuing, apprehending, imprisonment, banishment, death, and torture; this increasing rage, oppression, cruelty, and bloodshed, being no more than what they might look for, agreeable to the spirit and principles of that popish incendiary, to whom such trust was committed.

11. The poor wrestling remnant, besides their other grievous calamities and sufferings, being now obnoxious to much censure, in their appearances for truth

reproached, and invidiously misrepresented, both at home and abroad, by those that were at ease in Zion, as having forsaken the right way, and run into wild, extravagant, and unhappy courses; and, withal, being at this time destitute and deprived of their public standard bearers; their series of witnesses (since the death of Messrs. *Cameron* and *Cargill*) maintaining the testimony against the public national defections being in all appearance interrupted, except by martyrdom and sufferings; they were obliged to exert themselves, both for their vindication from those calumnies and slanders, wherewith they were loaded by their enemies, to foreign Protestant churches especially, and for obtaining a supply of gospel ministers. Wherefore, sending some of their number abroad, to represent the righteousness of their cause to the churches there, and crave their sympathy, in helping them to a supply of gospel ministers; the LORD was graciously pleased to countenance and bless their endeavors so, that they obtained access for the instruction and ordination of young men for the ministry, at a university in the *United Provinces*; and, in process of time, gave them a great reviving in their bondage, by sending forth his faithful embassador, Mr. *James Renwick*, who, while he stood on Zion's watch-tower, ceased not night and day to give faithful warning of the danger approaching the city of GOD, evidently discovering his being clothed with his Master's commission, in bearing faithful testimony and witness, both against the avowed enemies of truth and backsliders from it. And notwithstanding all the malicious rage of deadly foes, ranging and keenly pursuing him, through open or more secret places, the reproach of tongues and cruel mockings he endured, by the divine blessing, on his painful labors, amidst his many hardships, the number of Zion's friends were greatly increased, by the incoming and joining of many to the fellowship of their settled societies, who resolutely chose rather to suffer affliction with the people of GOD than to enjoy the pleasures of sin, which are but for a season. Upon this further attack upon Satan's interest, his emissaries issue forth fresh orders, and give commission to soldiers, foot and dragoons, to hunt, search, and seek them out of all their most secret dens, caves, and lurking places, where they might hide themselves, in the most remote and wildest glens and recesses in the mountains and deserts, allowing them to kill, slay, destroy, and any way to make an end of them, wherever they might be found; commanding the whole country, at their peril, to assist them, and raise the hue and cry after the poor wanderers, and not to reset, harbor, succor, or correspond with them any manner of way, under the highest pains, but to do their utmost in informing against them. Thus, without regard to any of their unlawful forms of legal procedure, they defiled and besmeared the high places of the field with innocent blood. These unprecedented methods and measures obliged the sufferers, for their own preservation, stopping the deluge of blood, and to deter the insolence of intelligencers and informers, to publish the apologetic declaration, which they affixed on several market crosses, and parish church doors, upon the 28th of *October*, 1684; wherein they declare their firm resolution of constant adherence to their covenanted engagements; and to the declaration disowning the authority of *Charles Stuart*, warning all bloody Doegs and flattering Ziphites, to expect to be dealt with as they deal with them; to be regarded as enemies to GOD, and the covenanted reformation, and according to their power, and the degree of their offense, punished as such, &c. After this declaration, these enemies were still more enraged, and their fury flamed more than ever formerly. They framed an oath, commonly called the oath of abjuration, renouncing and abjuring the same, and by a venomous bloody proclamation, enjoined this oath to be taken by all universally, from sixteen years and upward, women as well as men, under pain of death; and many prisoners who having the oath tendered them, refused or declined it, were sentenced, and executed all in one day, according to the tenor of their proclamation. And, moreover, they, on this occasion, renewed their orders and commission to the soldiers, for pursuing and chasing after the rebels (as they designed them) more vigorously and violently, and to shoot, or otherwise put them to death wherever they did light upon them. In the midst of this confusion of slaughter and bloodshed, GOD cut off by death, *February* 6th, 1685, that vile person, the author and authorizer of all this mischief, *Charles II*, who, *Antiochus* like, came in peaceably, and obtained the kingdom by flattery (*Dan.* xi), reigned treacherously and bloodily, and like that wicked king, *Jehoram* (2 *Chron.* xxi), died without being desired or lamented, poisoned, as was thought, by his unnatural popish brother. And, notwithstanding of all his bastards, begotten in adultery and fornication, at home and abroad, he died without any to succeed him, save him that was said to have murdered him. GOD pursued him with the curse of *Hiel* the *Bethelite*, for his rebuilding of that cursed *Jericho*, prelacy; and of that impious and wicked tyrant, *Coniah* (*Jer.* xxii), for his treachery and cruelty; "Thus saith the LORD, Write ye this man childless, a man that shall not prosper in his days, for no man of his seed shall prosper, sitting any more upon the throne of *Israel*."

12. Notwithstanding the abundant proof that the duke of *York* had given, in many instances, and in both kingdoms, of his being a vassal of antichrist, and notwithstanding of his open and public profession of papistry, upon his brother's death, fairly warning all what they might expect, yet were not those, who sat at the helm of affairs, deterred from committing the reins of government into his hands; but contrary to the word of God, and fundamental laws of the lands, this professed and excommunicate papist *James*, duke of *York*, was, *anno* 1685, proclaimed king of these once covenanted, but now treacherous and apostate lands, whereby they appointed themselves a captain to return into their anti-christian bondage. To this grievous yoke our infamous, perjured, and apostate state and council in *Scotland*, heartily and voluntarily subjected themselves and the nation, while others did it with reluctancy, caressing and embracing with their dearest and best affections, this enemy to GOD, and CHRIST, and his church, swearing implicit and unlimited obedience unto him, and asserting his absolute power and supremacy, indefeasible and hereditary right, without ever so much as requiring him to take the coronation oath, or give the least security for, any thing civil or religious (a depth of degeneracy, parallel to that eminency in reformation purity, from which they were fallen!) but laid the reins on his own neck, that he might have full freedom for the satisfying of his lusts, and fulfilling his wicked designs. This laid religion, liberty, and all, at the mercy of absolute power and popish tyranny; and still more and more cut off the people of God from having any hopes of mercy from their bloody enemies; on the contrary, the duke of *York*, in his letter to his first parliament, rec-

ommends and requires them to leave no means unattempted, for the extirpation of the poor wandering sufferers, whom he brands with the odious names of murderers and assassins, wild and inhuman traitors, &c. And these his ready servants and bloody executioners, came nothing short of his orders in the execution of them; so that there were more murdered in cold blood in the open fields, without all shadow of law, trial or sentence, more banished and sold as slaves, condemned and executed, &c., in the time of this usurper, than in all the time of the former tyrant.

As the honest sufferers, consistent with their testimony for truth, in opposition both to the secret and open subvertors of the cause and state of Zion's quarrel with her enemies, could not concur in *Argyle's* declaration (although there were many things in it materially good, and commend-worthy), nor join in a military association with him, on account (among other things) of the too promiscuous admission of persons to trust in that party, who were then, and afterward discovered themselves to be, enemies to the cause. Yet, against this usurpation of a bloody papist, advancing himself to the throne in such a manner, they published another declaration at *Sanquhar, May* 28, 1685; wherein, approving of, and adhering to all their former, and considering that *James*, duke of *York*, a professed and excommunicated papist, was proclaimed: they protest against said proclamation, with reasons subjoined at length for their so doing—against all kinds of popery, general and particular heads, as abjured by the national covenant—against its entry again into this land, and every thing that doth, or may directly or indirectly, make way for the same, &c. After this, Mr. *Renwick* and his followers were exposed to the greater fury of their adversaries; more cruel edicts were given forth against them, approving and ratifying of former acts, for raising the hue and cry, &c., whereby their calamities were very much increased, besides the slanders of professed friends, on account of their not associating and joining with them in their compliances, although, to the conviction of all unbiassed minds, they fully vindicated themselves from all their injurious reflections.

The extirpation of the Presbyterian interest—nay, the suppression of the Protestant religion in general, the reintroduction of popery, and plunging the nations in anti-christian darkness and tyranny, being the long concerted design of this popish bigot now got into the throne; he resolves to lose no time, and leave no stone unturned, for the prosecution and accomplishment thereof. And having made tolerable progress in the execution of this his favorite scheme (although not without opposition), in *England*, he turns himself to *Scotland*, expecting an entire acquiescence in his pleasure there, having found the first parliament, which began, 23d *May*, 1685, so much according to his own heart, in their hearty and sincere offer of their lives and fortunes, to assist, defend, and maintain him in his rights, prerogatives, sacred, supreme, and absolute power and authority, &c.

Wherefore, the parliament being to meet again *April* 29, 1686, in his letter to them, "he heartily recommends to their care his innocent Roman Catholic subjects, to the end, that as they have given good experience of their true loyalty and peaceable behavior, they may have the protection of his laws, without lying under obligations their religion could not admit of; that all penal laws made against them might be repealed, &c." But though many were for obliging their king in this particular, yet it could not be carried without debates and strong objections; so that, dissolving the parliament, what he could not obtain there, with any show or face of law, he effectuates, by virtue of the prerogative royal and absolute power, in a letter to his privy council, and proclamation inclosed, bearing date *February* 12, 1687, granting a royal toleration to moderate Presbyterians, clogged with a number of grievous Erastian conditions and restrictions, as usual. Secondly, to Quakers and other enthusiasts. Thirdly, to Papists, abrogating all penal statutes made against them, and making them in all respects free. And so devoted were the privy council to his interests, that without demur they published the proclamation, and wrote back to the king, "that his orders were punctually obeyed, thanking him for this further proof of his favors to all his subjects." Thus, this champion for Satan and antichrist proceeded with his wicked design, and so far succeeded; all kinds of papistry were publicly practiced, and many churches converted to mass chapels. For, before this, by the king's letter to his privy council, of *August* 21st, 1686, Papists were allowed the free exercise of their religion, the council required to support and maintain them therein, and the royal chapel at *Holyrood-House* ordered to be repaired for popish service. By which means a door was opened for that swarm of Jesuits and priests, ascending as locusts out of the bottomless pit, which quickly overspread the lands. But notwithstanding of all this indulgence and royal toleration granted to these three forementioned parties, yet there is no favor nor mercy for the honest and faithful sufferers, and honorable contenders for the interests and prerogatives royal of JESUS CHRIST, against his sacrilegious and blasphemous usurpation of the same. But while he thinks fit to give ease (as himself says) by this means, to tender consciences, he at the same time signifies his highest indignation against those enemies of Christianity (he means Popery) as well as government, and human society, the field-conventiclers, whom he recommends to the council to root out, with all the severity of the laws, and the most rigorous persecution of the forces, it being equally his, and his people's concern to get rid of them. In consequence of this, all their artillery is directed against the Rev. Mr. *James Renwick* only, and that poor, afflicted, and persecuted people that adhered to him (all others being comprehended in the pretended liberty granted), so that they were prosecuted with fire and sword, and according to the utmost severity of their wicked laws made against them, and a reward of a hundred pounds *sterling* offered by the bloody council to any that should bring in Mr. *Renwick* to them, either dead or alive. But he having his generation work allotted and cut out for him by GOD, was preserved and kept from falling into their hands, until that he had finished the work his Master had given him to do, notwithstanding all this hellish and anti-christian rage and fury wherewith they did pursue him. About the beginning of the year 1686, he, in conjunction with Mr. *Alexander Shields*, who had lately joined him, wrote the Informatory Vindication, by way of reply to various accusations in letters, informations and conferences, given forth against them and their people, wherein they vindicate, clear and justify themselves from the heavy and false charges, slanders and reproaches, cast upon them by their enemies, as may be seen in said book. About this time, also, Mr. *Shields* set about writing his *Hind let loose* (which was published next year), or, A Historical Representation of the Testimonies of the Church of *Scotland* for the interest of CHRIST, with the true state thereof in all its periods; wherein he also solidly, soundly, and judiciously vindicates the present testimony, in all the principles thereof, as stated, against the popish, prelatical, and malignant enemies of that church, for the prerogatives of CHRIST, privileges of the church and liberties of mankind, and sealed by the sufferings of a reproached remnant of Presbyterians there, witnessing against the corruptions of the time.

Whilst these two loving and faithful fellow-laborers were thus industriously exerting themselves for the propagation and vindication of the persecuted gospel, and cause of CHRIST; that fiery Jesuit, popish tyrant, and enemy to GOD and man, the duke of *York*, and his popish party, were equally industrious on the other hand, to promote their grand design of utterly extinguishing the light of the gospel, and bringing in Antichrist, with all his poisonous and hellish vermin, and abominable idolatries; and that, with all the murdering violence, diabolical subtilty and malignant rage that hell and *Rome* could invent and exert. He had formerly published a proclamation (as is noticed above), granting a lawless liberty to several sorts of persons therein specified, called his first indulgence; but breathing nothing but threatenings and slaughter against the people of GOD, who stood firm to his cause. But withal, this proclamation, enjoined an oath in the room of all oaths formerly imposed, to be taken by all that minded to share in his royal favor; wherein they swore, not only absolute subjection and passive obedience, never to resist him, not only on any pretense, but for any cause, let him do, or command to be done what he would; but also, absolute, active obedience, without reserve: "That they shall, to the utmost of their power, assist, defend, and maintain him, his heirs and successors, in the exercise of their absolute power and authority, against all deadly." This was so palpably gross and odious, that it was disdained and abhorred by all that had common sense. Wherefore, finding that this proposal did not take, nor answer his design, in a letter to the council, bearing date about a month after the former, he endeavors to mend the matter, and set it out in another dress, pretending that they had mistaken his meaning in the former, and so lets them know, that it is his pleasure now, that if the Presbyterian preachers do scruple to take the oath (contained in the proclamation), or any other oath whatsoever, they, notwithstanding, have the benefit of his indulgence (without being obliged to take the oath), provided they observe the conditions on which it was granted. But this not having the desired effect neither, it is followed with the third indulgence or toleration, emitted by proclamation, dated 28th *June*, 1687, excellently well calculated for obtaining his end; wherein, after a solemn declaration of his intention to maintain his archbishops and bishops, he does, by his sovereign authority, prerogative royal, and absolute power, suspend, stop and disable, all penal and sanguinary laws, made against any for non-conformity to the religion established by law — granting liberty to all the subjects to meet and serve GOD, after their own way, in private houses or chapels, or places purposely hired or built for that use, with an injunction to take care that nothing be preached or taught, that might any way tend to alienate the hearts of the people from him and his government: but, notwithstanding the premises, strictly prohibiting all field meetings, against all which all his laws and acts of parliament are left in full force and vigor; and all his judges, magistrates and officers of forces, commanded to prosecute such as shall be guilty of said field conventicles, with the utmost rigor; and all this under pretense, that now, after this his royal grace and favor, there is not the least shadow of excuse left for these meetings. Wherefore, he is confident, that none will, after these liberties and freedoms given to all, to serve God in their own way, further presume to meet in these assemblies, except such as make a pretense of religion, to cover their treasonable designs against his royal person, and peace of his government.

The most of the Presbyterian ministers in *Scotland* took the benefit of this wicked and boundless toleration, chiefly designed in favor of Papists. And a large number of them, being met at *Edinburgh*, agreed upon, and, in name of all the rest, sent an address of thanks to the tyrant for his toleration, stuffed with the most loathsome and blasphemous flatteries, to the dishonor of GOD, the reproach of his cause, and betraying of his church. For, in this address, dated *July* 21st, 1687, designating themselves the loyal subjects of this true religion and liberty destroyer, they offer him their most humble and hearty thanks for his favor bestowed, and bless the great GOD who put it into his heart to grant them this liberty, which they term a great and surprising favor, professing a fixed resolution still to maintain an entire loyalty, both in their doctrine and practice (consonant to their known, principles, which, according to the holy Scriptures, are contained in the *Confession of Faith*); and they humbly beseech, that any who promote disloyal principles and practices (as they disown them) may not be looked upon as any of theirs, whatever name they may assume to themselves; and that, as their address comes from the plainness and sincerity of loyal and thankful hearts, so they were much engaged by his royal favor, to continue their fervent prayer to the King of kings, for divine illumination and conduct, and all other blessings, both spiritual and temporal, ever to attend his person and government. Thus these men made themselves naked to their shame, and declared to the world, that they did only presumptuously arrogate to themselves the name of Presbyterians; whereas, in reality, they were quite another kind of creatures, acting diametrically opposite to Presbyterian principles, in congratulating, extolling and justifying a tyrant, for assuming to himself a blasphemous, absolute power, whereby he suspends and disables all penal laws against idolators, and gives a toleration for all errors.

But while these pretended Presbyterians, who all along loved peace better than truth, and preferred their own ease before the concerns of their Master's glory, were thus sheltering themselves under this refuge of lies; true Presbyterians, who kept by presbyterian principles, and acted a faithful part for CHRIST, refusing to bow down to the idol of supremacy, which the tyrant had set up, or pay any regard to his blasphemous toleration, were pursued, persecuted, and slain, without pity or compassion, all the engines of the court being leveled against them for their destruction, because they would still reserve to themselves the liberty wherewith CHRIST had made his people free, and not exchange it for one from Antichrist, restricted with his reserves and limitations; so that (as Mr. *Shields* tells us in his account of Mr. *James Renwick's* life), in less than five months after the toleration, there were fifteen most desperate searches particularly for him, both of foot and horse: and, that all encouragement might be given to any who would apprehend him, a proclamation was issued, dated *October* 18th, "Authorizing all officers, civil and military, to apprehend and secure in firmance his person, with some others; and for encouragement, insuring the sum of *100£ sterling* for taking him, or them, dead or alive." In the midst of all these hazards, this unwearied and faithful laborer did notwithstanding continue at his work, in preaching, catechising, &c., and the Lord still preserved him from falling into the enemy's hand, until he had finished that piece of generation work, in drawing up a full and faithful testimony against *York's* toleration, and for the covenants and work of reformation, &c., which he gave in to a meeting of Presbyterian ministers at *Edinburgh*, on the 17th *January*, 1688; and going thence to *Fife*, whither he was called to preach, in his return, was apprehended at *Edinburgh*, and called to seal his above testimony, with all his other contendings against Popery, Prelacy, Erastianism, and all defection from the land's attainments in reformation, with his blood, which he did in the *Grass market* of *Edinburgh*, 17th of *February*, 1688, with a remarkable and extraordinary measure of the Lord's gracious presence and spirit, not only in this part of his sufferings, but all the time of his imprisonment. The Lord hereby bearing witness, both to the truth of that cause for which he suffered, and also testifying his gracious acceptance of his sufferings, and of the free-will-offering of his life, which he laid down for his sake. And as neither the violence nor flattery of enemies could prevail with this faithful confessor and martyr himself, to quit with one hair or hoof of what belonged to Christ, so he recommended to the poor scattered remnant which he left, as part of his dying counsel, to keep their ground, and not to quit nor forego one of these despised truths, which he was assured the Lord, when he returned to bind up the breach of his people, and heal them of their wound, would make glorious in the earth. Thus that worthy minister, and now glorified martyr of Jesus, through a chain of sufferings, and train of enemies, fought his way unto an incorruptible and immortal crown of endless glory. He was the last that sealed the testimony for religion and liberty, and the covenanted work of reformation, against Popery, Prelacy, Erastianism, and tyranny, in a public manner, on the scaffold, with his blood. After the death of this renowned martyr, he was succeeded by the eminent Mr. *Alexander Shields*, who carried on, and maintained, the testimony, as it was stated, in all the heads and clauses thereof, continuing to preach in the fields. On which account, he, and the people who attended his ministry, were exposed for some time longer to the fury and resentment of their enemies. But their power, which they had so long perverted and abused, quickly came to a period. For in a few months, God, in his righteous judgment and adorable providence, overturned that throne of iniquity on which they depended, and expelled that inhuman, cruel monster, from his tyrannical and usurped power, upon the prince of Orange's coming over into *England*, in the beginning of *November* that same year. But, although the Lord at this juncture, and by this means, rescued and delivered our natural and civil rights and privileges in a national way from under the oppression and bondage of anti-christian tyranny, arbitrary and absolute power, yet the Revolution, at this time, brought no real deliverance to the church of God. But Christ's rights, [1] formerly acquired for him by his faithful servants, lay still buried under the rubbish of that anti-christian building of Prelacy, erected on the ruins of his work in this land; and the spiritual liberties and privileges of his house remained, and do still remain under the bondage of Erastianism, supremacy, toleration, &c. For it is well known, that although this man, Jehu-like, "destroyed *Baal* out of *Israel*, yet he departed not from the sins of *Jeroboam*, wherewith he made *Israel* to sin."

About this time, the united societies (having no actual minister since Mr. *Renwick's* death, Mr. *Shields* being only preacher) sent over some commissioners from their general meeting to *Embden*, one of the United Provinces, to bring over Mr. *Thomas Linning*, a young man whom they had sent thither some years before in Mr. *Renwick's* time, to the university there, and for ordination. In consequence hereof, the said Mr. *Linning* came home, with testimonials of his ordination to the ministry by the classes at *Embden*; and in conjunction with Mr. *Shields* and Mr. *William Boyd* (another of their ministers, who had also come from Holland about this time), renewed the Covenants National and Solemn League, and dispensed the sacrament of the Lord's supper near Lesmahago, in Clydesdale, and continued to preach to the people for about four months, until the first General Assembly (so called) met at Edinburgh 1689-90. At which time, he, with his two brethren, in their own name, and the name of their people, presented a paper to that Assembly, bearing on what terms they and their people would join in communion with them; only craving that they might all join in humbling themselves before the Lord, and acknowledge and bewail their fathers', their own, and the land's many and heinous iniquities, and breaches of Covenant, before they proceeded to any other business, and so have their public sins and scandalous compliances washed away by repentance, and calling upon the name of the Lord Jesus. That they would purge out from among them, all ignorant, insufficient, heterodox, and notoriously scandalous ministers, such as, by information, accusation, or otherways, were guilty of the blood of the saints, &c. But these proposals were reckoned unseasonable and impracticable, tending rather to kindle contention, than compose division, and so were thrown over their bar. The generality of these men were so plunged and puddled in the ditch of defection and apostasy, that they could not think of the drudgery of cleansing themselves in God's way, by a particular and public confession of, and humiliation for their own and the land's public sins, but chose rather to sit down filthy and polluted as they were, and presume, in the midst of their abominations unrepented of, to approach God's holy things, which, how provoking to heaven, let God in his word be judge, *Isa.* lii, 11; *Hag.* ii, 13, 14; 2 *Chr.* xxx, 3; *Ezek.* xliv, 10. Nay, it is but too, too evident, that for this cause, God then laid them under that awful sentence, *Rev.* xxii, 11: "Him that is filthy, let him be filthy still;" or that, *Isa.* xxii, 14. For as their hearts were then hardened against God's call by his word and providence to that important and most necessary duty; so, ever since, they, have been so much the more so, and have gone on from evil to worse.

---

[1] *Christ's rights, &c.* By these are not meant the rights of Christ personal. It is not in the power of mortals, or any creature, to acquire and secure these to him; but the rights of Christ mystical, that is, of the church, or, of his truth, true worship, and religion, and professors of it as such.

But to return to our purpose: the two brethren, Messrs. *Linning* and *Boyd*, upon the rejection of the above said paper of proposals, intending to unite with them at any rate, gave in another, importing their submission to the assembly; which paper, Mr. *Shields* also, through their influences, insinuations, and persuasions, was drawn in to subscribe and adhere to; which he had never done, had he not fallen by the means of these false brethren, and which, it is said, he sadly repented afterward. Thus, the poor people were again left destitute of ministers, and public gospel ordinances, until the Rev. Mr. *John, McMillan* acceded to them, from the public judicatories of the revolution church, in the year 1706. And their kind friend, Mr. *Linning*, to make amends for all his misdemeanors, and in return for the charges the societies were at about his education, at home and abroad, did them that good office, to write, and load them with calumnies and slanders, to the universities in the *Netherlands*, whither they had recourse formerly in like cases; so that all access for having their loss retrieved from that quarter, was blocked up.

What is thus briefly hinted above, may suffice to afford some cursory view of the rise and progress of religion and reformation in these lands, especially in *Scotland*; until, as a church and nation, our kingdom became the Lord's, by the strictest and most intimate federal alliance, and the name almost of every city, was, *the Lord is there*: together with the general state and condition of the church and land, from the fatal juncture of our woful decline, unto the end of the above mentioned bloody period; the faithfulness of some, in this time of trial and temptation: the defection and backsliding course of others; and the great and avowed wickedness of the rest, extended unto an exhorbitant hight of savage inhumanity, irreligion and impiety. Upon all which, the presbytery, in duty to God, the present and succeeding generations find themselves obliged to testify:

1, Their hearty approbation of the faithfulness of such ministers and others, who opposed, and faithfully testified against the public resolutions of church and state, framed in the year 1651, for receiving into places of power and trust, malignant enemies to the work of reformation, contrary to the word of God, *Exod.* xviii, 21; *Deut.* i, 13; *2 Chron.* xix, 2; and to all acts of assembly and parliament in the reforming period; the assembly disclaiming the resolutions, as appears from their act, *June 17th*, 1646, session 14th, entitled, *Act for censuring the compilers with the public enemies of this church and kingdom*: and their seasonable and necessary warning *June 27th*, 1640, session 27th; where "they judge it a great and scandalous provocation, and grievous defection from the public cause, to comply with, these malignants, &c." As also, *Act 11th*, Triennial Parliament of, Charles I, entitled, *Act for purging the army of disaffected persons to the Covenant and work of Reformation.* And the faithful warnings, given by general assemblies and parliament, even against the admission of Charles II to the regal dignity, when so evidently discovering his disingenuity, until once he should give more satisfying proof of hid sincerity; see act of the commission at the *West Kirk, August* 13th, 1650, where the commission of the general assembly, considering, that there may be just ground of stumbling, from the king's majesty's refusing to emit the declaration offered him by the committee of estates, and the commission of the General Assembly, concerning his former carriage, and resolution for the future, in reference to the cause of God, and enemies and friends thereof; doth therefore declare "That this kirk and kingdom do not espouse any malignant party, quarrel, or interest, but that they fight merely upon their former grounds and principles, and in the defense of the cause of GOD, and of the kingdom, as they have done these twelve years past: and therefore as they disclaim all the sin and guilt of the king and of his house, so they will not own him nor his interest, otherwise than with a subordination to GOD, and so far as he owns and prosecutes the cause of GOD, and disclaims his, and his father's opposition to the work of GOD and to the covenant," &c. The which declaration being seen and considered by the committee of estates, was the same day approven by them. Thus, both church and state exerted themselves in the discharge of their duty, in order to obtain a settlement, according to the word of God, and the covenants, which were now become the *magna charta* of the privileges and liberties of the nations, both civil and religious; and therefore, were sworn to and subscribed by Charles II, as was also the coronation oath, for the security and preservation of the true religion, at his receipt of the royal power.

2. The presbytery testify and declare their approbation of the conduct of the faithful, before the restoration, who, adhering to the aforesaid fundamental constitutions of the nations, both refused subjection unto, and testified against, the usurpation of *Oliver Cromwell* and his accomplices, his invading the land, his anti-christian toleration of all sectarian errors and heresies, threatening the ruin and destruction of the true religion, as well as liberty. This was particularly testified against by the synod of *Fife*, and others in conjunction with them, as wicked and intolerable; as opposite unto, and condemned by, the Scriptures of truth, *Job* xxxiv, 17; *Deut.* xiii, 1-12; *Zech.* xiii, 3; contrary to acts of assembly and parliament, made against malignants, their being received into places of power and trust, with whom these sectarians were compliers, such as *Act* 16th, of *Assemb.* 1646, *Sess.* 13th; *Act* 26th, *Sess.* 2d, parliament *Charles* I, &c.

3. The presbytery do hereby heartily approve and homologate the testimony borne unto the truths and royal prerogatives of Christ, as King of Zion, by the witnesses and martyrs for the same, from the restoration, *anno* 1660, to the late revolution, by protestations, declarations, confiscation of goods, bonds, imprisonment, banishment, all kinds of cruelty and suffering, even unto the death (as noticed above), by the impious revolters from the righteous laws of God, and overturners of the just and equitable laws of men, both sacred and civil; to the maintenance whereof, the greatest part of these transgressors had bound themselves by the most sacred and inviolable obligations, which made their wickedness the more daring and aggravated, and the testimony of the saints against such as had made themselves so vile in the sight of God and all good men, the more justifiable. *Psalm* cxix, 139: "My zeal hath consumed me, because mine enemies have forgotten thy words." And as the doers of the law have the promise of justification by the great Legislator, *Rom.* ii, 13, so they ought to have the approbation of his people for doing his will.

And as the Spirit discovers the church's duty not to consist only in bearing witness unto the truth, and justifying Christ's confessors and martyrs, in their faithful adherence unto it, but also in testifying against sin, and condemning the wicked for their wickedness; for which, also, we have the precedent of the reformed and covenanted church of *Scotland*, both before and during the defection and wickedness of the forementioned period. Likeas, the presbytery did, and hereby do declare and testify particularly:

1. Against that prime and leading step of defection, the public resolutions, a scheme projected by that arch hypocrite and traitor to God, Charles II, for the reintroduction of men of the same wicked and malignant spirit with himself, into places of public trust in the nation—men, the most of whom had been formerly excommunicated by the church, and excluded from all office-bearing in the commonwealth, by the states, in their act of classes, as being avowed and obstinate enemies to God and to their country. Which scheme, approven of and put in execution, with the consent of a corrupt part of the ministry of the church, called afterward resolutioners, made way for that sad and bloody catastrophe, which after befel the poor church of Christ in this land.

2. They declare and testify against the usurpation of *Oliver Cromwell*, with those who subjected themselves unto, and owned, his authority; against his treacherous invasion of this land, contrary to the public oaths and vows, and covenant union of the nations; together with his sectarian principles, and wicked toleration, then obtruded upon them.

3. They declare and testify against the restoration of *Charles* II, 1660, unto the government of these covenanted lands, after he had so plainly discovered his spirit and designs, in the matter of the public resolutions. On account of which treacherous and double dealing with God and man, he was, in the Lord's holy and adorable providence, justly secluded from the government, and lived an exile for the space of ten years; but, by means of his malignant public resolution friends, he was again, by might, though not of right, restored, without so much as his adherence sought to those oaths, which he had formerly so solemnly sworn. Add to this the church's sinful silence, through the influence of the backslidden resolution party therein, so that, at the convention of the pretended parliament, *anno* 1661, consisting mostly of persons of known disaffection to the true religion, elected of purpose to serve the king's traitorous designs, there was not so much as a protestation for civil or religious liberties and privileges offered thereunto; but the vile person (as be afterward fully declared himself) was peaceably, though illegally, exalted.

4. As the presbytery find themselves in duty bound to testify against this most unhappy restoration of *Charles* II, so, of necessary and just consequence, they declare against the whole of his usurped and tyrannical administration—particularly against his blasphemous and heaven-daring ecclesiastical supremacy; against the act rescissory, declaring null and void the covenants, presbyterian church government, and all the laws made in favor of the true religion since the year 1638; the wicked anniversary thanksgiving day, in memory of the restoration; the re-establishment of diocesan and Erastian Prelacy; his publicly and ignominiously

burning of our solemn covenants, after pretending to nullify their obligation; with all his cruelty, tyranny, oppression and bloodshed, under color, and without form, of law, exercised upon the Lord's people, during the whole of his reign.

5. They again testify against the treachery of these covenanted lands, in their advancing (contrary to our solemn covenants and all law and reason) *James*, duke of *York*, a professed Papist, and avowed malignant to the throne of these realms. As also, they testify against his Christ-dethroning supremacy, and anti-christian indulgences and toleration, flowing from that wicked fountain; his horrid and cruel massacreing and murdering of the saints and servants of the Most High; with all his other wickedness briefly specified in the foregoing narrative.

Upon the whole, the presbytery declare and testify against all the affronts done unto the Son of God, and open attacks made upon his crown and kingdom; all the different steps of apostasy from a work of reformation, and all the hellish rage and cruelty exercised against the people of God during the foresaid period of persecution, carried on by these two impious brothers.

PART II.

Containing the grounds of the Presbytery's testimony against the constitutions both civil and ecclesiastical at the late Revolution, anno 1689: as also, against the gross Erastianism and tyranny that has attended the administration both of church and state, since that memorable period: with various instances thereof, &c.

After the Lord, for the forementioned space of twenty-eight years, had, because of their manifold sins, sorely plagued this church and nation with the grievous yoke of prelatical tyranny, bloodshed, oppression and fiery persecution, and thereby had covered the daughter of Zion with a cloud in his anger, and cast down from heaven unto the earth the beauty of Israel, and had thrown down in his wrath the strong holds of the daughter of Judah, yea, brought them down even to the ground; he was pleased, in his holy sovereignty, to put a stop to that barbarous cruelty that was exercised upon his people, at the last national Revolution, by the instrumentality of the prince and princess of *Orange*; which is the more remarkable, in that those whom the Lord employed as the rod of his anger, to strike off that monstrous tyrant *James* duke of *York* from the *British* throne, were natural branches sprung up from the same stock: and this at a juncture when not only the church of Christ was in the greatest danger of being totally extirpated, but the whole land in hazard of being again overwhelmed with popish darkness and idolatry. But although a very fit opportunity was then offered the nations for reviving the long buried work of a covenanted reformation both in church and state, and re-establishing all the ordinances of God in purity, according to their scriptural institution: yet, alas! how deeply is it to be lamented, that, instead thereof, the multitude of his tender mercies being forgotten, there was a returning, but not to the Most High; yea, a turning aside like a deceitful bow; so that, in many respects, our national guilt is now increased above what it was in former times: wherefore, as the presbytery desire with the utmost gratitude to acknowledge the divine goodness, in giving a respite from the hot furnace of persecution; so they likewise find themselves, in duty to their princely Master and his people, obliged to testify and declare against foresaid revolution settlement, in a variety of particulars, with the many defections and backslidings flowing therefrom. Likeas they hereby do testify against the constitutions, both civil and ecclesiastic, at the Revolution, *anno* 1689, in those respects, and for these reasons:

1. Because that in the civil constitution, these nations once united together in

a scriptural and covenanted uniformity, unmindful of their former establishment upon a divine footing, wherein king and people were to be of one perfect religion, and the supreme magistrate obliged by solemn oath to maintain and preserve the same inviolable, did call and invite *William* and *Mary*, prince and princess of *Orange*, unto the possession of the royal power in these lands, in a way contrary to the word of God, as *Deut.* xvii, 15: "Thou shalt in any wise set him king over thee whom the Lord thy God shall choose: one from among thy brethren shalt thou set king over thee: thou mayest not set a stranger over thee, which is not thy brother." *2 Sam.* xxiii, 3: "The God of Israel said, the Rock of Israel spake to me, He that ruleth over men, must be just, ruling in the fear of God."

In opposition to these clear precepts, the nations did choose the foresaid persons to sway the civil scepter over them, who were neither brethren by birth, nor religious profession, being educated in a church where Erastianism prevails, as appears from their ascribing such an extensive power to the civil magistrate, as is inconsistent with the intrinsic power of the church. Accordingly, by these principles, said prince of *Orange* did regulate his conduct, in the assumption of his regal authority, consenting to swear two distinct oaths, whereby he obliged himself to preserve and maintain the two distinct and contrary religions (or modes of religions worship), Presbytery and Prelacy, and so betrayed both to God and man his politic, worldly views, and proclaimed himself destitute of that truth and religious fear, which is the essential character of every person who may warrantably be invested with supreme authority over the Israel of God. And as they wanted scriptural, so likewise covenant qualifications, namely, known integrity, approven fidelity, constant affection, and zeal to the cause and true church of God; and therefore could not in a consistency with the covenanted constitution, and fundamental laws of the crown, be set up as king and queen of these covenanted lands.

Again, as during the persecuting period the nations generally were involved in the guilt of perjury and deep apostasy, by the many sinful contradictory tests, oaths and bonds then imposed; so, in a particular manner, those who, by virtue of their birth and dignity, ought to have been the defenders of the nation's privileges, both sacred and civil, on the contrary, as privy councilors to the two impious brothers in their rage against the Lord and his Anointed, and as members of their iniquitous parliaments (where perverting equity and justice, they framed the most heaven-daring and abominable mischiefs into a law, and then with the utmost cruelty prosecuted the same), had many of them brought themselves under the fearful guilt of these atrocious crimes of murder, perjury, tyranny and oppression, and thereby, according to the law both of God and man, not only forfeited their lives, had the same been duly executed; but also divested themselves of all just right and title to act the part of the nations' representatives, in choosing and installing any in the office of supreme civil governor, until at least they had given suitable evidence of their repentance. Yet such were the constituent members of that committee of estates, and first parliament, employed in the Revolution settlement, without so much as making any suitable public acknowledgment of their wickedness in the active hand the generality of them had in the former bloody persecution, as appears from a comparative view of the lists of the members of parliament, and particularly the duke of *York's* last parliament, with act second of the acts and orders of the meeting of estates, *anno* 1689. Yea, by viewing the lists of *James* VII, his privy council, annexed by *Wodrow* to the second volume of his history, it is evident, that a great number of the nobility alone, members of that bloody council, were also members of foresaid convention of estates, the members of which convention (seven bishops excepted) were exactly the same with the members of the first parliament at the Revolution. For this, compare second act of the meeting of estates, with act first, parliament first, of *William* and *Mary*. By all which it is evident, that from princes who had thus removed the bound, and discovered no just remorse for their sins, there was little ground left to expect a happy establishment of religion, in restoring the flock of Christ to the full possession of those valuable privileges and liberties wherewith he had made them free.

The character of the constituent members being considered, the constitution itself, and wherein it is inconsistent with our covenanted establishment, and is therefore hereby testified against, comes next to be considered. Although the declaration of the meeting of estates in this kingdom, containing their claim of right, comprehended much more of their civil liberties, and formal rights of government, than was enjoyed under the former monstrous tyranny, yet by no means sufficiently provided for the legal establishment of our former happy reformed constitution, which necessarily obliged the civil rulers to employ their power to maintain and defend, not only the doctrine, but also the Presbyterian worship, discipline and government, as the only and unalterable form instituted by Christ in his house. Whereas this craves the abolition of prelacy, and the superiority of any office in the church above presbyters in *Scotland*, simply as it hath been a great and insupportable grievance and trouble to this nation, and contrary to the inclinations of the generality of the people ever since the reformation from Popery, without regarding the divine right of Presbytery, and the contrariety of Prelacy to scripture revelation. In agreeableness to which demand, when the first parliament met in *Scotland* immediately after the Revolution, which began the ____ day of *April*, 1689, in *Act* 3d, *Sess.* 1st, entitled *Act abolishing Prelacy*, they abolished Prelacy for the foresaid reason, and further declare, that they will settle by law that church government in this kingdom, which is most agreeable to the inclinations of the people. Accordingly, in the second session of the same parliament, *Act* 5th, *June* 7th, 1690, the parliament establishing the Presbyterian church government and discipline, as it had been ratified and established by the 14th *Act, James* VI, *Parl.* 12th, *anno* 1592, reviving, renewing and confirming the foresaid act of parliament, in the whole heads thereof, except that part of it relating to patronages, afterward to be considered of. Likewise, in the above mentioned act at the Revolution, the thirty-three chapters of the *Westminster* Confession of Faith (exclusive of the catechisms, directory for worship, and form of church government formerly publicly authorized, and Covenants National and Solemn League) were ratified and established by the parliament. And the said Confession being read in their presence, was voted and approven by them, as the public and avowed Confession of this church, without taking any notice of its scriptural authority. And further, in the same session of parliament, by the royal power allenarly, the first meeting of the general assembly of this church, as above established, was appointed to be held at *Edinburgh*, the third *Thursday* of *October* following, the same year, 1690. And by the same civil authority and foresaid act, many of the churches in *Scotland* were declared vacant.

2. The presbytery testify against the ecclesiastical constitution at the Revolution; particularly, in regard, 1st—That the members composing the same were no less, if not much more exceptionable, than those of whom the state consisted; the whole of them one way or other being justly chargeable with unfaithfulness to CHRIST, and his covenanted cause, by sinful and scandalous compliance with the public defections of the former times, or actively countenancing the malignant apostasy of the lands, which will appear evident, by considering, that the Revolution Church consisted of such office-bearers, as had, in contradiction to their most solemn covenant engagements, fallen in with, and approven of the public resolutions. And these public resolutioners, who had betrayed the LORD'S cause, which they had in the most solemn manner sworn to maintain, were, without any public acknowledgement demanded or offered, or adequate censure inflicted (even, after that the LORD had remarkably testified his displeasure against that leading step of defection, by suffering these vipers, which we thus took into our bosom, to sting us almost to death) for this their scandalous defection and perjury, admitted and sustained members of the Revolution Church. Again, the Revolution assembly consisted of such ministers as had shamefully changed their holding of CHRIST, and sinfully submitted, in the exercise of their ministry, to an exotic head, *Charles* II, who had, by virtue of his blasphemous supremacy, and absolute power, taken the power of the keys from Christ's ministers, and afterward returning only one of them (viz.: the key of doctrine) to such as accepted his anti-christian, church-destroying, and Christ-dethroning indulgences, attended with such sinful limitations and restrictions, as were utterly inconsistent with ministerial freedom and faithfulness, declaring the acceptors to be men-pleasers, and so not the servants of Christ (of which above). Of this stamp were the most of them, who, without any public acknowledgment of that horrid affront they had put upon the church's true Head, dared to constitute and act as the supreme judicatory of the church of Christ, *anno* 1690. Again, the foresaid assembly was almost wholly formed of such as had petitioned for, accepted of, and pretended to return a God-mocking letter of thanks for that blasphemous unbounded toleration, which that popish tyrant, the duke of *York* (as is noticed formerly), granted, with a special view to reintroduce abjured popery; and therefore while it extended its protection to every heresy, did exclude the pure preaching of the gospel in the fields; which toleration (according to *Wodrow*) was joyfully embraced by all the Presbyterian ministers in Scotland, the honored Mr. Renwick only excepted, who faithfully protested against the same.

But further, the Revolution assembly did partly consist of such members as, contrary to our solemn covenants, had their consciences dreadfully polluted, by consenting unto, subscribing, and swearing some one or other of the sinful wicked oaths, tests and bonds, tyrannically imposed in the persecuting period, or by persuading others to take them, and declining to give warning of the danger of them, or by approving the warrantableness of giving security to the bloody council, not to exercise their ministry, but according to their pleasure. Moreover, they were all, generally, manifestly guilty of the sin of carrying on and maintaining schism and defection from the covenanted church of CHRIST in *Scotland.* As also (which from the history of these times is evident), the ruling elders in that assembly, being generally noblemen, gentlemen, and burgesses, were mostly such as had an active hand in the tyranny and persecution that preceded, and in one respect or other, were stained with the blood of the martyrs of Jesus. Thus, that assembly was packed up, chiefly, of such blacked compilers, as, one way or other, were deeply involved in the apostasy, bloodshed and cruelty of the preceding period, yet had not broke off their iniquities, by a public confession of these crying sins, before that meeting; nor can it be found, that any adequate censure was inflicted on any of them for the same. Therefore, the presbytery testify against the Revolution church, as consisting mostly of such scandalous schismatical members, as could not, in a consistency with the scriptural rule, and laudable acts of this reformed church, have been admitted to church privileges, far less to bear office in the house of God; until, at least, they had been duly purged from their aggravated scandals, and given evident signs of a real repentance, according to the Word of God, 2 *Chron.* xxx, 3: "For they could not keep the passover at that time, because the priests had not sanctified themselves sufficiently." And *Ezek.* xliv, 10: "And the Levites that are gone away far from me, when Israel went astray, which went astray away from me after their idols, they shall even bear their iniquity;" v. 13: "And they shall not come near unto me, to do the office of a priest unto me, nor to come near to any of my holy things, in the most holy place; but they shall bear their shame, and their abominations which they have committed."

Next, the presbytery declare and testify against the Revolution church, because plainly Erastian, and utterly inconsistent with the covenanted constitution of the reformed church of *Scotland, anno* 1648: the truth of which charge will appear obvious, from considering the act of parliament, on which the civil power settled the constitution of the Revolution church, viz., *Act* 114, *James* VI, *Parl.* 12th; where, *inter alia*, it is expressly declared, "That it shall be lawful to the kirk ministers, every year at least, and oftener, *pro re nata*, as occasion and necessity sall require, to hald and keepe general assemblies, providing that the king's majesty, or his commissioner with them, to be appointed be his highness to be present at ilk general assembly, before the dissolving thereof, nominate and appoynt time and place, quhen and quhair the next general assemblie sall be halden: and in case neither his majesty nor his said commissioner beis present for the time, in that town, quhair the said general assemblie beis halden, then, and in that case, it shall be lesum for the said general assembly be themselves, to nominate and appoint time and place, quhair the next general assembly of the kirk sall be keeped and halden, as they have been in use to do these times by-past." Here, in this act, a manifest invasion and traitorous attack is made upon the headship and supremacy of Christ, as a Son in, and over his own house. He who is God's annotated King in Zion, and sits on the throne of his holiness, is hereby robbed of his crown rights; the intrinsic power, the spiritual liberty and freedom, granted by Christ to his church, is encroached upon. It is a received opinion among all true Presbyterians, that the church hath an intrinsic power to meet in the courts of Christ's house, from the lowest to the highest, by virtue of the power committed to her by the Lord Jesus Christ, without dependence on the civil power. This is agreeable to scripture, *Matth.* xvi, 19, and xviii, 18, 19, where the apostles receive the keys immediately from the hands of Christ their Lord and Master. And as one principal part of that trust Christ has committed to his church, this has been the constant plea of the reforming and re-formed Presbyterian church of *Scotland*. Let us hear what that renowned and faithful minister, and venerable confessor for Christ, the Rev. Mr. John Welsh, says to this particular, in his letter to the Countess of *Wigton* from *Blackness*, 1606, when a prisoner for this same truth. Having asserted the independence of the church, the spiritual kingdom of Christ, upon any earthly monarch, and her freedom to meet and judge of all her affairs; he adds, "These two points, 1st, that Christ is Head of his church; 2d, that she is free in her government from all other jurisdictions, except Christ's. These two points, I say, are the special causes of our imprisonment, being now convicted as traitors for maintaining thereof. We have been ever waiting with joyfulness to give the last testimony of our blood in confirmation thereof, if it should please our God to be so favorable as to honor us with that dignity. Yea, I do affirm, that these two points above written, and all other things that do belong to Christ's crown, scepter and kingdom, are not subject, nor cannot be, to any other authority, but to his own altogether: so that I would be glad to be offered up as a sacrifice for so glorious a truth." So far he. But now this assembly of *treacherous* men, by settling themselves upon such a constitution have openly given up this scriptural truth and Presbyterian principle handed down to us, sealed with the sufferings and dearest blood of the faithful Confessors and Martyrs of Christ, and have consented that it is unlawful for the office-bearers in the Lord's house to exert their proper power in calling and appointing general assemblies, however loudly the necessity of the church may call for them, unless the king authorize their diet of meeting, which he may, or may not do, according to his pleasure.

Again, it is evident, that the revolution church is constituted in the same Erastian manner with the late Prelacy in *Scotland*. For proof of which, observe, that as Prelacy was never ecclesiastically asserted to be of divine authority, neither has Presbytery, by any explicit and formal act of Assembly, at or since the revolution. As the prelates' high ecclesiastical court was called, adjourned and dissolved, in the king's name, so likewise are the assemblies of the Revolution Church. As the Episcopalians owned the king, in the exercise of his Erastian supremacy over them, so the Revolution Church, instead of opposing, did take up her standing under the covert of that anti-christian supremacy, and has never since declined the exercise thereof. And, as the civil power prescribed limits unto, and at pleasure altered, the prelatic church, so this church has accepted of a formula, prescribed by the civil power, requiring that all the ordinances within the same be performed by the ministers thereof, as they were then allowed them, or should thereafter be declared by their authority, as *Act* 23d, *Sess.* 4th, *Parl.* 1st, 1693, expressly bears. By what is said above, it may appear, that this church is Erastian in her constitution.

But it is further to be observed, that the present constitution is no less inconsistent with the scriptural and covenanted constitution of the church of *Scotland*, in regard that the retrograde constitution, to which the church fled back, and on which she was settled at the revolution, was but an infant state of the church, lately after her first reformation from Popery, far inferior to her advanced state betwixt 1638 and 1649 inclusive. It was before the church had shaken off the intolerable yokes of Erastian supremacy and patronages; before she had ecclesiastically asserted, and practically maintained, her spiritual and scriptural claim of right, namely, the divine right of presbytery, and intrinsic power of the church, the two special gems of Christ's crown, as King on his holy hill of Zion; before the explanation of the national covenant, as condemning episcopacy, the five articles of *Perth*, the civil power of churchmen; before the Solemn League and Covenant was entered into; before the *Westminster* Confession of Faith, the Catechisms, larger and shorter, the Directory for worship, Form of Presbyterian church government and ordination of ministers, were composed; and before the acts of church and state, for purging judicatories, ecclesiastical and civil, and armies from persons disaffected to the cause and work of God, were made; and all these valuable pieces of reformation ratified with the full and ample sanction of the supreme civil authority, by the king's majesty and honorable estates of parliament, as parts of the covenanted uniformity in religion, betwixt the churches of Christ in *Scotland, England* and *Ireland*. And therefore, this revolution constitution amounts to a shameful disregarding—yea, disclaiming and burying—much (if not all) of the reformation attained to in that memorable period, and is a virtual homologation and allowance of the iniquitous laws at the restoration, *anno* 1661, condemning our glorious reformation and sacred covenants as rebellion; and is such an aggravated step of defection and apostasy, as too clearly discovers this church to be fixed upon a different footing, and to be called by another name, than the genuine offspring of the true covenanted church of Christ in *Scotland*.

Besides what has been already noticed, respecting the sinfulness both of the members constituent, and the constitutions at the revolution, it is to be further observed, as just matter of lamentation, that, at this period, when such a noble opportunity was offered, no suitable endeavors were made for reviving the covenanted cause and interest of our REDEEMER; no care taken that the city of the Lord should be built upon her own heap, and the palace remain after the manner thereof; but, on the contrary, a religion was then established, not only exceedingly far short of, but in many particulars very inconsistent with, and destructive of, that blessed uniformity in religion, once the glory of these now degenerate isles. The presbytery, therefore, in the next place, do testify against the settlement of religion made at the revolution, and that in these particulars following:

1. Instead of abolishing Prelacy in *England* and *Ireland*, as it had been abjured in the Solemn League and Covenant, and stands condemned by the word of God, and fundamental laws of the nations, conform to the divine law, it was then, with all its popish ceremonies, anew secured, confirmed and established, in both these kingdoms, as the true religion, according to the word of God, to be publicly pro-

fessed by all the people; and the supreme civil magistrate solemnly sworn, at his inauguration, both that he himself shall be of the Episcopal communion, and that he shall maintain inviolably the settlement of the church of *England*, in the kingdoms of *England* and *Ireland*, and territories thereunto belonging. Thus the revolution has ratified the impious overthrow, and ignominious burial, of the covenanted reformation in these two kingdoms, that was made in the persecuting period, and has fixed a legal bar in the way of their reformation, in agreeableness to the sacred oath the three nations brought themselves under to God Almighty.

2. As to the settlement of religion in *Scotland*, the presbytery testify against it: because it was a settlement, which, instead of homologating and reviving the covenanted reformation between 1638 and 1650, in profession and principle, left the same buried under the infamous act rescissory, which did, at one blow, rescind and annul the whole of the reformation, and authority establishing the same, by making a retrograde motion, as far back as 1592, without ever coming one step forward since that time, and herein acted most contrary to the practice of our honored reformers, who always used to begin where former reformations stopped, and after having removed what obstructed the work of reformation, went forward in building and beautifying the house of the Lord.

That this backward settlement at the revolution, was a glaring relinquishment of many of our valuable and happy attainments, in the second and most advanced reformation (as said is), and consequently, an open apostasy and revolt from the covenanted constitution of the church of *Scotland*, is sufficiently evident, from the foresaid act of settlement 1690; where (after having allowed of the *Westminster* confession) they further add, "That they do establish, ratify and confirm, the Presbyterian church government and discipline, ratified and established by the 114th *Act, James* VI, *Parl.* 12th, *anno* 1592." So that this settlement includes nothing more of the covenanted uniformity in these lands, than only the thirty-three articles of the Confession of Faith, wanting the scripture proofs. Again, that the Revolution settlement of religion did not abolish the act rescissory, nor ratify and revive any act, between 1638 and 1650, authorizing and establishing the work of reformation, is clear from the same act: wherein, after abolishing some acts anent the late prelacy in *Scotland*, they declare: "that these acts are abolished, so far allenarly, as the said acts, and others, generally and particularly above mentioned, are contrary or prejudicial to, inconsistent with, or derogatory from, the Protestant religion, or Presbyterian church government, now established." Where observe, that this general clause is restricted to acts and laws, in so far only, as they were contrary to the religion settled in this act; and therefore, as this act includes no part of the covenanted reformation between 1638 and 1649, so this rescissory clause abolishes laws, not as against foresaid reformation, but only in so far as they strike against the revolution settlement, which the act rescissory could not do. Again, in another clause of the same act, it is added: "Therefore, their majesties do hereby revive and ratify, and perpetually confirm, all laws, statutes and acts of parliament, made against Popery and Papists." The only reason that can be given for the revival of laws, not against Prelacy, but Popery, when abolishing Prelacy, is, that the parliament, excluding the covenanted reformation from this settlement of religion, resolved to let the whole of it lie buried under the act rescissory. For as, in reality, there were no laws made expressly against Prelacy before 1592, but against Popery and Papists; so, had they said, laws against prelacy and prelates, they thereby would have revived some of the laws made by the reforming parliaments, between 1640 and 1650; wherein bishops and all other prelates, the civil places and power of kirkmen, &c., are expressly condemned. Again, in the foresaid act, they confirm all the article of the 114th *Act*, 1592, except the part of it anent patronages, which is to be afterward considered. Now, had the revolution parliament regarded the reforming laws to have been revived, and so the act rescissory to be rescinded, by their *Act* 5th, 1690, they would not have left this particular to be again considered of, seeing patronages were entirely abolished by an act of parliament 1649; but, having the ball at their foot, they now acted as would best suit with their political and worldly views. Once more observe, that when the revolution parliament ratified the act 1592, they take no notice of its having been done before, by a preceding parliament in 1649. All which plainly says, that the reforming laws and authority of the parliaments by which they were made, are not regarded as now in force. To conclude this particular, if the settlement of religion, made in 1690, had revived and ratified the authority of our reforming parliaments, and laws made by them; then, as these obliged the king to swear the covenants before his coronation, and all ranks to swear them, and obliged to root out malignancy, sectarianism, &c., and to promote uniformity in doctrine, worship, discipline and government, in the three nations, so the revolution settlement would have obliged all to the practice of the same duties, and that, before ever king, or any under him, could have been admitted to any trust; while all that would not comply therewith, would have been held as enemies, not only to religion, but to their king and country also, as was the case when reformation flourished. But, as the very reverse of this was authorized and practised at the revolution, it convincingly discovers, that the settlement of religion, made in 1690, left the whole of the reformation attained to, ratified and established by solemn oaths and civil laws between 1640 and 1649, buried under that scandalous and wicked act rescissory, framed by that tyrant, *Charles* II, after his restoration. Nor is there to be found, in all the acts, petitions, supplications and addresses, made by the assemblies at or since the revolution, any thing importing a desire to have that blasphemous act rescinded, which stands in full force, to the perpetual infamy and disgrace of the revolution settlement of religion, so much gloried in, by the greatest part, as happily established.

2. The presbytery testify against the Revolution settlement of religion, not only as including avowed apostasy from the covenanted constitution of the reformed church of *Scotland*, and a traitorous giving up of the interests and rights of Christ, our Lord and REDEEMER, in these, and especially in this land; but also, as it is an Erastian settlement, which will appear, by considering 1_st_. The scriptural method then taken, in establishing religion: instead of setting the church foremost in the work of the Lord, and the state coming after, and ratifying by their civil sanction what the church had done; the Revolution parliament inverted this beautiful order, both in abolishing Prelacy, settling Presbytery, and ratifying the Confession

of Faith, as the standard of doctrine to this church; 2_d_, In abolishing Prelacy, as it was not at the desire of the church, but of the estates of *Scotland*, so the parliament did it in an Erastian manner, without consulting the church, or regarding that it had been abolished by the church, *anno* 1638, and by the state, 1640, in confirmation of what the church had done. Thus, *Act* 3d, 1689, 'tis said, "The king and queen's majesties with the estates of parliament, do hereby abolish Prelacy." Again, when establishing presbytery, *Act* 5th, 1690, they act in the same Erastian manner, whereby the order of the house of God was inverted in the matter of government; in regard that the settlement of the government of the church in the first instance, properly belongs to an ecclesiastical judicatory, met and constituted in the name of the Lord Jesus Christ; and it is afterward the duty of the state to give the sanction of their authority to the same. This Erastianism further appears in the parliament's conduct with respect unto the Confession of Faith: see *Act* 5th, *Sess.* 2d, *Parl.* 1st, wherein thus they express themselves: "Likeas they, by these presents, ratify and establish the Confession of Faith, now read in their presence, and voted and approven by them, as the public and avowed confession of this church." Hence it is obvious, that the parliament, by sustaining themselves proper judges of doctrine, encroached upon the intrinsic power of the church: they read, voted, and approved the Confession of Faith, without ever referring to, or regarding the act of the general assembly 1647, or any other act of reforming assemblies, whereby that confession was formerly made ours, or even so much as calling an assembly to vote and approve that confession of new. That the above conduct of the state, without regarding the church in her assemblies, either past or future, is gross Erastianism, and what does not belong, at first instance, to the civil magistrate, but to the church representative, to whom the Lord has committed the management of the affairs of his spiritual kingdom, may appear from these few sacred texts, besides many others, namely, *Numb.* i, 50, 51: "But thou shalt appoint the Levites over the tabernacle of testimony, and over all the vessels thereof, and over all the things that belong to it: they shall bear the tabernacle and all the vessels thereof, and they shall minister unto it, and shall encamp round about the tabernacle; and when the tabernacle setteth forward, the Levites shall take it down, and when the tabernacle is to be pitched, the Levites shall set it up, and the stranger that cometh nigh shall be put to death." See also chapters iii, and iv, throughout; also *Deut.* xxxiii, 8, 10; 1 *Chron.* xv, 2; 2 *Chron.* xix, 11; *Ezra* x, 4. So *David*, when he had felt the anger of the Lord, for not observing his commandments in this particular, says, 1 *Chron.* xv, 12, 13, to the *Levites*, "Sanctify yourselves that ye may bring up the ark of the Lord God of Israel. For because ye did it not at the first, the Lord our God made a breach upon us, for that we sought him not after the due order." Likewise Hezekiah, a reforming king, did not himself, at first instance, set about reforming and purging the house of God; but having called together the priests and Levites, says to them, 2 *Chron.* xxix, 5: "Sanctify yourselves and sanctify the house of the Lord God of your fathers, and carry forth the filthiness out of the holy place;" compared with *ver.* 11; *Mal.* ii, 7; *Matth.* xvi, 19. "I will give unto thee the keys of the kingdom of heaven." And xxviii, 18, 19, 20: "All power is given unto me, go ye therefore and teach all nations, teaching them to observe all things whatsoever I have commanded you." From all which it may safely be inferred, that as the Lord

Jesus Christ, the King and Lawgiver of his church, has committed all the power of church matters, whether respecting the doctrine or government thereof, to church officers, as the first, proper receptacles thereof; so, for civil rulers, at first instance, by their own authority, to make alterations in the government of the church, and to settle and emit a standard of doctrine to the church, is a manifest usurpation of ecclesiastical authority, and tyrannical encroachment upon the ministerial office. It needs only to be added, that this Revolution conduct stands condemned by the Confession of Faith itself, in express terms (as well as in the holy scriptures), *chap.* xxiii, *sect.* 3, "The civil magistrate may not assume to himself the administration of the word or the keys." And also, by the beautiful practice of our reformers, betwixt 1638 and 1649, who observed the scriptural order, the church always going foremost, in all the several pieces of reformation attained to, and then the state coming after, by exerting their authority, in ratification and defense of the church's acts and deeds, in behalf of reformation.

3. The Erastianism of this settlement of religion, appears plain from the act of parliament 1592, noticed above, upon which the Revolution parliament did found it, as in *Act* 5th, *Sess.* 2, 1690, by which the forementioned act 1592, is ratified, revived, renewed and confirmed, in all the heads thereof, patronage excepted. Now, in regard that act 1592 contains an invasion upon the headship of Christ, and intrinsic power of the church, and ascribes an Erastian power to the civil magistrate over the church, making it unlawful for the church to convocate her superior judicatories, but in dependence upon the king for his licence and authority; and in regard the Revolution parliament did revive and renew this clause in foresaid act 1592, as well as other heads thereof, it must needs follow, that this settlement of religion cannot be freed of the charge of Erastianism. Nor is it very strange that statesmen, who had been educated in the principles of Erastianism, should be fond of reviving an act that robbed Christ of his crown rights, and the church of her spiritual liberty; but most surprising, that professed Presbyterian ministers should so greedily embrace and approve of Erastianism, as a valuable and glorious deliverance to the church of Christ! In agreeableness to this Erastian article of the above act the parliament, in their act 1690, indicted and appointed the first general assembly, as a specimen of their Erastian power over their newly constituted church; and it has ever since been the practice of the sovereign, to call, dissolve and adjourn her assemblies at his pleasure, and sometimes to an indefinite time. It is further observable, that the king's commission to his representative in assembly, runs in a style that evidently discovers, that he looks upon the assembly's power and right of constitution as subordinate to him. Thus it begins, "*Seeing by our decree that an assembly is to meet,*" &c. Yet notwithstanding of this, the assembly 1690 (nor any after them, so far as was ever known to the world) did not by any one formal act and statue expressly condemn Erastianism, and explicitly assert the alone headship of Christ, and the intrinsic, independent power of the church, in opposition to these encroachments made thereupon, and therefore may be justly construed consenters thereto. To conclude this particular, of the Erastianism of the present settlement of religion, it may be observed that although the Revolution parliament, from political views, did by *Act* 1st, *Sess.* 2d, rescind the first act of the

second parliament of Charles II. entitled *Act asserting his majesty's supremacy over all persons and in all causes ecclesiastical*; yet, from what is above hinted, it may be inferred, that the Revolution state has still preserved the very soul and substance of that blasphemous supremacy (though possibly they may have transferred it from the person of the king, abstractly considered, and lodged it in the hand of the king and parliament conjunctly, as the more proper subject thereof): for, in the words of Mr. John Burnet, in his testimony against the indulgence, quoted by Mr. Brown in his history of the indulgence, "To settle, enact and emit constitutions, acts and orders, concerning matters, meetings and persons ecclesiastical, according to royal pleasure (and parliamentary is much the same), is the very substance and definition of his majesty's supremacy, as it is explained by his estates of parliament." But the Revolution act of parliament settling religion, is just to settle, enact and emit such constitutions, acts and orders concerning matters, meetings and persons ecclesiastical, according to parliamentary, instead of mere royal pleasure: and therefore the act authorizing the Revolution settlement of religion, is the very substance and definition of a royal parliamentary supremacy. The truth of this will further appear by the sequel.

4. The presbytery testify against the Revolution constitution and settlement of religion, as it is not a religious, but a mere civil and political one; "not built upon the foundation of the apostles and prophets, Jesus Christ himself being the chief corner stone;" but upon the fluctuating inclinations of the people, as the formal foundation thereof. For proof of which, consider the acts of parliament relative to the abolition of Prelacy, and the establishment of presbytery. In consequence of an article of the claim of right made by the estates of Scotland, the *Act* 3d, *Sess.* 1st, *Parl.* 1689, declares, "That whereas the estates of this kingdom, in their claim of right, declared that Prelacy, and the superiority of any office in the church above presbyters, is and hath been a great and insupportable grievance to this nation, and contrary to the inclinations of the generality of the people ever since the reformation, they having been reformed from Popery by presbyters, and therefore to be abolished: our sovereign lord and lady, with advice and consent of the estates of parliament, do hereby abolish Prelacy, and all superiority of any office in the church in this kingdom above presbyters; and do declare, that they, with advice aforesaid, will settle by law that church government in this kingdom, which is most agreeable to the inclinations of the people." Agreeable to this, one of king William's instructions to the parliament 1690, is, "You are to pass an act establishing that church government which is most agreeable to the inclinations of the people." Accordingly we have the *Act* 5th, *Sess.* 2d, 1690, settling Presbyterian church-government in the same form, and on the same footing. And so much king William, who, doubtless, was perfectly acquainted with the true intent and meaning of that act, declares in his letter to the assembly indicted by him that same year. From all which (without noticing the Erastian form of these acts, &c.) it may be observed, that there is somewhat done that is materially good; but then there is nothing importing the contrariety of Prelacy to the scriptures of truth, nor the divine right of Presbyterian church government, so that the whole of this settlement is purely political, done for the pleasure of the good subjects of Scotland: for, 1st, the only

reason why Prelacy is complained of and abolished, is, because it was grievous and contrary to the inclinations of the generality of the people. It is not so much as declared contrary to law, though well known that it was condemned by many of the reforming laws; far less is it declared contrary to the word of God, and reformation principles founded thereupon. Neither is it said to be a grievance to the nations, though it is manifest, by the nations entering into a solemn covenant to extirpate it, that it was an insupportable burden to all the three. And the great reason assigned for the people's dissatisfaction to Prelacy, is *antiquity*, "they having been reformed from Popery by presbyters," as if our reformers had only contended for a church government merely human; whereas they strenuously maintained the divine right of presbytery, and condemned Prelacy as contrary to the word of God. This reason would be equally strong against presbytery, on supposition that prelates had got the start of presbyters in the reformation from Popery. Again, 2d, upon the same, and no better ground, was Presbytery established, namely, because it was more agreeable to the inclinations of the people, and as it was of a more ancient standing in Scotland than Prelacy. Further, that the divine right of presbytery is not acknowledged in this settlement, appears from the express words of the act itself, wherein it is designated, "the only government of Christ's church in the nation;" not the only government of Christ's church laid down in the word of God, received and sworn to by all the three nations, ratified by both civil and ecclesiastical authority. A clear evidence, that church government was regarded as ambulatory only, and what might be altered at pleasure. Hence, while the king was settling presbytery in Scotland, he was also maintaining, as bound by oath, Prelacy in England, &c. And so Presbytery, for peace's sake, as most agreeable to the inclinations of the people, was settled in Scotland as the government of Christ's church there. Thus, there is a settlement of religion, and yet not one line of scripture authority, or reformation principles legible therein: and, as one said (though a strenuous defender of the settlement), "The glory of that church is at a low pass, which hangs upon the nail of legal securities by kings and parliaments, instead of the nail which God has fastened in a sure place;" which, alas! is the case with the church of Scotland at this day. It is true, that the parliament call their settlement, "Agreeable to God's word;" but it is as true, that, from their conduct toward both (abolishing Prelacy, and establishing Presbytery, from these political motives above mentioned), it is abundantly plain, that they believed neither of them to be formally and specifically agreeable to, and founded upon the word of God; but that they regarded all forms of church government as indifferent, and thought themselves at liberty to pick and choose such a particular form as best suited the humors and inclinations of the people, and their own worldly advantage. Accordingly, we find the parliament 1689, appointing a committee to receive all the forms of government that should be brought before them, to examine them for this purpose, and then report their opinions of them to the house.

That the parliament at this time, or the king and parliament conjunctly, acted from the above latitudinarian principle, is further evident, from their establishing and consenting to the establishment of these two different and opposite forms of church government, Presbytery in *Scotland*, and Prelacy in *England* and *Ireland*,

and both of them considered as agreeable to the word of God, and the only government of Christ's church in the several kingdoms, where they were espoused; which, as it is self-contradictory and absurd, so it is impossible they could ever have done this, if they had believed the divine right of either of them. And finally, by this conduct of theirs, the state declared their approbation thereof, and resolution to copy after the 16th *Act, Sess.* 2d *Parl.* 1st of *Charles* II (yet in force), which ascribes an Erastian power to the king, of settling church government as he shall think proper. By all which it appears quite inconsistent with the Revolution settlement, to consider church power in any other light, than as subordinate to the power of the state. And yet with this political and Erastian settlement of religion, the Revolution Church have declared themselves satisfied; they have not condemned Episcopacy, as contrary to the word of God, nor positively asserted the divine right of Presbytery, and disclaimed the claim of right and act of settlement, as their right of constitution; but, on the contrary, approved of both, as appears from the commission's act, 1709, and their address to the parliament, 1711, both homologated by the succeeding assemblies. Whereby they declare, that they have dropped a most material part of the testimony of the reformed church of *Scotland*, and are not faithful to the Lord Jesus Christ, in maintaining the rights of his crown and kingdom. From the whole, it may too justly be concluded concerning the Revolution settlement of religion, what the prophet *Hosea* declares of the calf of *Samaria, Hos.* viii, 6: "For from Israel was it also, the workman made it, therefore it is not God; the calf of *Samaria* shall be broken in pieces." It is not a divine institution founded upon the word of God, and regulated by his revealed law; but a human invention, owing its original in both kingdoms to the inclinations of the people, and governed by laws opposite to the laws of Christ in the word.

Hence we have the idolatrous institutions of Prelacy, established in the one nation, and Erastianism, under the specious pretext of Presbytery, in the other; and both under an exotic head of ecclesiastical government.

From what is said above, respecting the Revolution constitutions, and settlement of religion in the nations, it will appear, that the same are opposite to the word of God, and covenanted constitutions of both church and state, and to the reforming laws, between 1638 and 1650, ratifying and securing the doctrine, worship, discipline, and government of the church, and all divine ordinances, sacred and civil, according to scripture revelation; and therefore cannot be acknowledged as lawful, by any that make the law of God their rule, and desire to go out by the footsteps of the flock of Christ.

The Presbytery proceed now to consider the administration since the late Revolution, as standing in immediate connection with the forementioned constitutions and settlement: only, in the entry, it may be observed, that as the mal-administrations, civil and ecclesiastical, are increased to almost an innumerable multitude, so that it would be next to an impossibility to reckon them all; the Presbytery propose only to observe so many of the most remarkable instances, as shall be sufficient to justify a condemnation of the present course of the nations, although the constitutions could not, be excepted against as sinful. And,

1. The Presbytery declare and testify against the gross Erastianism that has attended the administrations of both church and state, since the Revolution. As the constitutions of both (above noticed) were Erastian and anti-scriptural, so their conduct ever since has been agreeable thereto, tending evidently to discover that, while the state is robbing out Redeemer of his crown, and his church of her liberties, this church, instead of testifying against, gives consent to these impieties.

Particularly, 1, as at the forementioned period, so ever since, the king has continued, by his own authority, to call, dissolve, and adjourn the national assemblies of this church. The first Revolution Assembly was held, by virtue of an Erastian indictment, and by the same power dissolved. The nest was, by royal authority, appointed to be at *Edinburgh* 1691, but by the same power, adjourned to 1692, and then dissolved, without passing any act; and though again indicted to meet 1693, yet was not allowed to sit until *March* 1694, near a year after the parliament had made an humble address to the sovereign for granting that privilege. But it would be endless to attempt an enumeration of all the instances of the exercise of Erastianism in this particular, which is annually renewed. How often, alas! have the assemblies been prorogued, raised, and dissolved, by magistratical authority, and sometimes without nomination of another diet? How frequently also, have they been restricted in their proceedings, and prelimited as to members, and matters to be treated of, and discussed therein; depriving some members of their liberty to sit and act as members, though regularly chosen, merely, because such had not taken the oaths appointed by law? All which exercise of Erastian supremacy natively results from the parliamentary settlement 1690. And when no adequate testimony was ever given by the church against such Erastian usurpations, but they are still crouched under and complied with, it may justly be constructed a tame subjection and woful consent to this supremacy. That this is no forced inference from the continued practice of this church, appears from this (besides other evidences that might be adduced), viz., That as the Revolution parliament, when ratifying the Confession of Faith, entirely left out the act of Assembly 1647, approving and partly explaining the same (wherein these remarkable words are, "It is further declared, that the Assembly understands some parts of the second article of the 31st chapter, only of kirks not settled or constituted in point of government") as being inconsistent with the Erastian impositions of the magistrate. So this church, when they cause intrants into the ministry subscribe the Confession, do not oblige them to subscribe it with this explanatory act (which does by no means admit of a privative power in the magistrate, destructive of the church's intrinsic power), but they only do it as the parliament ratified it.

2. Another instance of Erastianism practiced by both church and state, is, that when the king and parliament did bind down episcopal curates upon congregations, forbidding church judicatories the exercise of discipline upon the impenitent, and enjoining the Assembly to admit such, without any evidence of grief or sorrow for their former apostasy, upon their swearing the oath of allegiance, and subscribing a *formula*, homologating the Revolution settlement, substituted in the room of the covenants; the church approved of this settlement, and protection

granted by the civil powers to such curates all their lifetime in their churches and benefices, who yet were not brought under any obligation to subject themselves to the government and discipline of the church. The truth of this is manifest, from sundry of king *William's* letters to the Assemblies, together with after acts of parliament, relative thereto. In his letter, dated *February* 13th, 1690, to the commission of the Assembly, he says, "Whereas there has been humble application made to us by several ministers, for themselves and others, who lately served under episcopacy; we have thought good to signify our pleasure to you, that you make no distinction of men, otherwise well qualified for the ministry, though they have formerly conformed to the law, introducing Episcopacy, and that ye give them no disturbance or vexation for that cause, or for that head: and it is our pleasure, that, until we give our further directions, you proceed to no more process, or any other business." In another letter, dated *June* 15th, 1691, he says, "We are well pleased with what you write, to unite with such of the clergy, who have served under Episcopacy; and that you are sufficiently instructed by the General Assembly to receive them; from all which, we do expect a speedy and happy success, that there shall be so great a progress made in this union betwixt you, before our return to *Britain,* that we shall then find no cause to continue that stop, which at present we see necessary; and that neither you, nor any commission or church meeting, do meddle in any process or business, that may concern the purging out of the episcopal ministers." And in a letter to the episcopal clergy, he says, "We doubt not of your applying to, and concurring with, your brethren the Presbyterian ministers, in the terms which we have been of pains to adjust for you; the *formula* will be communicated to you by our commissioners," &c. See also the 27th *Act, Parl.* 1695, where it is declared, "That all such as shall duly come in and qualify themselves, shall have and enjoy his majesty's protection, as to their respective kirks and benefices, they always containing themselves within the limits of their pastoral charge, within their said parishes, without offering to exercise any part of government, unless they be first duly assumed by a competent church judicatory; providing, nevertheless, that as the said ministers are left free to apply, or not, to the foresaid church judicatories," &c. To which agree, *Act* 2d, *Parl.* 1700; *Act* 3d, *Parl.* 1702; *Act* 2d, *Parl.* 1703, &c. Behold here the civil magistrate, exercising the supremacy in matters ecclesiastical, in that he both establishes the old *Scots* curates in their respective parishes, upon their former footing, limits them in the exorcise of their function, discharging them from exercising any part of ecclesiastical polity, but upon their uniting with the Presbyterians, on the terms he had adjusted for them. And further, by his authority stops the exercise of church discipline against these curates (though the most of them were notoriously scandalous); nay, even discharges the Assembly from proceeding to any other business, until they received other directions from the throne. Which palpable instance of Erastianism in the state, was not only peaceably submitted to, but heartily acquiesced in by the church: for as they had declared they would censure no prelatical incumbent for his principles anent church government, however much disaffected to a covenanted reformation, and had given frequent discoveries of their readiness to receive into communion the episcopal curates, according to the terms prescribed by the parliament (as appears from the Assembly records); so the Assembly 1694, *Act* 11th, having framed a sham *formula*, for receiving in the curates, containing no such thing as any renunciation of abjured prelacy, the abominable test, and other sinful oaths these creatures had taken, but only an acknowledgment of the Revolution settlement of religion, as established by law, by the foresaid act, appointed their commission to receive all the episcopal clergy who applied, and being qualified according to law, would also subscribe their *formula*, and that without requiring the least show of repentance for their scandalous public sins, and their deep guilt of the effusion of the blood of God's faithful saints and witnesses during the tyranny of the two brothers. These instructions to the commission and other judicatories (as appears by their acts), were successively renewed by the Assembly upward of twenty times, from 1694 to 1716, and were indeed attended with good success, as is evident from their address to the queen, recorded *Act* 10th, 1712; where they declare, as an instance of their moderation, "That since the Revolution, there had been taken in, and continued, hundreds of the episcopal curates upon the easiest terms," viz., such as were by the royal prerogative adjusted to them. Which practice, as it declares this church homologators of Erastianism, so is directly opposite to Presbyterian principles, the discipline and practice of our reformed church of *Scotland*, and to the laws of Christ, the supreme lawgiver, *Ezek.* xliv, 10-15; *2 Cor.* vi, 17, 18, &c.

3. A *third* instance of the Erastianism practiced since the revolution, is, that the king and parliament have taken upon them to prescribe and lay down, by magistratical authority, conditions and qualifications, *sine qua non*, of ministers and preachers. For proof of which, see *Act* 6th, *Sess.* 4th, *Parl.* 1st, 1693, where it is enacted, "That the said oath of allegiance be sworn the same with the foresaid assurance, be subscribed by all preachers and ministers of the gospel whatever—certifying such of the foresaid persons as are, or shall be, in any public office, and shall own and exercise the same without taking the said oath and assurance in manner foresaid,—ministers provided to kirks shall be deprived of their benefices or stipends, and preachers shall be punished with banishment, or otherwise, as the council shall think fit." Also, *Act* 23d, 1693, it is ordained, "That no person be admitted or continued to be a minister, or preach within this church, unless that he have first taken and subscribed the oath of allegiance, and subscribed the oath of assurance in manner appointed. And further statute and ordain, that uniformity of worship be observed by all the said ministers and preachers, as the same are at present performed and allowed therein, or shall hereafter be declared by the authority of the same: and that no minister or preacher be continued and admitted hereafter, unless that he subscribe to observe, and do actually observe, the foresaid uniformity." The Erastianism in these acts seems screwed up yet a little higher, by *Act* 7th, *Sess.* 5th, *Parl.* 1st, 1695; where, after appointing a new day to such ministers as had not formerly obeyed, it is ordained: "With certification that such of the said ministers as shall not come in between and said day, are hereby, and by the force of this present act, *ipso facto*, deprived of their respective kirks and stipends, and the same declared vacant, without any further sentence." The Erastianism in these acts is so manifest at first sight, that it is needless to illustrate the same; only it may be remarked, that, by these acts, the civil magistrate prescribes new ministerial qualifications, viz., the oaths of allegiance and assurance; and these imposed

instead of an oath of allegiance to Zion's King, viz., the oaths of the covenants. As also, that ministers are hereby restricted from advancing reformation, being bound down to observe that uniformity at present allowed, or that shall hereafter be declared by authority of parliament. And further, Erastianism is here advanced to the degree of wresting the keys of government out of the hands of the church altogether—taking to themselves the power of deposing all such ministers as shall not submit to their anti-christian impositions, and of declaring and ascertaining, by their own authority, what mode of worship or government shall take place in the church hereafter. This Erastian appointment of ministerial qualifications, &c., is evidently injurious, both to the headship of Christ in his church, and to the church's intrinsic power. It pertains to the royal prerogative of Christ, to appoint all the qualifications of his officers, which he has done in the Word. And it pertains to the church representative, by applying the laws of Christ in his Word, to declare who are qualified for the ministry, and who are not. But here the civil power, without any regard to church judicatories, by a magisterial authority, judges and determines, the qualifications that gospel ministers must have, otherwise they cannot be acknowledged ministers of this church. At the same time, it must be regretted, that the church, instead of faithfully discovering the sinfulness of foresaid conduct, and testifying against it, as an anti-christian usurpation, have declared their approbation thereof, by taking the above named illimited oaths, according to the parliament's order; and also by the assembly's enjoining their commission to act conform to the parliament's directions respecting ministerial qualifications, in their admission of those that had formerly conformed to Episcopacy, and refusing to admit any into their communion without having these new ministerial qualifications.

4. A fourth piece of Erastianism exercised since the commencement of the revolution settlement, against which the presbytery testify, is, the civil magistrate, by himself and his own authority, without consulting the church, or any but his parliament, privy council, and diocesan bishops, his appointing diets and causes of public fasting and thanksgiving. A number of instances might here be condescended on. So an act of the states, *anno* 1689, for public thanksgiving. An act of parliament 1693, appointing a monthly fast, declares, "That their majesties, with advice and consent of the said estates of parliament, do hereby command and appoint, that a day of solemn fasting and humiliation be religiously and strictly observed, by all persons within this kingdom, both in church and meeting-houses, upon the third *Thursday* of the month of *May*, and, the third *Thursday* of every month thereafter, until intimation of forbearance be made by the lords of their majesties' privy council; and ordains all ministers to read these presents a *Sunday* before each of these fast days, nominated, by authority; and ordains all disobeyers to be fined in a sum not exceeding 100£., and every minister who shall not obey, to be processed before the lords of their majesties' privy council; and requiring sheriffs to make report of the ministers who shall fail of their duty herein, to the privy council." But it is to no purpose to multiply instances of this kind, seeing it has been the common practice of every sovereign since the revolution, to appoint and authorize national diets of fasting, with civil pains annexed. And as the state

has made these encroachments upon the royalties of Christ, so this church, instead of bearing faithful testimony against the same, have finally submitted thereto. In agreeableness to the royal appointment, they observed the monthly fast for the success of the war against *Lewis* XIV (of which above), and in favor of the Pope, which king *William* was bound to prosecute by virtue of a covenant made with the allies at the *Hague, February*, 1691, to be seen in the declaration of war then made against *France*, wherein it is expressly said, "That no peace is to be made with *Lewis* XIV, till he has made reparation to the Holy See for whatsoever he has acted against it, and till he make void all these infamous proceedings (viz., of the parliament of *Paris*) against the holy father, *Innocent* XI." Behold here the acknowledgment of the Pope's supremacy, and his power and dignity, both as a secular and ecclesiastical prince; and in the observation of these fasts, the church did mediately (*tell it not in Gath*—) pray for success to the *man of sin*—a practice utterly repugnant to Protestant, much more to Presbyterian, principles, and which will be a lasting stain upon both church and state. As this church did then submit, so since she has made a resignation and surrender of that part of the church's intrinsic right to the civil power, see *Act* 7th, *Assem.* 1710: "All ministers and members are appointed religiously to observe all fasts and thanksgivings whatever, appointed by the church or supreme magistrate; and the respective judicatories are appointed to take particular notice of the due observation of this, and *Act* 4th, 1722, *Act* 5th, 1725." From which acts it is manifest, that the Revolution Church has not only declared the power and right of authoritative indicting public fasts and thanksgivings for ordinary, even in a constituted settled national church, to belong, at least equally, to the civil magistrate, as to the church; but, by their constant practice, have undeniably given up the power of the same to the civil power altogether—it being fact, that she never, by her own power, appoints a national diet of fasting, but still applies to the king for the nomination thereof. And further, as a confirmation of this surrender, it appears from their public records, that when some members have protested against the observation of such diets, the assembly would neither receive nor record such protest. Now, the sinfulness of this Erastian practice still persisted in, is evident from the Scriptures of truth, where the glorious king of Zion assigns the power of appointing fasts, not to the civil magistrate, but to the spiritual office-bearers in his house. *Jer.* xiii, 18: "Say unto the king and queen, Humble yourselves." Here it is the office of the prophets of the Lord, to enjoin humiliation work upon those that are in civil authority, contrary to the present practice, when kings and queens, usurping the sacred office, by their authority, say to ministers, "Humble yourselves." See also, *Joel* i, 13, 14, and ii, 15, 16, compared with *Numb.* x, 8-10. Here whatever pertains to these solemnities, is entrusted to, and required of, the ministers of the Lord, without the intervention of civil authority. The same is imported in *Matth.* xvi, 19, and xviii, 18; *John* xx, 23—it being manifestly contained in the power of the keys committed, by the church's head, to ecclesiastical officers. Moreover, this Erastianism, flowing from a spiritual supremacy exercised over the church, is peculiarly aggravated by these particulars:

1. That commonly these fasts have been appointed on account of wars, in which the nations were engaged, in conjunction with gross anti-christian idolaters,

who have been most active in their endeavors to root out Protestantism. Now, it cannot but be most provoking to the Majesty of Heaven for professed Presbyterians to observe fasts, the professed design of which, includes success to the interest of the avowed enemies of our glorious REDEEMER. Again, the above practice is aggravated, from this consideration, that these diets of fasting, with civil pains annexed to them, are sent by public proclamation, directed to their sheriffs and other subordinate civil officers, who are authorized to dispatch them to the ministers, and inspect their observation thereof. And while professed ministers of Christ tamely comply with all this, it amounts to no less, than a base subjection of the worship of God, in the solemnity of fasting in a national way, to the arbitrament of the civil powers, when whatever time and causes they appoint, must be observed.

From all which, in the words of the ministers of *Perth* and *Fife*, in their testimony to the truth, &c., 1758, the presbytery testify against the above Erastian conduct, as being, in its own nature, introductory to greater encroachments, and putting into the hands of the civil powers, the modeling of the worship of God, and things most properly ecclesiastical.

5. Another piece of Erastianism, respecting the present administration, which the Presbytery testify against, is the king and parliament their arbitrarily imposing several of their acts and statutes upon ministers and preachers, under ecclesiastical pains and censures; while this Revolution Church, by their silent submission and compliance therewith, have, at least, interpretatively given their consent thereto. Thus, as the oaths of allegiance and assurance were enjoined upon all in ecclesiastical office, under the pain of church censure (of which above), so likewise, *Act* 6th, 1706, ordains, "That no professors and principals, bearing office in any university, be capable, or be admitted to continue in the exercise of their said functions, but such as shall own the civil government, in manner prescribed, or to be prescribed by acts of parliament." In consequence of which, there is an *Act* 1707, an act in the first year of king *George* I, and another in the fifth year of his reign; by all which statutes, ecclesiastical persons are enjoined to take the oath of abjuration, with the other oaths, under pain of having ecclesiastical censures inflicted upon them. And they ordain, "That no person be admitted to trials, or licensed to preach, until they have taken the public oaths, on pain of being disabled." The foresaid act, in the fifth year of *George* I, ordains, "all ministers and preachers to pray in express words for his majesty and the royal family, as in former acts." The king and parliament at their own hand prescribe a set form of prayer for the Church of *Scotland*, and that under Erastian penalties, upon the disobeyers. Again, by an act of 1737, framed for the more effectual bringing to justice the murderers of Captain *Porteous*, it is enacted, "That this act shall be read in every parish church throughout *Scotland*, on the first Lord's day of every month, for one whole year, from the first day of *August*, 1737, by the minister of the parish, in the morning, immediately before the sermon; and, in case such ministers shall neglect to read this act, as is here directed, he shall, for the first offense, be declared incapable of sitting or voting in any church judicatory; and for the second offense, be declared incapable of taking, holding or enjoying any ecclesiastical benefice in that part of

Great Britain called *Scotland*." The Erastianism of this act is very plain, the penalties thereof are ecclesiastical, and infer a kind of deposition; seeing the disobeyers are hereby disabled from exercising and enjoying what is essential to their office. Moreover, the wickedness of this act appears, in that it was appointed to be read on the Sabbath day, and in time of divine service; whereby ministers being constituted the magistrates' heralds to proclaim this act, were obliged to profane the Lord's day, and corrupt his worship, by immixing human inventions therewith, which was directly a framing mischief into a law. Yet, with all these impositions above noticed, this church has generally complied; and thereby declared that they are more studious of pleasing and obeying men, than God, seeing their practice therein infers no less, than a taking instructions in the ministerial function, and matters of divine worship, from another head than Christ.

6. The last piece of Erastian administration in church and state, the presbytery take notice of, and testify against, is that of patronages. When the parliament 1690, had changed the form of patronages, by taking the power of presentations from patrons, and lodging it in the hands of such heritors and elders as were qualified by law, excluding the people from a vote in calling their ministers, this Erastian act, spoiling the people of their just privilege, was immediately embraced by the church, as is evident from their overtures for church discipline, 1696, where they declare that only heritors and elders have a proper right to vote in the nomination of a minister. Also their overtures, 1705 and 1719, do lodge the sole power of nomination of ministers in the hands of the majority of heritors, by giving them a negative over the eldership and congregation. But, as if this had not been a sufficient usurpation of the people's right, purchased to them by the blood of Christ, by an act of parliament, 1712, the above act, 1690, is repealed, and patrons fully restored to all their former anti-christian powers over the heritage of the Lord; which yoke still continues to oppress the people of God. While again, this church, as if more careful to please the court, and court parasites, than Christ and his people, have not only peaceably fallen in with this change, daily practicing it in planting vacant congregations, but, as fond of this child of *Rome*, have further established and confirmed the power of patrons, by the sanction of their authority, as appears from several acts of assembly, thereby declaring their resolutions to have this epidemic evil continued, though it should terminate in the utter ruin of the church. Patronage was always by the Church of *Scotland* since the reformation, accounted an intolerable yoke; and therefore she never ceased contending against it until it was at last utterly abolished by acts both of reforming assemblies and parliaments; and that as one of the inventions of the whore of *Rome*.

As this anti-christian practice was unknown to the church in her primitive and purest times, until gradually introduced with other popish corruptions, so it has not the least vestige of any warrant in the word of truth: nay, is directly opposite thereto, and to the apostolical practice: Acts i, 15-24; chap. vi, 2-7: as also, xiv, 23, and xvi, 9, with other passages therein;—a book, intended to give us the apostolical practice and pattern, in the settlement of the Christian church: and 2 Cor. iii, 19, &c. Wherefore the presbytery testify against this Erastian usurpation, as most sinful in itself, most injurious to the church of Christ, and inconsistent with the great ends of the ministry; and against this church, for not only submitting unto, but even promoting this wickedness; which is evident, from her deposing some of her members, for no other reason but because they could not approve of this pernicious scheme. Witness Mr. *Gallespie*, minister at Carnock, who was deposed May, 1752: and against all violent intruders, who, not entering by the door, can be regarded only as thieves and robbers; John x, 1.

These are a few of the many instances of the Erastian usurpations of the head-ship of Christ, as a Son, in and over his own house, and of the church's intrinsic power assumed by the state, and consented to by this church since the Revolution. [2] And without condescending upon any more, the presbytery concludes this part,

---

[2] Besides the above instances of that unholy, tyrannical, and church-robbing policy, which has been exercised by the supreme civil powers in these nations with reference to religion and the worship of God, all of which existed when the presbytery first published their testimony, there has, of late, a very singular instance of the same kind occurred, in the course of administration, which the presbytery cannot forbear to take notice of, but must embrace the present opportunity to declare their sense of, and testify against; and especial-ly, as it is one that carries a more striking evidence than any of the former, of our public national infidelity and licentiousness, and of our being judicially infatuated in our national counsels, and given up of heaven to proceed from evil to worse, in the course of apostasy from the cause and principles of the reformation. We particularly mean the instance of a late bill or act, which has been agreed upon by both houses of parliament, and which also, June, 1774, was sanctioned with the royal assent, entitled "An act for making more effectual pro-vision for the government of the province of Quebec in North America." By which act, not only is French despotism, or arbitrary power, settled as the form of civil government, but, which is still worse, Popery, the *Religion of Antichrist*, with all its idolatries and blasphemies, has such security and establishment granted it, as to be taken immediately under the legal protection of the supreme civil authority of these nations in that vast and extensive region of *Canada*, lately added to the British dominions in North America—a province so large and fertile, that it is said to be capable of containing, if fully peopled, not less than thirty millions of souls. This infamous and injurious bill, before it passed into a law, was publicly repro-bated and declaimed against by sundry members of both houses. It has been petitioned and remonstrated against by the most respectable civil body corporated in Britain, or its dominions, the city of London; by all the provinces of North America south of Quebec; and even by the inhabitants of the city of Quebec itself. It has been, in the most public manner, in open parliament, declared to be "a most cruel, oppressive, and odious measure—a child of inordinate power," &c. All which are sufficient indications how scandalous, offensive, and obnoxious this act was. There was afterward, in the month of May, 1775, a bill brought into the house of lords, in order to effectuate the repeal of the foresaid disgraceful act, when, in the course of public debate, it was represented by those few members of the house who appeared in the opposition, as "one of the most destructive, most despotic, most nefarious acts that ever passed the house of peers." But all in vain—the repeal could not be effected.

And moreover, let it be further observed here, that the bench of bishops in the house of peers, who assume the anti-christian title of *spiritual lords*, and pretend to claim a seat in parliament for the care of religion, during the whole course of this contest, instead of appearing for the Protestant interest, have, to their lasting infamy, publicly distinguished themselves in opposition to it, by—"Standing forth the avowed supporters of Popery."

The presbytery, therefore, find themselves in duty obliged, in their judicative capacity, principally in behalf of the rights and interests of the great God and of his Son Jesus Christ our Redeemer—that is to say, in behalf of the rights of truth, true religion, and righteousness among men, which he ever owns as his, to add, as they hereby do, their public testimony against this nefandous national deed, so manifestly injurious to all these.

The presbytery do not, as some others, found their testimony against this extravagant act establishing Popery, &c., in Canada, solely or simply on its injuriousness to the private interests of men—their bodily lives, goods, or outward privileges; nor do they declare against and condemn it merely because *that* religion which is sanctioned with this national decree and engagement for its defense is a sanguinary one: "Has deluged our island in blood, and dispersed impiety, persecution, and murder, &c., through the world." (See an address from the general congress to the people of Great Britain.) These are all indeed incontestable proofs that it is not the religion of the divine Jesus, but of antichrist. Nevertheless, the same have been known to be the staple and constant fruits of Prelacy too, which, to the extent of its reach and influence, has as much Christian blood wrapped up in its skirts as Popery, if not more. Nor yet is it merely on account that it is greatly injurious, as indeed it is, and a notorious breach of the public faith to the British Protestant settlers in that province. The presbytery's particular objections against this extraordinary measure are of a different quality. They are briefly such as follow:

1. The *iniquity* of it against God. It is certainly a deed highly provoking and dishonoring to the God of heaven. For (1), it is a giving that public protection and countenance to a *lie*, i.e. to idolatry and false worship (and to anti-christian idolatry, the worst of all other), which is only due to the truth of God. It is a devoting and giving our national power to the preservation of the life of the Romish beast, after the deadly wound given it by the Reformation. And therefore (2), a most wretched prostitution of the ordinance of civil power, sacred by its divine institution, to be *a terror* and restraint *to evil doers, and a praise to them that do well*, Rom. xiii,—to the quite contrary purposes. What right have open idolaters and blasphemers to be protected and supported by any ordinance of God in the public acts of their idolatry? And how awful is it to think (3), that it is a setting ourselves openly to fight against God, in a national engagement to support and defend what God has declared and testified to us in his word, he will have destroyed; and wherein he expressly forbids giving the least countenance to idolatry. And shall we thus harden ourselves against God and prosper? (4), As this last instance of our profane national policy is a still more open discovery of our incorrigibleness in our apostasy, so it is also the most striking of all the former of that Erastianism and spiritual supremacy exercised by the civil powers in these lands over the church and kingdom of Christ. Herein we have an open and avowed justification of that anti-scriptural right and power claimed by them to settle and establish whatever mode of religion they please, or is most agreeable to the inclinations of the people, or which best answers their worldly political purposes, although it should be the religion of Satan in place of that of Christ. This has been the great leading principle all along since the Revolution, but never more openly discovered than in this instance. Upon all which it may appear how sinful and provoking to the divine Majesty this act must be.

2. The *folly and shamefulness* of it as to ourselves. How disgraceful and dishonorable is this public act in favor of Popery, even to the nation itself, and its representatives, who me the authors of it. How palpably inconsistent is it with our national character and profession as Protestant, and with our national establishments, civil and ecclesiastical (both which are professedly built upon reformation from Popery), to come to take that idolatrous religion under our national protection, and become *defenders* of the *anti-christian* faith; nay, were it

with observing upon the whole, that when Henry VIII of England did cast off the authority of the see of Rome, and refused to give that subjection to the pope formerly paid by him and his predecessors; he did, at the same time, assume to himself all that power in his dominions, which the pope formerly claimed; and soon afterward procured to have himself acknowledged and declared, by act of parliament, to be head of the church—head over all persons, and in all causes, civil and ecclesiastical. And which anti-christian supremacy has, ever since, continued an essential part of the English constitution, and inherent right of the crown; so that all the crowned heads there, have ever since been as little popes over that realm: and that all such still appropriate unto themselves that blasphemous anti-christian title of the head of the church, and supreme judge in all causes, is undeniably evident from the known laws and canons of England: and further appears from a declaration made by King George I, June 13th, 1715, where he styles himself *Defender of the faith, and supreme Governor of the church in his dominions*; declaring, that before the clergy can order or settle any differences about the external policy of the church, they must first obtain leave under his broad seal so to do. Which title or authority for man, or angel, to assume, is a downright dethroning and exauctorating of Christ, the only and alone Head and Supreme Governor of his church. From this spiritual anti-christian supremacy, granted by English laws to the king of England, confirmed and established, by virtue of the incorporating union, in British kings, by acts of British parliament, do flow all the forementioned acts im-

competent for the presbytery as a spiritual court, and spiritual watchmen, to view this act in a civil light, they might show at large, that it is a violation of the fundamental national constitutions of the kingdom, and reaches a blow to the credit of the legal security granted to the Protestant religion at home. We need not here mention how contrary this act is to the fundamental laws and constitutions of the kingdom of Scotland, which are now set aside. But it is contrary to, and a manifest violation of the Revolution and British constitution itself; contrary to the Claim of Right, yea, to the oath solemnly sworn by every English and British sovereign upon their accession to the throne, as settled by an act of the English parliament in the first year of William III. By which they are obliged to "profess, and to the utmost of their power maintain, in all their dominions, the laws of God, the true profession of the gospel, and the true reformed religion established by law." But these things the presbytery leave to such whom it may more, properly concern. Let it, however, be observed that the presbytery are not here to be interpreted as approving of the abovesaid oath, as it designedly obliges to the maintenance of the abjured English hierarchy and popish ceremonies, which might better be called *a true reformed lie*, than the true reformed religion. Nevertheless, this being the British coronation oath, it clearly determines that all legal establishments behoove to be Protestant, and that without a violation of said oath, no other religion can be taken under protection of law but what is called Protestant religion only.

The presbytery conclude the whole of this additional remark with observing, That as in the former instances of the exercise of this Erastian power above mentioned, the present church of Scotland never gave evidence of her fidelity to Christ, so far as to testify against them; so their assembly has, in a like supine, senseless manner, conducted themselves with reference to this last and most alarming instance. Notwithstanding all that has been remonstrated against it, and in favor of the reformed religion, they have remained mute and silent, which indeed evidences them not to be truly deserving of the character of *venerable* and *reverend*, which they assume to themselves, but rather that of an association; or, in the words of the weeping prophet, *an assembly of treacherous men*: Jer. ix, 2.

posed upon the Revolution Church of Scotland. And as these acts and laws declare, that the British monarch confines not his spiritual supremacy to the church of England, but it extends it also over the church of Scotland: so this Revolution Church, having never either judicially or practically lifted up the standard of a public, free and faithful testimony, against these sinful usurpations, flowing from the fountain of said supremacy, and clothed with the authority of an anti-christian parliament, where abjured bishops sit constituent members, but, on the contrary, has submitted to every one of them; therefore, this church may justly be constructed, as approvers and maintainers of Erastian supremacy. And hereby, indeed, the revolt of these degenerate lands from their sworn subjection and obedience to the Lord Jesus Christ, as supreme in his own house, is completed, when they have these many years substituted another in his place, and framed supremacy into a standing law, to be the rule, according to which their kings must lord it over the house and heritage of the Living God. Again:

The presbytery testify against the manifold, and almost uninterrupted opposition to the ancient glorious uniformity in religion between the nations, that has appeared in the administrations of both church and state, since the last Revolution. The revolution constitution and settlement of religion, as has been already observed, laid our solemn covenants and work of reformation, sworn to therein, in a grave, and many stones have since been brought and cast upon them: many ways and measures have both church and state taken to make sure the revolution sepulcher of a covenanted work of reformation, and prevent, if possible, its future resurrection: against all which, the presbytery judge themselves bound to lift up their testimony. Particularly,

1. The presbytery testify against the incorporating union of this nation with *England*; and as being an union founded upon an open violation of all the articles of the Solemn League and Covenant, still binding upon the nations; and consequently, destructive of that uniformity in religion, once happily attained to by them: which will at first view appear, by comparing the articles of the union with those of the Solemn League. All associations and confederacies with the enemies of true religion and godliness, are expressly condemned in scripture, and represented as dangerous to the true *Israel* of God: *Isa.* viii, 12; *Jer.* ii, 28; *Psal.* cvi, 35; *Hos.* v, 13, and vii, 8, 11; 2 *Cor.* vi, 14, 15. And if simple confederacies with malignants and enemies to the cause of Christ are condemned, much more is an incorporation with them, which is an embodying of two into one, and, therefore, a straiter conjunction. And taking the definition of malignants, given by the declaration of both kingdoms joined in arms, *anno* 1643, to be just, which says, "such as would not take the covenant, were declared to be public enemies to their religion and country, and that they are to be censured and punished, as professed adversaries and malignants;" it cannot be refused, but that the prelatical party in *England*, now joined with, are such. Further, by this incorporating union, this nation is obliged to support the idolatrous Church of *England*; agreeable whereto, the *Scottish* parliament, in their act of security, relative to the treaty of union, declares, "that the parliament of *England* may provide for the security of the Church of *England*, as they

think expedient." Accordingly, the *English* parliament, before entering upon the treaty of union with *Scotland*, framed an act for securing the Church of *England's* hierarchy and worship, as by law established. Which act, they declare, "Shall be inserted, in express terms, in any act of parliament which shall be made for settling and ratifying any treaty of union, and shall be declared to be an essential fundamental part thereof." Hence, the act of the *English* parliament for the union of the two kingdoms, contains the above act for securing the Church of *England*. Which act being sent down to *Scotland*, stands recorded among the acts of the last *Scottish* parliament. Moreover, the last article of said union contains, that all laws and statutes in either kingdom, so far as they are contrary to, or inconsistent with the terms of these articles, or any of them, shall, from and after the union, cease and become void; which, as in the act of exemplification, was declared to be, by the parliaments of both kingdoms. Thus, this nation, by engrossing the *English* act, establishing Prelacy, and all the superstitious ceremonies, in the act of the union parliament, and by annulling all acts contrary to the united settlement, have sealed, as far as men can do, the gravestones formerly laid upon the covenanted uniformity of the nations. To all which the revolution church, by consenting, and practically approving this unhallowed union, have said Amen; though, at first, some of the members opposed and preached against it, yet afterward changed, and (if some historians may be credited) by the influence of gold, were swayed to an approbation. This church's consent to the union is evident, from their accepting of the act of security, enacted by the *Scots* parliament, as the legal establishment and security of the Church of *Scotland*; and from the assembly 1715, utterly rejecting a proposal to make a representation to the king, that the incorporating union was a grievance to the Church of *Scotland*; though it ought still to be regarded as such, by all the lovers of reformation principles, because it is a disclaiming of our sworn duty, to endeavor the reformation of *England* and *Ireland*. It is a consenting to the legal and unalterable establishment of abjured Prelacy in them, obliges the sovereigns of *Great Britain* to swear to the preservation of the prelatical constitution, and idolatrous ceremonies of the episcopal church, and join in communion therewith; and, therefore, for ever secludes all true Presbyterians from the supreme rule. This union establishes the civil, lordly power of bishops, obliging the Church of *Scotland* to acknowledge them as their lawful magistrates and ministers, to pray for a blessing upon them in the exercise of their civil power, and is therefore a solemn ratification of anti-christian Erastianism. It has formally rescinded, and for ever made void any act or acts, in favor of a covenanted uniformity in religion, that might be supposed to be in force before this union: and therefore, while it stands, it is impossible there can be a revival of that blessed work, which was once the glory of the nations of *Scotland, England* and *Ireland*.

2. The presbytery testify against the sinful practice of imposing oaths upon the subjects, contradictory to presbyterian principles in general, and the oath of the covenants in particular, as the allegiance, and particularly the abjuration; all which oaths, imposed by a *British* parliament, exclude our covenanted uniformity, and homologate the united constitution. But, to prevent mistakes, let it be here observed, that the presbytery do not testify against any of these oaths, out of the re-

motest regard to the spurious pretended right of a popish pretender to the throne and crown of these kingdoms; for they judge and declare, that, by the word of God, and fundamental laws of the nations, he can have no right, title or claim, to be king of these covenanted kingdoms—seeing, by our covenants and laws, establishing the covenanted reformation, which are well founded on the divine law, all Papists, as well as Prelatists, are forever excluded from the throne of these, and especially of this land. So that it is utterly inconsistent with the principles maintained by this presbytery, constituted upon the footing of the covenanted church of *Scotland*, and the oath of God they, with the nations, are under, ever to acknowledge and own the popish pretender, or any of that cursed race, as their king; but they testify against these oaths, because they bind to the acknowledgment of the lawfulness of a prelatic Erastian constitution of civil government, and homologate the incorporating union, in one article whereof, it is declared, that these words, "This realm, and the crown of this realm, &c," mentioned in the oaths, shall be understood of the crown and realm of *Great Britain*, &c.; and that in that sense the said oaths shall be taken and subscribed, and particularly the oath of abjuration, which whosoever takes, swears to maintain Erastian supremacy, Prelacy, and *English* popish ceremonies; and so, at least, by native and necessary consequence, the swearing thereof is an abjuring of our sacred covenants. But that which puts it beyond all dispute, that the oath of abjuration, in the literal sense thereof, obliges to maintain the prelatic constitution of *England*, both in church and state, as by law established, and secured by the union act, is the express words of that act of parliament, by which this oath was imposed, and to which it expressly refers, viz., the act of further limitation, where it is said: "On which said acts (viz., of limitation, and further limitation), the preservation of your majesty's royal person and government, and the maintaining of the church of *England*, as by law established, do, under God, entirely depend. To the intent therefore, that these acts may be forever inviolably preserved, it is hereby enacted, that magistrates and ministers shall take the following oath," namely, of abjuration. The above act, then, declaring that said oath was directly intended for the support and establishment of the prelatic church of *England*, it follows, that this oath is a solemn abjuration of the covenanted reformation, as it is also expressly repugnant to Presbyterian principles. But though the above oath is so manifestly sinful, yet the ministers of this church did neither faithfully warn others of the sin and danger thereof, nor faithfully oppose it when imposed on themselves; but, agreeing that every one should act therein as he thought proper, they who refused it may be reputed *socii criminis* with the generality, who, contrary to their professed principles, did take and subscribe the same, and that (as says the oath) heartily and willingly; whereby they not only engaged to maintain a prelatic government, Prelacy, with all its popish ceremonies, but to maintain *only* a prelatic government, and to oppose all others, even though Presbyterian, in their accession to the throne; and this by virtue of the sinful limitations and conditions, wherewith the oath is clogged. And hereby, these nominal Presbyterians discover that they are not possessed of a zeal for the advancement of the true Presbyterian cause and principles, proportionable to that which the *English* discover for their will worship and superstition.

3. The presbytery testify against a sinful and almost boundless toleration, granted *anno* 1712, a woful fruit of the union; by which toleration act, not only those of the Episcopal communion in *Scotland* have the protection of authority, but a wide door is cast open, and ample pass given to all sects and heretics (popish recusants and antitrinitarians some way excepted, who yet are numerous in the nation), to make whatever attacks they please upon the kingdom and interest of our glorious Redeemer, in order to the advancement of their own and the devil's, and all with impunity. The foresaid act warrants the Episcopal clergy publicly to administer all ordinances, and perform their worship after their own manner, with all the popish canons and ceremonies thereof, and obliges all magistrates to protect and assist them, while it destroys the hedge of church discipline against the scandalous and profane, and is, therefore, a settling and establishing of Prelacy in *Scotland*, giving it a security, little, if anything, inferior to that which the established church has. Again, by a clause in the toleration bill, the security given by former laws to Presbyterian church government and discipline, is undermined and taken away, at least rendered ineffectual, and made the subject of ridicule to the openly profane, by the civil magistrate's withdrawing his concurrence, in as much as it declares the civil pain of excommunication to be taken away, and that none are to be compelled to appear before church judicatories. There is nothing in religion of an indifferent nature; "For whosoever [saith Christ] shall break one of the least of these commandments, and shall teach men so, shall be called least in the kingdom of heaven." It must, then, be the most daring wickedness, and an affronting of the Majesty of Heaven in the highest manner, for an earthly monarch to pretend to enact a toleration of religions, and thereby give a liberty where the divine law has laid a restraint; it implies an exalting of himself, not only to an equality with, but to a state of superiority above, the God of glory. Whatever principles are of divine authority require no toleration from man; it is wickedness to pretend to do it, seeing whatever comes under the necessity of a toleration, properly so called, falls, at the same time, under the notion of a crime. And no less wicked is it for a magistrate to protect, by a promiscuous toleration, all heretics, heresies and errors; yea, it is a manifest breach of trust, and plain perverting the end of his office, seeing he is appointed to be *custos et vindex utriusque tabulae*, intrusted with the concerns of God's glory, as well as the interests of men. Experience has, in every age, taught, that a toleration of all religions is the cut-throat and ruin of all true religion. It is the most effectual method that ever the policy of hell hatched, to banish all true godliness out of the world. But however manifold the evils be that toleration is big with, this church, instead of opposing, seems to have complied therewith, and to be of toleration principles; which is evident, not only from their receiving into communion the *Scots* curates, of which above; but from their joining in communion with Mr. *Whitefield (an English* curate and member of that church, and ring-leader of the Methodists there), when he is in *Scotland*. Again, it is known, that when the *Scots* gentlemen are sent to attend the *British* parliament, or at any time in *England*, they do, many of them, join in communion with the prelatic church—nay, are guilty of taking the sacramental test (that is, taking the sacrament after their superstitious manner, to qualify them for any public post); yet this church receives them into the closest communion, without requiring any satisfaction for these evils; whereby

they act contrary to Christ's example, in purging and keeping his house pure, and contrary to the Scripture; *Rev.* ii, 14, 15, 20.

4. In like manner, the presbytery testify against the tyranny that has frequently appeared in the administration since the revolution, both in church and state. The civil powers have discovered not a little of tyrannical and arbitrary power, in imposing their laws, statutes and injunctions, upon the church, as in the instances of the particulars formerly noticed. But further, it has appeared in their fining and imprisoning persons, because (though endeavoring to live peaceably, as far as possible, with all men) they could not, in conscience, and in a due regard to the covenanted cause, own the lawfulness of their authority, by swearing fidelity to the present constitution. Again, in their dispensing with, and counteracting, the law of God in a variety of instances. Thus, while, without any divine warrant, the crime of theft is capitally punished, yet the grossest adulterers, who are capitally punishable by the divine law, pass with impunity. And frequently reprieves, and sometimes pardons (as in the case of *Porteous*), have been granted to murderers, expressly contrary to the law of God, which declares that "Whosoever sheddeth man's blood, by man shall his blood be shed." Another astonishing and full evidence of the above charge, is in the act repealing the penal statutes against witches, &c., 1735, where it is enacted, "That no prosecution, suit or proceeding, shall be carried on against any person or persons, for witchcraft, sorcery, enchantment or conjuration," &c. This act, in plain terms, flatly contradicts and opposes the law of God, in the very letter thereof. See *Levit.* xx, 6, 27; *Deut.* xviii, 10-12; *Exod.* xxii, 18. Not only has the state, in these and other instances (as the imposing almost intolerable taxations upon the impoverished subjects, for supporting the grandeur of useless and wicked pensioners, and for carrying on wars, often not only sinful in respect of their rise and causes, but in their nature and tendency unprofitable to the nations), been guilty of this evil, but also the Revolution Church has exercised a most tyrannical government. As many of the constituent members of the Revolution Church had shown a persecuting, tyrannizing spirit, against the faithful contenders for the truth, in the matter of the public resolutions, so the same spirit has still continued since the revolution, and frequently exerted itself in a most arbitrary manner, against all who have made any appearance for a covenanted work of reformation. Accordingly, soon after the revolution, this church raised some processes against Mr. *John Hepburn*, minister at *Orr*, under pretense of some irregularities, but in reality, for his making some appearance against their abounding defection, and for a covenanted work of reformation, and continued their prosecution to suspension and deposition; and further, applied to the civil magistrate, to apprehend said Mr. *Hepburn*, who accordingly was imprisoned in *Edinburgh*, and then, because of his preaching to the people out of a window, was carried to *Stirling* castle, and kept close prisoner there for a considerable time, as a book, entitled *Humble Pleadings*, fully discovers. They likewise exercised their tyranny against Messrs. *Gilchrist* in *Dunscore*, and *Taylor* in *Wamphray*, whom they prosecuted, not only to deposition, but even excommunication, for no reason but their bearing testimony against that ensnaring oath of abjuration, and a number of other defections. Again, this church, still fond of suppressing the good old cause

and owners thereof, framed and prosecuted a libel, most unjustly (some even of themselves being judges), against Mr. *John McMillan*, minister in *Balmaghie*, for presenting, in a regular manner, a paper of real and acknowledged grievances; and, because he would not resile from it, but continued to plead for a redress, was at last deposed. As also Mr. *John McNeil*, preacher, for the same reason, had his license taken from him; and, by the authority of the assembly, both of them were prosecuted and censured, not for scandal, insufficiency or negligence, error in doctrine, &c., but only on account of their pleading for the covenanted reformation of the Church of *Scotland*, and maintaining a necessary testimony against the prevailing corruptions and defections of former and present times, as appears from their paper of grievances and joint declinature, printed 1708. Nay, such was their mad zeal against reformation principles, that, by the *Act* 15th of *Assem.* 1715, the commission was not only empowered to censure all the forementioned persons, but also enjoined to apply to the civil magistrate for suppressing and punishing them; and accordingly sundry of them were proclaimed rebels over public market crosses, only for their continued adherence to reformation. And besides other instances, their magisterial and lordly power exercised over the flock of Christ, in the violent intrusion of ministers into vacant churches over the belly of the people, and then excommunicating from sealing ordinances such as cannot in conscience submit to the ministry of these intruders, is a most glaring one; while at the same time, severe censures are inflicted upon such ministers as have the honesty to oppose these anti-christian measures. Loud complaints have likewise been made against their arbitrary and tyrannical conduct, with reference to Mr. *Ebenezer Erskine*, and others with him, designated by the name of the *Associate Presbytery*, because of their remonstrating against, and endeavoring to rectify, some of the forementioned evils in the church; the justness of which grievances and complaints may be instructed from their own writings on that head.

It must not be here omitted to remark, that as this church is justly charged with tyranny in government, so she is equally guilty of partiality in discipline. Though all that discover any measure of faithfulness in the concerns of Christ's glory, are sure to meet with most severe treatment, yet the loose, profane and erroneous, have seldom any church censures put in execution against them. This church never made any suitable inquiry into the sinful compliances, and sad defections of her members and office-bearers, during the persecuting period: and that unfaithfulness in the exercise of church discipline is still copied after. How few, guilty of the most gross scandals, are censured, such as notorious drunkenness, blasphemy, cursing, swearing, sabbath-breaking, uncleanness, especially among the rich, who are capable to give pecuniary mulcts to free them from church censure? (Thus, in conformity to the prelatical and anti-christian example, setting to sale the censures of the church, and dispensing with the laws of Christ for money.) Nay, not only are such overlooked, but many guilty of these gross sins, together with oppression, neglecters of family worship, and the grossly ignorant, are without any public acknowledgement of these sins, admitted to the highest and most solemn ordinances, viz., both sacraments. And this may be thought the less strange, when persons chargeable with most of these sins, are admitted, and continued to be office-bearers in the house of God. Persons, and even teachers maintaining most dreadful blasphemous errors connived at, patronized, or but slightly censured, and still kept in communion, without any open renunciation of these heresies. Play-houses, the seminaries of vice and impiety, erected in the principal cities of the nation, and stage players, commonly among the most abandoned of mankind, escape with impunity. Yea, this pagan entertainment of the stage is countenanced by the members and office-bearers of this church, and that to such a degree, that one of the ministers thereof has commenced author of a most profane play, called *The Tragedy of Douglas*, wherein immorality is promoted, and what is sacred exposed to ridicule. Oh! how astonishing! that a minister in the once famous church of Scotland should be guilty of such abominations, and yet not immediately sentenced to bear the highest of all church censure!

5. The Presbytery testify against this established church, for unfaithfulness of doctrine; which will appear by a few instances: although before the Revolution, the Lord Jesus was openly, as far as human laws could do, divested of his headship and sovereignty in and over his church; although the divine right of presbytery had been publicly and nationally exploded, derided and denied, yet this church has never by any formal act, declared that our Lord Jesus Christ is sole king, the alone supreme head of his church—nor in the same manner declared that the presbyterian form of church government is of divine right, and condemned all other forms as contrary to the word. Such a testimony was the more necessary, when the civil powers have arrogated Christ's power to themselves, and continue to exercise it over his church; and the want of it is an evidence of the church's unsoundness in the doctrine of government, and of Christ's kingly office. This church's error in doctrine further appears from their condemnation of a book entitled *The marrow of modern divinity*, as containing gross antinomian errors; whereby they condemned many great gospel truths as errors, particularly, that believers are altogether set free from the law, as a covenant of works, both from its commanding and condemning power, together with others; whereby they have made way for, and encouraged that legal, moral way of harranguing, exclusive of Christ and his most perfect righteousness (which is so common and frequent in all parts of the land), and opened a door for introducing *Baxterian* principles, which, in consequence hereof, have since very much prevailed. Another evidence of this church's unsoundness and unfaithfulness in doctrine, is their excessive, sinful lenity toward the most gross heretics. Notwithstanding *Arminian* and *Pelagian* heresies, and *Arian* blasphemies, have been publicly taught; and although true godliness, and the effectual working of the Spirit on the souls of men have been publicly exposed as enthusiasm, and many other damnable heresies vented, yet this church has never lifted up the faithful standard of a judicial testimony, in condemnation of these heresies, and in vindication of the precious truths of Christ thereby impugned. And when the ministers and members of this church have been processed before her assemblies, and convicted of maintaining many gross errors, no adequate censure has been inflicted. This particularly appears in the case of Mr. Simpson, professor of divinity in the college of Glasgow, when processed before the judicatories of this church, in the years 1715 and 1716, for several gross errors; such as, "That

regard to our own happiness, in the enjoyment of God, ought to be our chief motive in serving him, and that our glorifying of God is subordinate to it: that Adam was not our federal head;" and other *Arminian, Socinian* and *Pelagian* heresies, all to be found in his answers to Mr. Webster's libel given in against him, and clearly proven: yet was he dismissed with a very gentle admonition. Which sinful lenity encouraged him, not only to persist in the same errors, but also to the venting of *Arian* heresies among his students.

Accordingly, he was again arraigned before the assembly's bar in the years 1727-28-29, when it was found clearly proven that he had denied the necessary existence of our Lord Jesus Christ, and the numerical Oneness of the Three Persons of the Trinity in substance and essence, with other damnable tenets. Yet when these articles, whereby he had attempted to depose the Son of God from his supreme deity, were proven, and when (as one of the members of this church, in his protest against the assembly's sentence, said) the Son of God was, as it were, appearing at the bar of that assembly, craving justice against one who had derogated from his essential glory, and blasphemed his name, at which every knee should bow. Yet such was the corruption and unfaithfulness of this church, that the blasphemer was dismissed without any adequate censure passed upon him, and still continued in the character of a minister and member of this church.

Again, when Mr. Campbell, professor of church history at St. Andrews, was processed before the judicatories of this church, for maintaining a scheme of dangerous and most pernicious principles, which he published to the world, having a manifest tendency to subvert revealed religion, and expose the exercise of serious godliness, under the notion of enthusiasm; to advance self-love, as the leading, principle and motive in all human actions whatever, and to destroy the self-sufficiency of God, making him a debtor to his creatures: yet though these, with a number of God-dishonoring, creature-exalting, and soul-ruining errors, were notorious from his books, and were defended by him; the heretic, instead of being duly censured, was countenanced and carressed: whereby this church has given a most deep wound to some of the most important truths of the Christian religion, and becomes chargeable with the guilt of all the errors maintained by that erroneous professor.

A third instance of this church's unfaithfulness, appears in the case of Mr. Glas, and others, who openly vented, by preaching and printing, independent schemes of church government, with some new improvements; attacked our Confession of faith and Covenants, unhinging all order and government in the church, pulled up the hedge of discipline, to introduce all errors in doctrine, and corruption in worship; and, at last, openly renounced presbytery, name and thing (denying that there is any warrant for national churches under the New Testament), and asserted, that our martyrs, who suffered for adhering to the covenanted reformation, were so far in a delusion, with many other sectarian tenets: for which, the church at first suspended, and then deposed some of them. But afterward, as if this church repented of doing so much in favor of presbytery, they were reponed, to the great danger of the church: for having discovered no remorse for their errors, they immediately employed all their parts to shake presbytery, by setting up independent churches and ordaining several mechanics to be their ministers; and nothing done by the church for putting a stop to these errors, and for reviving and vindicating the precious truths they had impugned.

Likewise, when Mr. Wishart was staged for error vented by him in some of his sermons, with respect to the influence of arguments taken from the awe of future rewards and punishments, and other erroneous notions; he was dismissed without any renunciation of his heterodox principles, and assoilzied by the judicatories of this church: and, as easy absolutions encourage error, so no sooner was he assoilzied, but he had the assurance to recommend erroneous books, such as Doctor Whitchcot's sermons, to his students. It is indeed no small evidence of the unsoundness of this church, when the heads of colleges are suffered, *impune*, to recommend such books for students and probationers to form upon.

Again, when professor Leechman was quarreled with for his deistical sermon on prayer, by the presbytery of *Glasgow*, and afterward carried before the assembly; yet although in all his sermons, he presents God as the object of prayer, merely as our Creator, without any relation to Christ, as Mediator; but recommends to his hearers, as the only acceptable disposition of mind, an assured confidence in the goodness and mercy of their Creator: not only has that Christless sermon been very much extolled, but the author dismissed from the assembly's bar in such a manner, as if thereby he had merited their applause. From all which it sufficiently appears, that this church is unsound and unfaithful, in point of doctrine; especially, if it is considered, that she has been frequently addressed by representations, declaring the necessity of an assertory net, affirming and ascertaining the precious truths injured and impuned, and that publicly, by the above mentioned errors; and that a solemn warning should be emitted, discovering the evil and danger of them: yet that necessary duty has still been contemned and disregarded.

The great truths of God, have, for many years, lain wounded and bleeding in our streets, trampled upon by their open and daring enemies; while this church has entirely forgotten and slighted the divine command, to contend earnestly for the faith once delivered to the saints. And though the *Westminster* Confession of Faith continues to be subscribed by intrants into the ministry (the covenants owned by the Reformed Church of *Scotland*, as a part of her confession, being abstracted from the confession of this present church), yet how little of that system and order of doctrine is now taught? the generality having just as much of Christ, and the doctrines of his cross, in most of their discourses, as is to be found in the writings of *Plato, Epictetus* and *Seneca*, and the rest of the Pagan moralists. So that this church appears orthodox, in little (or no) other sense than the church of *England* is so, viz., by subscribing the thirty-nine articles, which are *Calvinistical* in the doctrinal parts; while yet the *Arminian* system of doctrine is generally received and taught by her clergy. Add to what is above, that this church maintains no suitable testimony against sins of all sorts, in persons of all stations; neither emits faithful warnings anent the snares and dangers of the nation, nor full and free declarations of present duty, as church judicatories, like faithful watchmen did in former times.

But such faithfulness in God's matters is not now, alas! to be expected; seeing this church has made a formal concert, or mutual paction, binding up one another from preaching against, and applying their doctrines to the sins, corruptions and scandals of the times: see *Acts of Assem.* 16th, 17th, *anno* 1712; *Act* 6th, 1713; *Act* 8th, 1714; *Act* 6th, 1715. The Presbytery cannot also here omit observing, and that with deep regret, that although the most damnable principles, which have a direct tendency to deny the being of God, and so to propagate opinionative atheism, to subvert all religion, to extol the power of corrupt nature, and exalt Popery, as the best form of religion, to deny the subjection of the world to the providence of God, to destroy all distinction between virtue and vice, and consequently affirm, that there is no moral evil in the world, and to ridicule Christianity, as destitute of divine authority, have been lately vented by *David Hume*, Esq.; and another designated by the name of *Sopho*: yet this church has passed no suitable censure upon the authors of these impious and blasphemous principles, though they justly deserve the very highest: nor have they done anything to testify their dislike, or put an effectual stop to the spreading of these abominable tenets. The presbytery therefore, as they declare their abhorrence of these, and the other errors formerly mentioned, so testify against the church's notorious unfaithfulness, in suffering these wretches to pass with impunity; and as being, on all these accounts noticed, unsound and corrupt, in the matter of doctrine, &c. It may also be here remarked, as an undoubted evidence of the corruptness of the state, that, although there are civil laws presently in being, which declare the maintaining of antitrinitarian, atheistical principles, to be not only criminal, but capital; yet the civil powers in the nation have not so much regard to God, and the Son of God, as to punish treason openly acted against them.

6. The presbytery testify against both church and state, for their sinful associations with malignants: as declared enemies to the covenanted interest have engrossed the civil power wholly to their hands, since the public resolutions, that a door was opened for their admission; so such is the nature of the laws presently extant and in force, that one cannot be admitted to any office, civil or military, but by swearing away all friendship to a covenanted reformation. And, moreover, all along since the late Revolution, the nations have been the most earnest pursuing after friendship with the grossest idolators; and, in express contradiction to the word of God, have confederated in the closest alliance with God's declared enemies abroad; nay, have exhausted their strength and substance, in maintaining the quarrel of such as have been remarkable for their hatred at, and persecution of the protestant interest. The Revolution Church has also said a confederacy with such as have, on all occasions, shewed a rooted enmity and hatred at reformation principles: which appears from their admitting such (noticed above) to be office-bearers in the church: from their observing fasts, and praying for success to the allied armies, though almost wholly composed of such, and many of them oftentimes gross Popish idolaters: from their going in with, and approving of the sinful incorporating union with *England*: from their acknowledging the civil power of church men as lawful: from their joining in religious communion with Mr. *Whitefield*; and in many other instances. Not to insist further in enumerating par-

ticulars, the Presbytery finally testify against church and state, for their negligence to suppress impiety, vice, and superstitious observance of holy days, &c. The civil powers herein acting directly contrary to the nature and perverting the very ends of the magistrate's office, which is to be *custos et vindex utriusque tabulae*; the minister of God, a revenger, to execute wrath on him that doeth evil. Transgressors of the first table of the law may now sin openly with impunity; and, while the religious observation of the sabbath is not regarded, the superstitious observation of holy-days, even in *Scotland*, is so much authorized, that on some of them the most considerable courts of justice are discharged to sit. Stage-plays, masquerades, balls, assemblies, and promiscuous dancings, the very nurseries of impiety and wickedness, are not only tolerated, but even countenanced by law. And as these, with other evils, are permitted by the civil powers; so this church seems to have lost all zeal against sin. No suitable endeavors are used to prevent the growth of atheism, idolatry and superstition: and though Prelacy, as well as Popery, is growing apace in the lands, and organs publicly used in that superstitious worship; yet no testimony is given against them, but new modes introduced into the worship of God, for carnal ends, as a gradual advance toward that superstition. Yea, so unconcerned about suppressing vice and extravagant vanity, &c, that not only are the forementioned nurseries of sin frequented by ministers' children, but ministers themselves have countenanced them by their presence, to the great scandal of their office, and manifest encouragement of these seminaries of immorality. And notwithstanding that by the late proclamation, the penal laws against vice and profanity seem to be revived (which is in itself so far good), yet this cannot supersede or remove the ground of the Presbytery's testimony against church and state complexly, on the above account, or even against the thing itself, in the manner that it is gone about. For besides that, notwithstanding of all former endeavors of this kind, since the overthrow of our scriptural and covenanted reformation, immorality and wickedness have still increased and overflowed all these banks; partly, because, after all their pretenses, the laws were not vigorously put in execution (and as good, no law nor penalty, as no execution), and partly, because these law-makers, being also themselves the law-breakers, have entrusted the execution to such as are generally ringleaders in a variety of gross immoralities; it is not likely, that ever God will countenance and bless such attempts, whereby (contrary to scripture and all good order) the ecclesiastical power is subjected to the civil, and ministers made the bare inspectors of men's manners, and informers to inferior judges, without having it in their power to oblige such transgressors (if obstinate) to compear before church judicatories, and conform and submit to the laws of Christ's house. Nay, so far will God be from approving such Erastian methods of reformation, that he will certainly visit for this, among all our other iniquities, and in his own due time make a breach upon us, because we sought him not in the due order. Wherefore, and for all these grounds, the Presbytery testify against both church and state, as in their constitutions Erastian and anti-scriptural, including the substitution and acknowledgement of another head and governor over the church than Christ, as may be sufficiently evident from proofs above adduced. And particularly, because the British united constitution is such as involves the whole land, and all ranks therein, in the dreadful guilt of idolatry, communicating with idolators, apostasy, perjury, &c. [3] They declare they can have no communion therewith; but that it is such an association as that God's call to his people, concerning it, is, "Come out from among them. Be ye separate, and touch not the unclean thing, and I will receive you, saith the Lord."

* * * * *

SUPPLEMENT TO PART SECOND.

For as much as a good number of people in the north of *Ireland* have acceded, and submitted themselves to the Presbytery, and one of their number is fixed among them as their proper pastor; the Presbytery intended to have subjoined something by way of appendix to the above Testimony, with relation to the state of religion in that kingdom, especially with regard to the settlement of the presbyterian religion there. But as diocesan Episcopacy is the religion there established by law, against which the Presbytery has declared and testified (as above) as an anti-scriptural, anti-covenanted and merely a human and political settlement (whether considered abstractly or complexly with that in the kingdom of *Scotland*), there needs nothing be further said anent it. And as those called Presbyterians in *Ireland*, are equally enemies to the true covenanted Presbyterian cause with those of the Revolution Church of *Scotland*; so the above testimony equally strikes against them with the other. There seems, however, to be this considerable difference betwixt the Presbyterians in *Scotland* and *Ireland, viz.,* That although the settlements the same as to the matter of it, yet so it is not as to the form or manner of it, the Presbyterians in *Ireland* neither having, nor claiming any other security or foundation for their different mode of religious worship than the royal indulgence, or toleration Act. And therefore, as the Presbytery did and do testify against toleration, and toleration principles, disclaiming such an anti-scriptural shelter; they therein, of consequence, bear witness and testimony against all such as do in these lands (where God has given his people a claim of another kind) professedly dwell under such a shadow. But besides, the Presbytery view them (complexly considered) as unworthy of their regard or notice in these papers, as to engaging in any particular or explicit testimony against them, in as much as they have denuded themselves of almost any pretense to the Presbyterian name, by not only disclaiming and opposing the true Presbyterian cause, but having also fallen from the belief and profession of the most important and fundamental truths of Christianity; thereby plainly discovering themselves to be creatures of quite another species and spirit, than the ministers of Jesus Christ, and friends to the blessed spiritual Bridegroom; deserving rather to be termed a synagogue of *Libertines*, a club of *Socinians, Arians, Pelagians* &c., banded together against Christ, and the doctrines of his cross than a synod of the ministers of the gospel. Therefore, as the presbytery testify and remonstrate against them, their toleration, or indulgence footing, on which they professedly stand, together with their poisonous jumble and medley of errors, commonly called *Newlight*, adopted, and with the greatest warmth and diligence, spread and propagated by most of them, and connived at and tolerated <u>by the rest and all</u> their books or prints written by them, or others of the like spirit

[3] See pages 68, 69, preceding.

with them in defense of these dangerous and damnable tenets so they do hereby judicially warn and exhort all the people under their inspection there, to beware of such men, and such books, however they may varnish over the doctrines they bring, with fine words fair speeches and pretenses, in order to deceive the hearts of the simple; and this, as they would not incur the displeasure of a holy and jealous God, and have their souls defiled and destroyed by these error's. On the contrary to endeavor to have their minds and understandings enlightened with the knowledge of the truths of Christ, and mysteries of his gospel, and their hearts warmed with the love of them; so that being through grace established in the belief of the truth, they may not "be as children tossed to and fro, and carried about with every wind of doctrine, by the sleight of men, and cunning craftiness, whereby they lie in wait to deceive;" *Eph.* iv, 14, 15. "But speaking the truth in love may grow up in all things unto him, which is the Head even Christ;" and striving to refrain and keep themselves from every wicked, offensive and backsliding course, and to live soberly, righteously and godly, blameless and harmless as the sons of God, without rebuke, adorning the gospel of Christ with a conversation becoming the same; so shall they thereby glorify God, and transmit a faithful testimony for the despised truths of Christ to posterity, that so there may be a seed to do service unto him in these lands, and make his name to be remembered through all generations.

PART III.

The principles of some parties, who have made the most specious appearances for the Reformation, considered.—Particular grounds of testimony against that body of ministers and people known by the name of the Secession, wherein their partiality and unfaithfulness in their profession of the covenanted testimony of the Church of Scotland is discovered in various instances,—their loose and immoral doctrine about civil society and government—their corruption in worship, sinful terms of communion, &c., &c.

The Presbytery having in the preceding pages exhibited their testimony against both church and state, as now established in these isles of the sea, and therein discovered the reasons, why they are obliged to disapprove of both, proceed, next, to take notice of some of the parties that have made the most specious appearances for reformation in this land since the Revolution, of which that party commonly known by the name of the *Secession*, are not the least remarkable. It is vast pity, and it is with grief and lamentation, that the Presbytery find themselves, in point of duty, obliged to lift up a testimony against the forementioned party; considering, that they have made a professed appearance under a judicial banner displayed for truth, and a covenanted work of reformation, and have, in reality, showed much zeal in opposing a variety of errors in doctrine, corruption in discipline and government, most prevalent in the national Church of *Scotland*; have contributed to vindicate some of the most important truths and doctrines of the Christian faith, that have been openly impugned in this day of blasphemy, and may have been instrumental in turning many to righteousness, and reviving the exercise of practical godliness among not a few. But as *Paul* withstood *Peter* to the face, and testified against his dissimulation, though both of them apostles of our common Lord and Savior; so it still remains duty to testify against the most godly, and such as may have been very useful to the church in many respects, in so far as they have not showed themselves *earnest contenders for the faith once delivered to the saints*, but have dealt treacherously with God in the concerns of his glory. It is therefore with just regret they proceed to observe, that they are obliged, to testify against this party designated, first, by the title of *The Associate Presbytery* (and then that of *The Associate Synod*)—and that particularly, for their error in doctrine, treachery in covenant, partiality and tyranny in discipline and government. It may at first seem strange, to see a charge of error advanced against those who made the countenancing of error in the judicatories of the established church, one principal ground of their secession therefrom. But by taking a narrower view of the principles and doctrines which they have roundly and plainly asserted, and endeavored to justify in their printed pamphlets anent civil government, the reception and belief of which they zealously inculcate upon their followers, it will appear, that their scheme is so far from tending to promote the declarative glory of God, and the real good of human and religious society, or the church of God, which are the very ends of the divine ordinance of magistracy, that it is not only unscriptural, but anti-scriptural, contrary to the common sentiments of mankind, and introductive of anarchy and confusion in every nation, should it be thoroughly adopted, and therefore ought to be testified against. The sum of their principles anent civil magistracy, may be collected from these few passages, to be found in a print entitled, *Answers by the Associate Presbytery to reasons of dissent, &c.*—*Page* 70. "This divine law, not only endows men in their present state with a natural inclination to civil society and government, but it presents unto them an indispensable necessity of erecting the same into some form, as a moral duty, the obligation and benefit whereof no wickedness in them can lose or forfeit.—*Page* 74. Whatever magistrates any civil state acknowledged, were to be subjected to throughout the same.—*Page* 50. Such a measure of these qualifications (viz., scriptural) and duties cannot be required for the being of the lawful magistrate's office, either as essential to it, or a condition of it *sine qua non*: I. It cannot be required as essential thereunto; for then it would be the same thing with magistracy, which is grossly absurd, and big with absurdities. In the *next* place, it cannot be a condition of it *sine qua non*, or, without which one is not really a magistrate, however far sustained as such by civil society; for then no person could be a magistrate, unless he were so faultlessly. The due measure and performance of scriptural qualifications and duties belong not to the being and validity of the magistrate's office, but to the well-being and usefulness thereof.—*P.* 87. The precepts, already explained, are a rule of duty toward any who are, and while they are acknowledged as magistrates by the civil society. Nothing needs be added for the clearing of this, but the overthrow of a distinction that has been made of those that are acknowledged as magistrates by the civil society, into such as are so by the preceptive will of God, and such as are so by his providential will only; which distinction is altogether groundless and absurd: All providential magistrates are also preceptive, and that equally in the above respect (viz., as to the origin of their office) the office and authority of them all, in itself considered, does equally arise from, and agree unto the preceptive will of God.—*P.* 88. The precepts already explained (*Prov.* xxiv, 21; *Eccl.* x, 4; *Luke* xx, 25; *Rom.* xiii, 1-8; *Tit.* iii, 1; *1 Pet.* ii, 13-18), are a rule of duty equally toward any who are, and while they are acknowledged as magistrates by the civil society; they are, and continue to be a rule of duty in this matter, particularly, to all the Lord's people, in all periods, places, and cases." These few passages, containing the substance of Seceders' principles on the head of civil government, may be reduced to the following particulars: 1. They maintain the people to be the ultimate fountain of magistracy, and that as they have a right to choose whomsoever they please to the exercise of civil government over them; so their inclinations, whether good or bad, constitute a lawful magistrate, without regard had to the divine law. 2. That the law of God in the scriptures of truth, has no concern with the institution of civil government, but only adds its precept in forcing obedience upon the conscience of every individual, under the pain of eternal damnation, to whomsoever the body politic shall invest with the civil dignity; and that, without any regard to the qualifications of person or office. 3. Whomsoever the *primores regni*, or representatives of a nation, do set up, are lawful magistrates, and that not only according to the providential, but according to the preceptive will of God also, in regard that God, the supreme governor, has prescribed no qualifications in his word, as essential to the being of a lawful magistrate, nor told what sort of men they must be, that are invested with that office over his professing people, though it is confessed there are many that are necessary to the well-being and usefulness of that office: and therefore, 4. That no act, or even habitual series of the greatest wickedness and mal-administration can forfeit the person's right to the people's subjection, for conscience sake, considered as individuals, while the majority of a nation continue to recognize and own his authority. The absurdity of this scheme of principles may obviously appear at first view to every unbiassed mind that is blessed with any competent measure of common sense and discretion, and tolerable knowledge of divine revelation. That magistracy is a divine ordinance, flowing originally from Jehovah, the supreme and universal Sovereign of Heaven and earth, as the ultimate fountain thereof, cannot be denied. Neither is it to be doubted, but that the Lord has lodged a power and right in the people, of choosing and setting up those persons that shall exercise civil government over them, and to whom they will submit themselves. But then, while God has lodged this power in the people, of conveying the right of civil authority to their magistrates, he has at the same time given them positive and unalterable laws, according to which they are to proceed, in setting up their magistrates; and, by the sovereign authority of the Great Lawgiver, are they expressly bound to act in agreeableness to these rules, without any variation, and that, under the pain of rebellion against him, who is King of kings, and Lord of lords. The Presbytery, therefore, testify against this scheme of Seceding principles, calculated, in order to inculcate a stupid subjection and obedience to every possessor of regal dignity, at the expense of trampling upon all the laws of God, respecting the institution, constitution, and administration of the divine ordinance of magistracy. Particularly, this opinion is,

1. Contrary to the very nature of magistracy, as described in the scriptures of truth, where we are taught, that all authority to be acknowledged of men, must be of God, and ordained of God. The divine ordination of magistracy is the alone formal reason of subjection thereto, and that which makes it a damnable sin to resist. So the apostle teacheth, *Rom.* xiii, 1, &c.: "There is no power but of God; the powers that be, are ordained of God." Not only is it the current sentiment of orthodox divines upon the place, but the text and context make it undeniably evident, that by *power* here, is understood, not a natural, but a moral power, consisting not only in an ability, but in a right to command. Which power is said to be ordained of God, as importing, not merely the proceeding of the thing from God providentially, but such a being from God, as carries in it his instituting or appointing thereof, by the warrant of his word, law, or precept. So that that power which is to be owned as of God, includes these two particulars, without which, no authority

can be acknowledged as God's ordinance, viz., institution and constitution, so as to possess him, who is God's minister, with a moral power. In the divine institution of magistracy is contained, not only the appointment of it, but the defining the office in its qualifications and form, in a moral sense, prescribing what shall be the end, and what the measure of its authority, and how the supreme power shall rule and be obeyed. Again, the constitution of the power, or the determination of the form, and investiture of the particular person with the government, is of God: hence our Savior, *John* x, 35, in his application of these words in the *Psalms*, "I said, ye are gods," to magistrates, shows how they were gods, "because unto them the word of God came;" that is, by his word and warrant he authorized them; his constitution is passed upon them, who are advanced by men, according to his law in his word. When therefore a nation acts according to divine rule, in the molding of government, and advancing of persons to the exercise of it; there the government and governors may be said to be ordained of God. But that government that is not consonant to the divine institution, and those governors, that are not advanced to the place of supreme rule, in a Christian land, by the people, regulating themselves by the divine law, cannot be said to be the powers ordained of God. It is not merely the conveying the imperial dignity by men unto any particular person, that constitutes the power to be of God; but because, and in so far as this is done by virtue of a warrant from God and in agreeableness to his law that the action has the authority of God upon it.

Hence, if in this matter there is a substantial difference from, or contrariety to the divine rule, then there is nothing but a contradiction to God's ordinance: this must needs be granted, unless it is maintained that God has wholly left the determination of this ordinance to men, absolutely and unlimitedly, giving them an unbounded liberty to act therein, according to their own pleasure, which is most absurd. From the whole, it follows, that more is requisite than the inclinations of any people, to constitute a lawful magistrate, such as can be acknowledged God's ordinance. That power which in its institution and constitution is of God, by his law, can alone challenge subjection, not only for wrath, but for conscience sake.

2. The Presbytery testify against this scheme of principles, as being anti-scriptural, and what, in its tendency, is destructive to the authority of the sacred oracles. *Seceders* maintain, that the people, without regard to scriptural qualifications, have an essential right to choose whom they please to the exercise of civil government, and that whomsoever they choose are lawful magistrates; and thus make the great ordinance of magistracy dependent on the uncertain and corrupt will of man. But that this annarchical system is not of divine authority, but owes its origin to their own invention, appears from the following texts of holy writ, besides others, *Exod.* xviii. 21: "Moreover, thou shalt provide out of all the people, able men, such as fear God, men of truth, hating covetousness; and place such over them to be rulers." This counsel of Jethro, was God's counsel and command to Moses, in the choice of magistrates, supreme and subordinate; and discovers, that people are not left to their own will in this matter. It is God's direction, that the person advanced to rule, must be *a man in whom is the spirit; Numb.* xxvii, 18; which *Deut.*

xxxiv, 9, interprets to be *the spirit of wisdom*, (i.e.) the spirit of government, fitting and capacitating a man to discharge the duties of the magistratical office, to the glory of God and the good of his people; without this, he ought not to be chosen. *Deut.* i, 13: "Take ye wise men and understanding, and known among your tribes, and I will make them rulers over you." Here is a precept, directing the people in their choice: they must not be children nor fools; if so, they are plagues and punishments, instead of scriptural magistrates, who are always a blessing. And they must be men of known integrity and affection to the real welfare of *Israel*, not such as are known to be haters of, and disaffected to the *Israel* of God. Again, the express law of the king, is, that he must be one of the Lord's chosing; *Deut.* xvii. 14, 15: "When thou art come unto the land which the Lord thy God giveth thee, and shalt possess it, and shalt dwell therein, and shalt say, I will set a king over me, like as all the nations about me: thou shalt in anywise set him king over thee, whom the Lord thy God shall choose: one from among thy brethren shalt thou set king over thee, thou mayest not set a stranger over thee, who is not thy brother." Here, though Christians have a right to set a king over them, yet, it is evident, they are not left at liberty to choose whom they please, but are, in the most express and positive terms, limited and circumscribed in their choice to him, whom the Lord their God shall choose: and this divine choice must certainly be understood (in a large sense) of a person of such a character, temper of mind, and qualifications, as God pointed out to them in his law, particularly in the text before cited (for whatever God's word approves of and chooses, that God himself chooses). And in the text before, as the person is further described, both negatively and positively, he must be a brother; which relation is not to be confined to that of kindred or nation, but especially respects religion. He must not be a stranger and enemy to the true religion, but a brother, in respect of a cordial embracing, and sincere profession (so far as men can judge) of the same cause of religion, and so one, of whom it may be expected that he will employ his power and interest to advance the kingdom of Jesus Christ. This precept respects the office, and points at the very deed of constitution, and in the most positive manner, restricts not only the people of the *Jews*, but every nation blessed with the light of divine revelation, in their setting up of civil rulers, pointing forth on whom they may, and on whom they may not confer this honorable office. The same truth is confirmed by 2 *Sam.* xxiii, 2, 3, 4: "The spirit of the Lord spake by me—the God of *Israel* said,—he that ruleth over men must be just, ruling in the fear of God."—So *Job* xxxiv, 17, 18: "Shall even he that hateth right govern?—Is it fit to say to a king, Thou art wicked? and to princes, Ye are ungodly?" In which words, while *Elihu* is charging *Job* with blasphemy, in accusing God of injustice, declaring that if he made God a hater of right and impeached him of injustice, he did, in effect, blasphemously deny his government, universal dominion and sovereignty in the world. It is not only supposed, but strongly asserted and affirmed, that he that hateth right should not govern. Again, 1 *Cor.* vi, 1, 4, 5: "If then ye have judgments of things pertaining to this life, set them to judge—Is it so, that there is not a wise man among you? no, not one that is able to judge between his brethren?" All these texts, which are plain, positive, moral precepts, whereby God hath set boundaries about his own ordinance; that it be not corrupted by men, as they demonstrate what magistrates ought to be, and prove that they cannot be of God's ordaining who have not these qualifications: so they evince, that scriptural qualifications are nothing less necessary and essential to the being of a lawful scriptural magistrate, than the consent of the people; and consequently, do sufficiently overturn this anti-scriptural scheme. *Seceders* indeed grant, that God hath declared his will, concerning the choice of magistrates in the above, and such like precepts; but, from their granting these scriptural qualifications to be only advantageous to those that have them, and necessary to the well-being and usefulness of lawful magistrates, and at the same time denying them to be necessary to the being thereof; it necessarily follows, as the consequence of their sentiments, that they allow civil society a negative over the supreme Lawgiver in this matter; and in so doing, exalt the will and inclination of the creature above the will of the Creator, which is the very definition of sin. Say they in the fore-quoted pamphlet, page 80th, "It is manifest, that the due measure and performance of scriptural qualifications and duties, belong not to the being and validity of the magistrate's office, but to the well-being and usefulness thereof." How easy is it here to turn their own artillery against themselves, and split their argument with a wedge of its own timber? For if, as is granted, scriptural qualifications are essential to the usefulness of the magistrate's office, they must also be necessary to the being thereof, otherwise it is in itself quite useless. And if in itself useless, with respect to the great ends thereof, without the due measure of scriptural qualifications, it cannot then be the ordinance of God, in regard it must not be supposed, that a God of infinite wisdom and goodness, who does nothing in vain, has instituted an ordinance for the good of his people, in subserviency to his glory, which yet, in itself (as to its being and essence), is useless, and of no profit nor advantage to them. And as for their comparison of the magistrate's office to other common and ordinary places and relations among men, the parallel will not hold, no not for illustration, far less for a proof of their doctrine. Nor is there any comparison, unless they can prove, that God in his word has as plainly and positively required men to be so and so qualified, before it is lawful for them to enter into, or for others to put them in such places and relations, as he has done, with regard to magistracy. This is indeed the scope and end of their whole scheme, to derogate from, degrade and lessen the dignity of this great ordinance of magistracy, allowing it no more than what is common to men in general, in other inferior states and ordinary business of life, alleging, "That these qualifications (which they grant God has prescribed in his word) are only advantageous to them that have them;" and that at the hazard of evidently opposing and contradicting the intention of the Spirit of God, in the above texts of scripture, which imply a specialty, and particular appropriation to kings and rulers in their office.

Again, this principle either, as above said, denies magistracy to be God's ordinance instituted in his word; or then says, that he hath instituted ordinances in his revealed will, without prescribing any qualifications as essential to their being, but entirely left the constitution of them to the will of man. But how absurd is this, and derogatory to the glory of God, in all his perfections, who is a God of order, once to imagine, that he hath set any of his ordinances, either as to matter or manner, upon the precarious footing of the pure will of wicked and ungodly men? The smallest acquaintance with divine revelation will readily convince, that he hath not. It may as well, and with the same parity of reason, be refused, that there are any qualifications requisite, as essential to the being and validity of the office of the ministry, but only necessary to its well-being and usefulness; and therefore, is as lawful (in its exercise) in the want of these qualifications, as the ordinance of magistracy is accounted to be. But how contrary is this to scripture, *Tit.* i, 7, 8; 1 *Tim.* iii, 2, 3, 4, 5, 6, 7, &c. Now, comparing these with the above-cited texts, respecting the qualifications of magistrates, it appears, that the qualifications of the magistrate are required in the same express and as strong terms (if not also somewhat more clearly,) as the qualifications of the minister; and seeing a holy God hath made no difference, as to the essentiality of the qualifications pertaining to these distinct ordinances, it is too much presumption for any creature to attempt doing it. Both magistrate and minister are, in their different and distinct spheres, clothed with an equal authority from the law of God,—have subjection and obedience equally, under the same pains, required to them respectively, (as *Deut.* xvii. 9 to 13; 2 *Chron.* xix, 5 to 11; *Heb.* xiii, 17, &c.)—and the qualifications of both, as above, stated and determined with equal peremptoriness, making them no less essential to the being and validity of the one than the other. And this being the case, it is not easy to understand how *Seceders* will reconcile their principles anent civil government, with their principle and practice, in separating from an established church or ministry, whose constitution they acknowledge to be good; and who being presbyterially ordained, are also still countenanced by the body of the people. Sure, had they dealt fairly, honestly and impartially in the matters of God, they would have acted in this case agreeably to their declared principle, page 79th of their pamphlet, viz.: "The passages holding forth these qualifications and duties of magistrates, do not by the remotest hint imply, that, if in any wise they be deficient in, or make defection from the same, their authority and commands, even in matters lawful, must not be subjected unto and obeyed," &c. Certainly, according to this, all the deficiencies, defections, and mal-administrations in the church, could never have been a warrantable ground (which yet they make the only ground) of their separation from her. "But on the contrary," they should still have continued in communion with her, and subjection to her in matters lawful, in a way of testifying "against the same, and essaying their reformation, by all means that were habile for them." *Seceders* must either grant, that such was their duty, and so of themselves condemn their separation as unwarrantable; or else deny, that the qualifications of the magistrate and minister are required in the same express terms in scripture; that both are clothed with an equal (though distinct) authority; and that subjection and obedience are under the same pains enjoined to both, and consequently say, that it is less dangerous to cast off, contemn and disregard the authority of a church, than that of the state; while yet (according to their scheme) civil authority is entirely resolved into, and depends purely upon the changeable will of civil society. But, it is presumed, they will allow, that ecclesiastical authority is derived, and flows from, and depends entirely upon the Lord Jesus Christ alone, the glorious Judge, Lawgiver, and King of his church; so that (according to them) this being of a far more noble extract and original, it must be of far more dangerous consequence, to contemn and cast off it, than the other.

Again, as this doctrine gives unto men a negative over the Holy One of Israel, it also opens a wide door for introducing and enforcing the cause of deism, already too prevalent: for, if all who are set up by civil society, however wicked, and void of the qualifications God has required, while they are acknowledged and submitted to by their constituents, must be equally regarded as God's ordinance, with those who have those qualifications; then it will follow, that the corrupt will of wicked men legitimates the magistrate's office and authority, not only without, but in contradiction to the preceptive will of God; and what is this (*absit blasphemia*), but to exalt man above God, in giving unto the universal Sovereign and Supreme Lawgiver, only a consultative power in the constitution of magistracy, while it ascribes unto man an absolute and definitive power, whereby they have power to receive or reject the law of God (at least respecting magistracy) at pleasure, and their deed of constitution be equally valid, when opposite, as when agreeable unto, and founded upon his righteous law. And sure, by the same reason, that man may take a liberty to dispense with the authority of God, in one point of his commanding will; he may also in another, until at last every part of it is rejected. It is but a contempt of the same authority, and he that offends in one point, is guilty of all. Such are the absurdities that this their scheme leads to, though it is hoped the authors do not intend so. It may here be only necessary further to observe, that among the other desperate shifts *Seceders* are driven to in defense of their favorite notion, they say, that scriptural qualifications cannot be essential to God's ordinance of magistracy, or necessarily required as a condition of it *sine qua non*; for then it would be the same thing with magistracy; nor can these qualifications be the condition (*sine qua non*, or), without which one could not be a magistrate; for then it would be necessary, that every one were possessed of them faultlessly, before he could be owned as a lawful magistrate; either of which they allege would be grossly absurd. But this plausible and fair-set argument of theirs, if it prove any thing, will prove more than it is supposed they themselves will grant, and consequently proves nothing at all. For the same gross absurdity may, with equal reason, be inferred from a maintaining, that a due measure and performance of scripture qualifications and duties are essential to any other of God's ordinances, and so that these are the ordinance itself. For instance, they might as well reason (as some have justly observed already), that scriptural qualifications are not essential to a lawful gospel minister, for then it would be the same thing with the ministry, itself; nor can it be a condition, without which one is not really a minister, unless he were so faultlessly. And thus they have at once stripped, not only all of the race of *Adam*, that ever exercised that office, but themselves also, of any real mission, as ministers, unless they have assumed the Pope's infallibility, and are advanced to the *Moravian* perfection. So, although the scripture declares it essential to the true church, that she hold the head, yet by their childish reasoning, this would infer a conclusion big with absurdities, even that this qualification of a true church, is the church itself. And, in like manner, it can no longer be admitted, that faith in Christ, and holiness, are essential to the being of a true Christian; for that would be to make faith the same thing with a Christian, and would infer, that as in heaven only holiness is in perfection, so there alone Christians are to be found. Upon the whole, as the Lord has given an indispensable law, respecting the constitution of kings, showing what conditions and qualifications are required of them; it undeniably follows, as an established truth, that Christianized nations must invest none with that office, but in a way agreeable to that law, and those alone according to scripture, are magistrates of God's institution, who are in some measure possessed of these qualifications. It is therefore an anti-scriptural tenet, that nothing is requisite to constitute a lawful magistrate, but the inclinations and choice of the civil society.

3. The Presbytery testify against this system of principles, because it has a direct tendency to destroy the just and necessary distinction that ought to be maintained between the perceptive and providential will of God, and necessarily jumbles and confounds these together, in such a manner, as a man is left at an utter uncertainty to know when he is accepted and approven of God in his conduct, and when not. That this is the scope of their principles, is confessed, p. 87, of their book of principles: "Nothing needs be added [say they] for the clearing of this, but the overthrow of a distinction that has been made of those who are acknowledged as magistrates by civil society, into such as are so by the preceptive will of God, and such are so by his providential will only; which distinction is altogether groundless and absurd. It will not be refused, that all such preceptive magistrates are also providential. But, moreover, all such providential magistrates are also preceptive. The office and authority of them all, in itself considered, does equally arise from, and agrees to the preceptive will of God." A doctrine most shocking in itself! How strange! that Christians, from any consideration, will obstinately maintain a favorite opinion, which is confessedly built upon, and cannot be established but at the expense of blending and confounding the preceptive and providential will of God, while the distinction thereof is clearly and inviolably established in the word of God! Although divine providence, which is an unsearchable depth, does many times, and, in many cases, serve as a commentary to open up the hidden mysteries of scripture revelation; yet, where the law of God in the scriptures of truth is silent, there providence regulates not, is neither institutive, nor declarative of God's will to be done by us; and where the said divine law does ordain or deliver a rule to us in any case, there providence gives no relaxation, allowance or countermand to the contrary. (See *Gee* on magistracy, in his excellent discourse on providence.) That an overthrow of this necessary distinction, for the sake of the above dangerous scheme, cannot be admitted of, in a consistency with a due regard to the authority of revealed religion, and that therefore the right and lawfulness of magistracy is not founded upon the providential will of God, though they are countenanced and supported by the majority of a nation, will partly appear from the following considerations:

1. If there is no distinction to be made between the preceptive and providential will of God, then is providence equally in all respects the rule of duty, as much as the precept is, and so man should be left at an utter uncertainty, what is duty, in regard of the opposition that is many times between providential dispensations and the precept. Nay, then it is impossible that man can be guilty of sin, in transgressing the divine will, because God infallibly brings to pass, by his holy and

over-ruling providence, whatever he has decreed by his eternal purpose. *Rom.* ix, 17. And thus the Jews, in murdering the Son of God, should be acquitted from the charge of guilt, and could not be said to transgress the divine will.

2. If no distinction is to be made between the preceptive and providential will of God, but providence is declarative of the precept, then is providence a complete rule without the written word. And this at once supersedes the necessity of divine revelation, and derogates from the sufficiency and perfection of the scriptures of truth. The written word is affirmed to be *perfect*: *Psal.* xix, 7. Sinners are reproved for doing that which the word gave no command for, *Jer.* vii, 31, and xix, 5; and challenged for following the promising appearances: *Isa.* xxx. 1, 2, 3, 11. It is therefore daring presumption to set up providence for a rule in opposition to the written law of God. Hence it must be concluded, either that the preceptive will of God in the scriptures is imperfect, or the laws therein repealable by providence; or then that providence cannot be the rule of human actions.

3. If the distinction between the preceptive and providential will of God is to be overthrown, then providence must be expressive of God's approbative ordination, equally as his revealed will is. For, without this (viz. the divine approbation), there can be no lawful title to what is possessed. But this is what providence of itself cannot do; it cannot without the precept discover either God's allowance or disallowance. If then this distinction is denied, and the providential will of God asserted to be declarative of his preceptive, and so of his approbative will; it remains to be manifested, where and how it has been appointed of God for such an end, an end that is by the Spirit of God denied unto it: *Eccl.* ix, 1, 2, 4. If this distinction is to be overthrown, then either the providential will of God, without any regard to the precept, in every case, and in every sort of tenure, gives a just and lawful right and title; or God has declared in his word that it shall be so in the matter of civil government only, viz. that whosoever gains the ascendancy in the inclinations of the people, by whatever sinful methods this is obtained, it matters not, and so is by the hand of providence raised up above all his rivals to the regal dignity, he is the lawful magistrate, God's ordinance according to his precept. The first cannot be said; it were impious to suppose it; for that would justify all robberies and violences, and legitimate every fraud; not the latter, for where is it to be found in all the book of divine revelation, that God hath made such a law touching magistracy? But how big with absurdities, to say, that a holy God has given to man a plain and positive law to be his governing rule in every particular that concerns him, this of magistracy only excepted. In this great ordinance he hath wholly left him to be guided, or rather misled and bewildered by his own corrupt inclinations: but the contrary of this has been in part discovered, and may further. 5. If, in order to establish their anti-government scheme, the foresaid distinction is to be destroyed, and all such as are providential powers, and acknowledged by man, are also preceptive, and therefore to be submitted to for conscience sake, then are the kingdoms of men necessarily obliged to own and submit unto the dominion of the devil. The devil not only claims to himself the possession of the power of all the kingdoms of this world, but it is certain that of the most of them he still retains an

actual predominancy, hence styled the god of this world. Now, it cannot be refused, but that the power he exercises is providential (or a power of permission); and it is most certain, that it is with the consent and good will of all the children of men, while in a natural state. But are men therefore obliged to acknowledge his authority, or submit to that providential power he maintains over them? If every providential power is also preceptive, the answer must be given in the affirmative. The like may be said of the Pope of *Rome*, the devil's captain-general, to display his hellish banner against the King of kings, and Lord of lords, with respect to those nations where he is acknowledged in his diabolical pretensions. It can be to no purpose for *Seceders* to allege that the Pope claims a power unlawful in itself, and therefore cannot be owned, in regard the person whom they make a pretended acknowledgment of, as their lawful sovereign, is by the act of his constitution invested with a similar power, a power both civil and ecclesiastical, and declared to be head of the church, as well as the state. Nothing, therefore, remains for them, but either to acknowledge this clear distinction between the providential and preceptive will of God, or then profess the lawfulness of both the above mentioned powers. 6. If the foresaid distinction is too big with absurdities to be received, and if the authority of all providential magistrates does equally arise from, and agree unto the precept, then it would be no sin to resist the powers ordained of God, provided that providence proves auspicious and favorable to the rebel, and advances him to the throne, with the good will of his fellow rebellious subjects, by expelling the lawful sovereign; at least such resistance could not be determined to be sinful, until once the event declared, whether providence would countenance the treasonable attempt or not. Thus what the apostle declares a damnable sin, *Rom.* xiii, 2, must be justified and made the foundation of subsequent duty, if patronized by a multitude. This they evidently maintain, as appears from their declaration of principles, page 82, where, pretending to obviate some difficulties anent their principles, arising from the people of God's disowning anti-scriptural magistrates: "The whole nature of any simple revolt [say they] lies in breaking off immediately from the civil body, by withdrawing from, or withdrawing part of their territories; and then it necessarily follows at the same time, that these revolters break off from the head of the civil body, without ever denying his authority over the members who still cleave unto the same." This, in connection with their grand foundation principle, and the scope of their discourse at the above citation, discovers that they grant, that if the whole civil society should reject the authority they had set up (however agreeable it should have been to the preceptive will of God, and should again set up another, though never so opposite thereto), their doing so would be lawful; but it is not lawful for a few to disown any authority (however wicked and anti-scriptural), unless they can at the same time withdraw from, or withdraw part of his territories. Nothing can be more absurd than to say, that a people are bound by the laws of God to give subjection for conscience sake, and yet at the same time are at liberty to cast off and reject the same authority at pleasure. If the magistrate be lawful, it is utterly unlawful to reject him; an attempt to divest him of his office, power and authority, though carried on by the *primores regni*, is rebellion against God. It is most ridiculous to allege, that a people considered as a body politic, are not under the same obligation to their rightful sovereign, as when they are considered as individuals, but may lawfully reject him, and set up another, if they please; so that he who one day is God's minister, next day hath no title to that office, but if he claim it, must be treated as a traitor, whereby all security that can possibly be given to the most lawful magistrate, is at once destroyed. Thus, if the Chevalier had succeeded in his late attempt, had gained the favor of the *primores regni*, and thereby mounted the *British* throne; *Seceders* must then, of necessity, either have quit their present principles, or then have subjected to his yoke for conscience sake, under the pain of eternal damnation. His being a professed Papist, and enslaved vassal of *Rome*, could not have warranted them to leave their place of subjection to him while owned by the civil society, and so they must have treated the present powers as usurpers and enemies to government, though they now flatter them with the pretensions of an ill-grounded loyalty. Again, how absurd and self contradictory to grant, that a minor part may not only revolt, but also withdraw part of a prince's territories; and yet that the same party may not, when residing in the nation, refuse to acknowledge the lawfulness of an anti-scriptural power. This is to say, that people are no longer obliged to submit to authority, than they are in capacity to withdraw from, or withdraw part of their prince's territories from him, and so to justify their rebellion, by that which can only be a terrible aggravation of their sin. These, with a number of other absurdities, natively flow from a denial of the distinction between the providential and preceptive will of God, making the title of the lawful magistrate depend solely upon the will of the people. Nothing is more evident than this, that if the inclinations of the people, exclusive of all other qualifications, constitute a lawful magistrate, then (though he rules ever so agreeable to God's preceptive will), so soon as this body (though in a most unjust and tyrannical manner) casts him off, he that moment for ever loses all title and claim to the office, and can no longer be regarded as a lawful magistrate. A principle that in its nature and tendency is introductive of all anarchy and confusion, and with the greatest propriety deserves the encomium of the *anti-government scheme.*

7. This anarchical system of principles, which destroys the above just and necessary distinction, is directly in opposition to the laudable and almost universal practice of all nations, in ordaining and enacting certain fundamental laws, constitutions and provisos, whereby the throne is fenced, the way to it limited, and the property thereof predisposed. The Scripture sufficiently discovers those restrictions and rules, which God himself has prescribed and laid down, for directing and determining of his people's procedure about the erection of magistrates. And profane history abounds in discovering certain fundamental laws and conditions to take place, almost in every nation, without conforming to which, none can be admitted to that dignity over them. But to what purpose are any such laws and constitutions, if this vague principle is once admitted, which cancels and disannuls all such provisos and acts? Why should *Moses* have been so solicitous about his successor in the government of *Israel, Numb.* xxvii, 15-17, if God had ordained the inclinations of the people alone should determine? Or to what purpose did *Israel*, after the death of *Joshua*, ask of God, who should be their leader, if their own inclinations alone were sufficient to determine it? If God has declared, that

the corrupt will of the people is the alone basis of civil power, then, not only are all state constitutions and fundamental laws useless, because, on every vacancy of the throne, they not only must all give place to the superior obligation, the incontrollable law, of the uncertain inclinations of the body politic, but they are in their nature unlawful; their proper use in every nation being to prevent all invasion upon the government by unqualified persons, and to illegitimate it, if at any time done. So that, if the consent of civil society is the only essential condition of government which God has authorized, not only are all scriptural conditions and qualifications useless and unlawful, but also all human securities, either from intruders or for lawful governors, are unlawful, in regard the very design of them all is to oppose this grand foundation principle, the jure-divinity of which *Seceders* have found out, and do confidently maintain. And thus, by the seceding scheme, is condemned, not only the practice of almost all other nations, determining by law, some indispensable qualifications that their rulers must have; but particularly the practice of these once reformed lands, when reformation had the sanction, not only of ecclesiastic, but also of civil, authority, is hereby condemned. Scripture and covenant qualifications were then made essential to the being of a lawful magistrate, by the fundamental laws and constitutions of the nations; so that however the inclinations of the people might run (as it soon appeared they were turned in opposition to these), yet, by these laws, and in a consistency with that constitution, none could be admitted to the place or places of civil authority, but such as professed, and outwardly practiced, according to reformation principles. See *Act* 15th, *Sess.* 2d, *Parl.* 1649. And how happy we had been, if we had constantly acted in conformity to these agreeable laws, experience, both former and latter, will bear witness. How much better had it been for us to have walked in God's statutes, and executed his judgments, than by our abhorrence of them, and apostasy from them, to provoke him to give us statutes that are not good, and judgments whereby we cannot live (*Ezek.* xx, 25), or have any comfortable enjoyment and possession of the blessings and privileges of his everlasting gospel, as it is with us at this day. And yet, this is what *Seceders* would have us caressing, embracing and (with them) blessing God for, under the notion of a present good; and so bless God for permitting his enemies (in anger against an ungrateful and guilty people) to overturn his work and interest, and establish themselves upon the ruins thereof; to bless him for making our own iniquities to correct us, and our backslidings to reprove us, until we know what an evil and bitter thing it is to depart from the LORD GOD of our fathers; to bless him (for what is matter of lamentation) that the adversaries of *Zion* are the chief, and her enemies prosper, *Lam.* i, 5: and all this abstractly, under the notion, of good, which comes very near the borders of blasphemy.

But, moreover, the civil settlement at the revolution is also condemned by this principle of theirs; not because of its opposition to a covenanted reformation, but in regard it includes some essential qualifications required in the supreme civil ruler. The nations are, by that deed of constitution, bound up in their election of a magistrate; and all Papists, such as marry with Papists, or do not publicly profess the Protestant religion, are declared incapable of the throne. So that we see the present law makes some other qualifications, besides the consent of the body politic, essential to the constitution of a lawful sovereign in *Britain*. From all which it is plain, that this principle of *Seceders* is neither a reformation nor a revolution principle; let then the impartial world judge whence it came.

Seceders, in consequence of their contradictory and self-inconsistent system of principles, declare they cannot swear allegiance to a lawful government. They maintain the present to be lawful, yet (in Dec. of their principles, *page* 55th) they say, "The question is not whether it be lawful for us to swear the present allegiance to the civil government, which the Presbytery acknowledge they cannot do, seeing there are no oaths to the government in being, but what exclude the oath of our covenants, and homologate the united constitution." But seeing they acknowledge that every constitution of government, that comprehends the will and consent of civil society, were it as wicked and diabolical as can be imagined, is lawful—yea, as lawful as any that is most consonant to the preceptive will of God, having all the essentials of his ordinance; and seeing, because of the will and consent of the people, they own the present to be lawful, it is most surprising why they cannot swear allegiance to it; their reasons cannot, in a consistency with their principle, be sustained as valid. That the present oaths of allegiance and the oath of the covenants are inconsistent, is readily granted; but seeing the oaths of allegiance bind to nothing more than what they confess they are bound to for conscience sake, namely, to own the lawfulness of the government, and to maintain it according to the constitution thereof (which is a duty owed by subjects to every lawful sovereign); and seeing that whatever is in the oaths of allegiance contrary to the covenants, does not flow from them, abstractly considered, but from the constitution to which they bind (which constitution is sanctified by the people's acknowledgement of it). If, therefore, the covenants forbid a duty, to which they are bound for conscience sake, their authority in that ought not to be regarded.

But certainly *Seceders*, who have found it duty to alter and model the covenants, according to the circumstances of the times they live in, might have found it easy work to reconcile the oath of the covenants with allegiance to a lawful government. The other part of their reason is no less ridiculous and self-contradictory, viz., "They cannot swear allegiance to the present government, because it homologates the united constitution." But is not this constitution according to the will, and by consent of, the body politic? and is it not ordained by the providential will of God? therefore, according to them, has all the essentials of a lawful constitution, which claims their protection, under pain of damnation. How great the paradox! they cannot swear allegiance, because they would bind them to acknowledge and defend a lawful constitution. Is not active obedience, is not professed subjection for conscience sake, an homologation of the constitution? Certainly they are, and that not in word only, but in deed and in truth. And what is the allegiance, but a promise to persevere in what they do daily, and what they hold as their indispensable duty to do? To grant the one, then, and refuse the other, is, in effect, to homologate or acknowledge the constitution, and not to acknowledge it, at the same time, which is a glaring absurdity.

But here, they would have people attend to their chimerical distinction between the king's civil and ecclesiastical authority. They have made a successless attempt (in order to establish their antigovernment scheme) for the overthrow of a distinction, which Heaven has irreversibly fixed, between the preceptive and providential will of God; and, for the same purpose, they will impose this distinction on the generation—a mere shift and artifice, which has no foundation nor subsistence any where else, but in their imagination, and serves for no purpose but to cheat their own and others' consciences, and betray the cause of God. It is plain, that as a power, both civil and ecclesiastical, belongs to the essence and constitution of an English diocesan bishop, so the same is declared to belong now to the essence and constitution of an English king, who is the head and chief prelate among them all; and it is their manner to call themselves his bishops (not Christ's), as having their power, both ecclesiastical and civil, immediately from him, as the fountain of all power within his dominions So that there is no room for this distinction of *Seceders* here, unless they are such expert logicians, as to distinguish a thing from that which is essential to it, and so from itself; but this is a destruction, not a distinction. *Seceders* indeed presume and depend very much upon their abilities of this kind; for they can distinguish between the magistrate's office and its essential qualifications, which God has inseparably joined together in his word. They can distinctly pray for the head, author, authorizer and prime supporter, of abjured Prelacy and Prelates, that God would bless him in his government, and yet not pray for the Prelates themselves. They can pray very fervently and distinctly for the British and Irish parliaments, and yet not at all pray for the bishops, necessary and essential members there. And what is all this but to pray for a nonentity, a mere creature of their own mind? They have neither king nor parliament in their abstracted and imaginary sense, but do clearly distinguish themselves out of both. We might refer them to that famous and faithful embassador, and renowned martyr for the cause and testimony of Jesus, Mr. *Donald Cargill*, in his last speech and testimony, and let him determine the controversy (in this particular) between us. They will not be so bold as to say, that this honorable witness died with a lie in his right hand. His words are these: "As to the cause of my suffering, the main is, not acknowledging the present authority as it is now established. This is the magistracy I have rejected, that was invested with Christ's power; and seeing that power taken from Christ, which is his glory, and made the essential of the crown, I thought it was as if I had seen one wearing my husband's clothes, after he had killed him. And seeing it is made the essential of the crown, there is no distinction we can make, that can free the conscience of the acknowledger from being a partaker of this sacrilegious robbing of God. And it is but to cheat our conscience, to acknowledge the civil power, for it is not the civil power only, that is made the essential of the crown. And seeing they are so express, we must be plain; for otherwise, it is to deny our testimony, and consent to his robbery." From these words it is evident, *first*, that Mr. Cargill was no *Seceder*, or of their mind, in this particular; and *second*, that, at the time, there were some who did cheat and impose upon their own consciences, by distinguishing (where there was no room for distinction) between the king's civil and ecclesiastical authority—which distinction was condemned and testified against by all who were truly faithful to Christ and their own consciences, and tender of his honor and glory, by their unanimous rejection of that anti-christian and unlawful power; and that when they had much more rea-son and temptation to fly to such a subterfuge for their safety, than *Seceders* now have. And, *third*, from these words it is also clear, that Mr. *Cargill* and that poor, distressed and persecuted people that adhered to him, rejected and disclaimed the then authority, not so much because of their tyranny and mal-administrations, as on account of the unlawfulness and wickedness of the constitution itself (which was the prime original and spring of all the wickedness in the administration), namely, because the king arrogantly and sacrilegiously assumed to himself that power, which was the sole and glorious prerogative of Jesus Christ. And as to the difference that *Seceders* make between that and the present time (since the revolu-tion), it is certain, that whatever greater degree of absolute supremacy was then assumed by *Charles* II, it does not vary the kind of that claimed, or rather conferred on and exercised, by the supreme powers, since the revolution (for *majus et minus non variant speciem*), nor acquit them of the guilt of robbing the Son of God, Jesus Christ, of his incommunicable prerogative and supremacy in and over his church, as the only king and head thereof. Nor will the difference of times, while the con-stitution remains the same, while God remains the same, and truth and duty re-main the same, nor yet any distinction that can be made, free the conscience of the acknowledger, more now than then, from being a partaker (art and part) with the civil power, in this sacrilegious robbery. *Psal.* l, 18: "When thou sawest a thief, then thou consentedst with him," &c.

But passing this: seeing the above mentioned reasons, which *Seceders* allege why they cannot swear allegiance to the present government, which they assert is lawful and scriptural, cannot be sustained, some others must be sought for them: and they may be either, because they judge allegiance itself unlawful; or rather, because then they would be bound by oath to continue faithful to this government in all changes that can happen. Whereas now, they are free, and equally ready, in a full consistency with their principles, to profess their subjection to another, were it even a popish pretender. For according, to them, an infidel or papist may have a just and lawful authority over us, notwithstanding all, both the reformation and revolution laws, to the contrary. If, therefore, the legislature would, in the oaths of allegiance, insert this limitation, viz. so long as the body politic is pleased to acknowledge the supreme magistrate, they would find it easier to come over their other pretended and inconsistent difficulties. For the truth is, they cannot, in a consistency with their anti-government scheme, and with safe consciences, swear to any government, but with such limitation, in regard they cannot be sure, but he that is now owned by civil society may be rejected, and another set up, who must be acknowledged. So they would be brought into an inextricable dilemma; either they must own them both to be God's ordinance, which is absurd; or then be perjured, by rejecting him to whom they had sworn; or then incur damnation, by refusing obedience to him, who is set up by the body politic. Such is the labyrinth of confusion and contradiction this anarchical system leads into; a system that cancels all constitutions by God and men anent civil government.

8. This anti-government Seceding principle, destructive of said distinction be-

tween the providential and preceptive will of God, is both contrary to, and confuted by many approven scriptural examples; in which the Spirit of God testifies, that the actual possession of the throne, under the favor of providence, and by the consent of a majority of a nation, may be in one, while the moral power and right of government is in another. The word of God acknowledges *David* the rightful sovereign over all *Israel*, for the space of forty years (1 Kings, ii, 11; 1 Chron. xxix, 26, 27); seven of these he is said to have reigned in *Hebron*, and thirty-three in *Jerusalem*. During the first seven years of his reign at *Hebron*, there is a positive confinement of his actual rule to the tribe of *Judah* only; 2 Sam. v, 5. And at the same time, *Ishbosheth* is said to be made king over all *Israel*, and to have reigned two years. In agreeableness to Seceding principles, there is no reconciling these different texts. According to their scheme *David* can with no propriety be said to have reigned forty years over all *Israel*, seeing seven of the years were elapsed before he was actually acknowledged by all *Israel*, before providence put him in the actual possession of all that extensive power. There is another known example, applicable to the present purpose, in the instance of *David*, during the rebellion of his unnatural son *Absalom*. According to the sacred story, 2 Sam. chap, xv, xvi, xvii, xviii, xix, it appears, that he was wholly ejected, both out of the hearts and territories of *Israel*, and not only the throne, but the will and consent of the people given up to *Absalom*. But was *David* therefore divested of his right and title? Though it is most contrary to scripture to suppose it; yet, according to *Seceders*, seeing *Absalom* was king, by possession of the throne, and had not only the power providentially put into his hand, but had it also by the consent of the people; it necessarily follows that *Absalom*, being a providential magistrate, his office and authority did equally arise from, and agree to the preceptive will of God, and subjection and obedience, for conscience sake, was equally due to him, as to *David*, by the *Israelitish* tribes. And so it was a damnable sin in *David* to fight against him, as it could be no less than a resisting the ordinance of God. The same may be said with respect to that other revolt, by the instigation, and under the conduct of *Sheba*; 2 Sam. chap. xx. But although, according to *Seceders*, he must also have been their lawful magistrate, the Spirit of God discovers the reverse, still acknowledging the right of government in all these changes to be in *David*. Another example is in the case of *Solomon*, who was ordained or designed by God expressly for the kingdom of *Israel*. *Adonijah* had obtained the ascendancy, both in respect of actual possession, and the inclinations and consent of the majority of the nation; the consent was general; 1 Kings, i, 5, 7, 9, 11, 18, 25, and ii, 15. He had all to plead for himself, which *Seceders* make essential to the constitution of a lawful king. He had got to the throne by providence, and had full admission and possession, by the inclinations of the people. If then there is no distinction to be made of those who are acknowledged by civil society, into such as are so by the preceptive will of God, and such as are so by his providential will only—then *Solomon* had no right nor title to the crown; and the enterprise of *David* and *Nathan*, &c., of setting him on the throne, was utterly unlawful. Both they and *Solomon* ought to have acquiesced in the duty of subjection to *Adonijah*, as being the ordinance of God. But this would have been opposite to the express direction of the Lord, appointing the kingdom to *Solomon*, "It was his from the Lord," as *Adonijah* himself confessed. To the same purpose might be adduced, the instance of *Joash*, the son of *Akaziah*, who was king *de jure*, even when *Athaliah* had not only the countenance of providence, but the consent of the people, in the possession of the kingdom; 2 Chron. xxii, 10, 12. Again, the practice of nations, in owning those for their lawful sovereigns, who, by providence, were put from the actual exercise of their rule and authority, contributes to confute this absurd notion. Thus, the people of *Israel*, who had risen up for *Absalom*, do even, when *David* was out of the land, own him for their king. So, during the *Babylonish* captivity, there are several persons noted as princes of *Judah*, whom the people owned, as having the right of government over them. With a variety of other instances, all discovering, in opposition to their anarchical system, that it is not by the dispensations of providence, that the right and title of the lawful magistrate is to be determined. Moreover, as the Associate Presbytery have so barefacedly belied the scriptures of truth, as to assert that there cannot be so much as an instance found in all the history of the Old Testament, of any civil members refusing, either by word or deed, an acknowledgment of, or subjection unto the authority of any magistrate actually in office, by the will of the civil body: besides what have been already adduced, take these few following examples of many. After that *Saul*, by his disobedience to the commandment of the Lord, had forfeited his title to the kingdom, he was no more honored as king, by *Samuel*, the prophet; but, on the contrary, he openly testified to his face, that the Lord had rejected him from being king; 1 Sam. xv, 26-35. Though he mourned over him as one rejected, yet he no more acknowledged him as clothed with the authority as a lawful king; nay, the Lord having rejected him, reproves his prophet for mourning for him, 1 Sam. xvi, 1. From which, and the command he received to anoint *David* in his stead, and that even while the civil society did acknowledge, and was subject unto *Saul*, it appears, that the throne of *Israel* was then regarded, both by the Lord and his prophet, as vacant, until *David* was annointed; from which time, in the eye of the divine law, he was the rightful king, and ought, in consequence of the public intimation made by the prophet of *Saul's* rejection, to have been acknowledged as the Lord's Anointed by the whole kingdom of *Israel*. In agreeableness whereto, the scripture informs, that not only *David* in expectation of the Lord's promise, resisted *Saul* as an unjust usurper, but many among the tribes of *Israel*, whom the Spirit of God honorably mentions, rejected the government of *Saul*, and joined themselves to him that was really anointed of the Lord; 1 Chron. xii, 1-23. Now, if the Lord did command, under pain of damnation, to give loyal obedience to all in the place of supreme authority, however wicked, while acknowledged by the body politic, he would not reject such, nor command to set up others in their room, nor approve of those who disowned and resisted them. But all this is done in this instance, which of itself, is sufficient to overthrow their scheme. Another instance is in 2 Chron. xi, 13, 16, where the authority of *Jeroboam* is rejected and cast off, even when acknowledged and submitted to by the nation of *Israel*, by the priests and *Levites*, and after them, by all such as did set their hearts to seek the Lord God of *Israel*, through all the ten tribes; and this, because of his abominable wickedness. Whereby it appears a commendable duty to refuse the lawfulness of the authority of wicked occupants, though acknowledged by the majority of a nation. A similar example there is in the reign of *Baasha*, who could not by all his vigilance prevent many from casting off his government; 2 Chron. xv, 9. Again, there is an express example of *Elisha's* disowning the king of *Israel*, even when the civil society owned him; 2 Kings, iii, 14, 15. He did not regulate his conduct by providence, and the will of the people, but, in opposition to both, refused him that honor that is due to all that are really kings. To these may be added that notable example of *Libnah*, a city of the priests, who could not but have knowledge by the law of their God what was their duty; 2 Chron. xxi, 10. Here is an instance of a people's casting off allegiance to a king, properly because of his apostasy and intolerable wickedness, whereby they bore testimony against him, and discovered what was the duty of the whole nation, on account of his apostasy from the Lord. Their so doing was a most positive, actual and express condemnation, both of *Jehoram* for his wickedness, and of the people for concurring, joining with him, and strengthening his hands in it (even as *Noah* by his faith and obedience is said to have condemned the antediluvian world; Heb. ix, 7.) And this their conduct and testimony the Spirit of God justifies, and records to their honor. These few of many that might be adduced, declare the impudence, as well as fallacy and imposture of *Seceders* in this matter, and also justify the principles which they maliciously nick-name the anti-government scheme; and that for no other reason, but because it establishes the ordinance of magistracy among a people favored by God with divine revelation, upon his preceptive will, in opposition to their anarchical notions of setting it wholly upon the tottering basis of the corrupt will of man. And, to conclude this particular, how ridiculously absurd is it in them to insinuate, that, in the examples above, or others to be found in sacred history, those persons did, notwithstanding their own practice in rejecting the authority of wicked rulers, still view it as the duty of the rest of the nation, to acknowledge them? This is pure jargon and nonsense, contrary both to reason and religion. By what law could the opposite practices of those that disowned, and those that still continued to own the authority of unlawful rulers, be justified? It could not by the divine law, which never condemns that as sin in one, which it approves as duty in others in the same circumstances. Seeing therefore these, in the instances above, are justified, the practice of those who continued to acknowledge the lawfulness of these wicked rulers, must be regarded as condemned, both by the divine law, and also by the practices of the above persons, which do all jointly concur in witnessing, that they viewed it the duty of all the rest of the nation, to have done as they did. And from the whole, it appears a commendable duty for the Lord's people to disown the right and lawfulness of rulers set up in contradiction to the divine law.

9. The iniquity of attempting to destroy the necessary distinction between the providential and preceptive will of God in the matter of magistracy, appears from God's express disallowance of some whom providence had actually exalted to the supreme command over a people; *Ezek.* xxi, 27: "I will overturn, &c." Although this may have an ultimate respect to Christ, yet it has also a reference to the rightful governors of *Judah*, when disposessed of their right by the providential will of God. And here the Lord threatens the execution of his judgments upon the unjust possessor. See also *Amos* vi, 13; *Hab.* ii, 5, 6; *Nah.* iii, 4, 5; and *Matth.* xxvi, 52. By all which it appears, that the supreme lawgiver states a real difference between those

who are only exalted by the providential will of GOD, and not authorized by his preceptive will; and therefore it is impossible that the office and authority of them both can equally arise from, and agree to the precept. Again, in *Hos.* viii, 4, "They have set up kings, but not by me; they have made princes, and I knew it not," is this distinction showed, as with the brightness of a sun-beam, so that he that runs may read it. The LORD by his prophet here charges this people with horrid apostasy, in changing both the ordinances of the magistracy and the ministry, particularly, although the LORD commanded, if they would set up kings, they should set up none but whom he chose; *Deut.* xvii, 15. Yet they had no regard to his law. This charge seems to have respect to the civil constitution among the ten tribes after their revolt from the house of David; not simply charging their revolt on them, but that after their secession, they did not consult GOD, nor act according to his precept, in their setting up of kings. As nothing can happen in the world, but by the course of providence; and as all things are known unto GOD, in respect of his omniscience, the text cannot respect either of these. The true import of the charge then is, they have set up kings, but not according to the law and preceptive will of GOD; and therefore he neither did nor would approve either them or their kings. Hence the prophet charges this as one cause of their national destruction. Here then it is undeniably evident that GOD himself establishes that distinction pleaded for; and it is therefore most wicked to assert, as *Seceders* do, that it is altogether groundless and absurd. Again, this text discovers, that all kings that are set up and acknowledged by civil society, are not agreeable to the preceptive will of GOD, or, as such, approven by him, as they have falsely asserted: for here the LORD declares, that *Israel* had set up kings that were not agreeable to his precept: and the charge respects their authority, the very deed of constitution. To say then, that all providential magistrates are also preceptive, is directly to give the GOD of truth the lie. Moreover, this plainly intimates, that all such providential magistrates as are not set up in agreeableness to the precept; are disallowed and condemned by GOD, and therefore GOD commands to put away the carcasses of such kings, as, because of the blind consent of civil society, were little better than adored by the people, *Ezek.* xliii, 9, "that he might dwell in the midst of them forever;" and therefore he declares it the sin, and so the cause of the people's ruin, as in the above text: and also in *Hos.* v, 11, "*Ephraim* is oppressed;" because he willingly walked after the commandment, deliberately and implicitly followed every wicked ruler set up by civil society. It is but a perverting and abusing the above text, to plead that it is only a condemnation of *Israel*, for not consulting the LORD in making choice of their kings, but no condemnation of them for setting them up, and acknowledging them, in contradiction to the LORD'S choice, as plainly laid before them in his preceptive will. And it is very contradictory, to acknowledge it a sin, not to consult God, and yet to assert that it is a matter of indifference as to the validity of their office, whether his counsel be followed or not, which it must be, if, as their principle bears, the being of the magistrate's office and authority is equally good and valid, when contrary, as when agreeable to the commanding will of God. But if, as is granted, it be a sin not to consult God in the choice of magistrates, it must needs be a great aggravation thereof, after consulting him, to reject and contemn his counsel, and openly contradict his positive command, by constituting kings in opposition to his declared will, which is evidently the sin charged upon *Israel*, and the reason why he disclaims all such; and therefore, according to that known and approven rule, that wherever any sin is forbidden and condemned in scripture, there the contrary duty is commanded and commended; it follows, that the setting up of rulers, in opposition to the express command of God, being here condemned, the contrary duty is commended, namely, a disowning of all such rulers; for, if it be a sin to set up rulers, and not by God, it must also be a sin to acknowledge them when so set up, in regard it is a continuing in, and approving of the sin of that wicked erection; although such an acknowledgment may indeed be agreeable to their principle, which gives to the creature a prerogative above the Creator. From the whole it may already appear, what reason the Presbytery have for testifying against *Seceders*, for maintaining such a corrupt doctrine; a doctrine, which they very justly acknowledge (p. 87) cannot be established, but by the overthrow of this distinction between the providential and preceptive will of God; a distinction, that as they shall never be able to overturn by all their impotent and impious attacks: so it will to all ages stand as a strong bulwark, inviolably defending the truth here contended for by the Presbytery.

4. The Presbytery testify against this anti-government principle of the *Secession*, as being contradictory to, and inconsistent with the reformation principles, and covenanted obligations, whereby these nations, in agreeableness to the law of God, bound themselves to maintain all the ordinances of God in their purity, according to their original institution in the scriptures of truth. The Seceding scheme (as has been noticed formerly) is, that whomsoever the bulk of the nation, or body politic, set up, and providence proves auspicious and favorable to, is the lawful magistrate, to be owned and submitted to for conscience sake. The inconsistency of which tenet with reformation principles, may appear from viewing and comparing therewith the coronation oath, *James VI, Parl.* 1, *cap.* 8, where it is ordained as a condition *sine qua non*, that all kings, princes, and magistrates, shall at their installment solemnly swear to maintain the true religion of Jesus Christ, and oppose all false religions. So also *James VI, Parl. 1, cap.* 9th, which ordains, that no person may be a judge or member of any court that professes not the true religion. Also *Charles I, Parl.* 2, *sess* 2d, *Act.* 14, it is ordained, that before the king be admitted to the exercise of his royal power, he shall give satisfaction to the kingdom anent the security of religion: and so the same parliament, *Act* 15th, 1649, express themselves (referring to the coronation oath above mentioned): "The estates of parliament judging it necessary, that the prince and people be of one perfect religion, appoint, that all kings and princes, who shall reign or bear rule within this realm, shall at the receipt of their princely authority, solemnly swear to observe in their own persons, and to preserve the religion, as it is presently established and professed. And they ordain, that before the king's majesty who now is, or any of his successors, shall be admitted to the exercise of his royal power, he shall, by and attour the foresaid oath, declare by his solemn oath, under his hand and seal, his allowance of the National Covenant, and of the Solemn League and Covenant, and obligation to prosecute the ends thereof in his station and calling; and that he shall consent, and agree to acts of parliament, enjoining the Solemn League and Cove-

nant, and fully establishing Presbyterian government, the Directory for worship, Confession of Faith, and Catechisms approved by the General Assembly of this kirk, and parliament of this kingdom—and that he shall observe these in his own practice and family,—and shall never make opposition to any of these, or endeavor any change thereof. Likeas, the estates of parliament discharge all the lieges and subjects of this kingdom to procure or receive from his majesty any commissions or gifts whatsoever, until his majesty shall give satisfaction, as said is, under the pain of being censured in their persons and estates, as the parliament shall judge fitting. And if any such commissions or gifts be procured or received by any of the subjects before such satisfaction, the parliament declares and ordains all such and all that shall follow thereupon, to be void and null." And the same session, *Act* 26th, it is in short ordained, that none shall bear any place of public trust in the nation, but such as have the qualifications God requires in his word. Thus, in the prefatory part of the act, they say, "The estates of parliament taking into consideration, that the Lord our God requires that such as bear charge among his people, should be able men, fearing God, hating covetousness, and dealing truly: and that many of the evils of sin and punishment, under which the land groans, have come to pass, because hitherto they have not been sufficiently provided and cared for," &c. (And afterward in the statutory part), "Do therefore ordain, that all such as shall be employed in any place of power and trust in this kingdom, shall not only be able men, but men of known affection unto, and of approved fidelity and integrity in the cause of God, and of a blameless Christian conversation," &c. To the same purpose, *Act* 11th, *Parl.* 2d, *Sess.* 3d, entitled *act for purging the army*. See also the coronation oath, of *Scotland*, as subscribed by *Charles II*, at *Scoon*, 1650. All which, and many other fundamental laws of the like nature, made in time of reformation, show the principles of our reformers to have been quite different from those of *Seceders* anent civil government: and that to constitute lawful magistrates, they must of necessity have scriptural and covenant qualifications, besides the consent of the people. With what face then can they pretend to have adopted a testimony for reformation principles, and to be of the same principles with our late reformers? The vanity of this pretense will further appear, by comparing their principles with the Solemn League and Covenant, with every article of which they are inconsistent. They profess the moral obligation of the covenants, and yet at the same time maintain the lawfulness of every providential government, whether popish or prelatic, if set up by the body politic. But how opposite this to the *first* article, obliging constantly to endeavor the preservation of the reformed religion? Can it be consistent therewith, to commit the government of the nations to a sworn enemy to the reformation? or, with that sincerity which becomes the professors of Christ, to plead the lawfulness of an authority raised upon the overthrow of the reformed religion? No less opposite is it to the *second* article, which obliges, and that without respect of persons, to endeavor the extirpation of popery, prelacy—to maintain and plead for the lawfulness of that which establishes or supports prelacy or popery in the nations. This appears rather like a sincere endeavor in them to promote whatever is contrary to sound doctrine, and the power of true godliness; and that, because an apostate people approves thereof, contrary to *Exod.* xxiii, 2: "Thou shalt not follow a multitude to do evil." Again, the *third* article binds to preserve the rights of parliaments, and the liberties of the kingdoms, and the king's authority in the preservation and defense of the true religion. But how inconsistent is it therewith, to own and defend an authority that in its constitution and habitual series of administration, is destructive of all these precious and valuable interests? It is full of contradiction, and a mocking both of God and the world, to pretend to own and defend the destroyers of the true religion, in the defense of religion, as *Seceders* do in their mock acknowledgment of such as are sworn to maintain Prelacy, in opposition to the reformed religion. The contradictoriness of this principle of theirs to the *fourth* article, needs no illustration. Again, the owning of an authority, which is reared up and stands upon the footing of the destruction of the covenanted union, and uniformity of the nations in religion can never be consistent with the *fifth*, article, which binds, to an endeavoring, that these kingdoms may remain conjoined in that firm covenanted union to all posterity. In like manner, as the *sixth* article obliges to a defending of all that enter into that League and Covenant, and never to suffer ourselves to be divided, and make defection to the contrary part; it must be a manifest contradiction thereto, not only to defend such as are enemies to that covenant, but even in their opposition thereto. And it is a making defection to the contrary part, and from that cause and covenant with a witness, to plead the lawfulness of the national constitution, which is established upon the ruins of a covenanted work of reformation, as *Seceders* do; whose principle and practice, in opposition to what is professed in the conclusion of the covenant, as well as what was the very design of entering into it, is, instead of a going before others, in the example of a real reformation, a corrupting of the nations more and more, and going before them in the example of a real apostasy and defection from the reformation, so solemnly sworn to be maintained in this covenant; and a teaching of them to appoint themselves a captain, to return to their anti-christian bondage.

Upon the whole, as the Presbytery ought to testify against this new scheme of principles, respecting the ordinance of magistracy; they therefore, upon all the grounds formerly laid down, did, and hereby do declare, testify against, and condemn the same, as what is, indeed, a new and dangerous principle, truly anti-government, introductory of anarchy and confusion, of apostasy and defection from the covenanted work of reformation, the principles by which it was carried on and maintained, and acts and laws, by which it was fenced and established; and what is flatly opposite to, and condemned by the word of divine revelation, in many express and positive precepts, and approven examples, agreeable thereto, as well as by our solemn national covenants, founded upon, and agreeable to the said word of divine revelation. And finally, let this be further observed, that as it was a beautiful branch of our glorious reformation, that the civil government of this nation was modeled agreeable to the word of God; and that the right of regal government was constituted, bounded and fixed by an unalterable law, consonant to the word of God, and sworn to be inviolably preserved both by king and people: so the *Associate Brethren*, by their doctrine on this head, which is inconsistent with our uncontroverted establishment, and fundamental laws, excluding from the throne all papists and prelatists, have counteracted a most important point of the covenanted reformation, and opened a wide door to *Jacobitism*. For, if every one is bound to acknowledge implicitly any government, in fact, that prevails: then, if a party in these nations should rise up, and set a *popish* pretender on the throne, according to their doctrine, all should be obliged to subject to him; and it would be sinful to impugn the lawfulness of his authority, although that, by being popish, he is destitute of the essential qualifications required of a king, not only by the word of God, but by the national constitution and laws, in order to make him a lawful sovereign to these nations.

2. The Presbytery testify against the Associate Presbytery, now called Synod, for their wronging, perverting and misapplying the blessed scriptures of truth in many texts, in order to support their erroneous tenet: namely, that the word of God requires no qualifications as essential to the being of a lawful Christian magistrate: but that whosoever are set up, and while they continue to be acknowledged by civil society, are lawful magistrates, though destitute of scripture qualifications, and acting in a manifest opposition to the revealed will and law of God.

The texts of scripture used by them, do prove this general proposition, viz., That it is the duty of the people of God to obey and submit to lawful rulers in their lawful commands: and that it is utterly unlawful and sinful to oppose such lawful authority. But none of these texts quoted by them, prove, that it is the duty of the people of God, blessed with the knowledge of his revealed will, to submit to, and obey, for conscience sake, an authority that is sinful, and opposite to the revealed will of God, both in its constitution and general course of administration. Nor do they prove, that a prelatical, Erastian or popish government, is a lawful government, either expressly, or by right of necessary consequence, over a people, who either do, collectively considered as a church and nation, or are bound to profess all the parts of the true religion, and to maintain all the divine ordinances in their purity: nor do they prove, that any can be lawful rulers over these Christian and covenanted nations, who want the essential qualifications required by the word of God, the covenants, and fundamental laws of the kingdoms: or that it is sinful in the people of God, to say so much, in testifying against the joint and national apostasy from God and the purity of religion. Particularly,

The first text they adduce is, *Prov.* xxvi, 21: "My son, fear, thou the Lord and the king, and meddle not with them that are given to change." It is granted, that this scripture enjoins all those duties that, in a consistency with the fear of the Lord, a people owe to their rightful kings. But nothing can be more absurd, than to extend the command to all that bear the name of kings, who are acknowledged by a nation as kings, and while they do so own them, though their constitution should be most anti-christian, and they justly chargeable with unparalleled evils not only in their private character, but in their public conduct: be they idolaters, adulterers, blasphemers, sabbath-breakers, murderers, invaders, and avowed usurpers of the throne, crown and scepter, and incommunicable prerogatives of Christ, the glorious King of Zion, setting themselves in the temple of God, and exalting themselves above all that is called God, by dispensing with his laws, and, in place thereof, substituting their own wicked laws, whereby they establish iniquity, and enjoin, under severe penalties, the profanation of the name, day and ordinances of the Lord. This command must certainly be understood in a consistency with the duty and character of one that is resolved to be an inhabitant of the Lord's holy hill, *Psal.* xv, "In whose eyes a vile person is contemned." It must be consistent with the fear of the Lord, which can stand very well with a fearing and honoring all who are really kings; but a flat contradiction thereto, to fear every vile person, because it is the will of civil society to set him up in the character of king. Till therefore Seceders prove, either that kings are under no obligation to obey the law of God themselves, and so not liable to its sanction and penalty, in case of disobedience; or then, that the favor and approbation of civil society can justify a dispensing with the law of God, they will never be able to prove from this, nor any other text, that such as are guilty of any crime declared capital in the word of truth have a right and title to that fear, honor and obedience, that is due to lawful kings, even though they are acknowledged by civil society. And so this text makes nothing for, but against their darling tenet; and their explication thereof is evidently a wresting of scripture, making it speak in their favor, contrary to the scope and meaning of the Holy Spirit therein. And their inviduous insinuation, that all who differ from their opinion, do likewise depart from the fear of the Lord, is but a further evidence of their abuse of scripture, while it is at the same time utterly false. See Mr. Knox's history, p. 422, 1st *Book of Discipline, cap.* 10, 11.

A *second* text abused, for supporting their forementioned principle, is *Eccles.* x, 4: "If the spirit of the ruler rise up against thee, leave not thy place, for yielding pacifieth great offenses." As formerly, so here they assert, that this text refers to any rulers presently acknowledged by the civil society, and that the rising of the ruler's spirit must be understood as groundless, and so sinful, and necessarily comprehends any wrath or wrong that a subject may meet with unjustly at the ruler's hand, upon personal or religious accounts. That yet, notwithstanding, the subject (in the use of lawful endeavors for his own vindication) must continue in subjection and obedience to the ruler, in lawful commands, while the civil state continues to acknowledge him; and this, as the only habile mean of convincing the ruler of his error, and preventing further evils.

But, as the reason which they there allege, does not necessarily conclude and prove this rising of spirit in the ruler to be sinful; so the whole of their application and gloss built upon it, is invalidated; and, moreover, is a condemnation of the principles and practice of our reformers, and sufferers for the cause and truths of Christ, in the late times, when they left their place of subjection, and took up arms in defense of their religion, liberties and lives.

Their explication is also self inconsistent; for, if this rising of spirit necessarily comprehends any wrath or wrong, on personal or religious accounts, then there must be a yielding, or keeping the place of subjection, not only in lawful commands, but in all matters, whether lawful or not; otherwise, this yielding cannot be supposed to answer the end designed. For though a subject should yield in all other particulars, yet, unless he also yield in that particular, on which the rising of the ruler's spirit is grounded, his yielding cannot pacify the ruler's wrath. So all the subjection, they contend, the sufferers gave, particularly in the beginning of the late persecution, to the then rulers, did not, nor could, pacify their wrath, because they would not give up with their conscience and all religion, which was the very foundation of the rising of his spirit against them; though, according to their explication of the text, this was what they should have done, and so have pacified the ruler's wrath. It is but a mere shift to tell the world, that it is only in lawful matters they are to yield; the yielding must surely correspond to the rising of the spirit spoken of. But with such deceitful shifts are they forced to cover over a doctrine, which, if presented in its native dress, would not meet with such ready reception. But in opposition to their strained interpretation of the text, the ruler must be understood a lawful ruler, who is the minister of God for good—one who has not only moral abilities for government, but also a right to govern. And as a subject may be keeping his place of subjection to a righteous ruler, and yet be guilty, in his private or public character, of what gives just offense, and occasions the ruler's spirit justly, and so not sinfully, to rise against him—thus, one may be guilty of many criminal mismanagements in the discharge of his public trust, guilty of profaning the name of God or his day, or of riot, excessive drinking, &c, without having any thought of casting off the authority of his ruler—so, when a person has hereby provoked the spirit of his ruler, this divine precept teaches the party offending not to aggravate his offense, by attempting (though able) to make good his part, or rebel against his sovereign, but to yield, acknowledge his guilt and trespass, and submit to such punishments as the lawful ruler shall justly inflict, according to the degree and quality of the offense; whereby only, the ruler will be satisfied. Agreeable to this, is that parallel text, *Eccles.* viii, 2, 3: "I counsel thee to keep the king's commandment, and that in regard of the oath of God: Be not hasty to go out of his sight; stand not in an evil thing." On the whole, it must be a great abuse of Scripture, to wrest a divine precept, which directs subjects to submit to such punishments as their lawful ruler shall justly lay them under for their offenses, to the support of this anti-scriptural notion, viz., that every wicked person, whom the majority of a nation advances to the supreme rule, is the minister of God, to whom obedience is due, under pain of eternal damnation, as is done with this text.

A *third* scripture, perverted to support the above principle, is *Luke* xx, 25: "Render therefore to *Caesar* the things which be *Caesar's*, and unto God the things which be God's." From this, *Seceders* imagine strongly to fortify their cause. But, from a just view of the text, it will appear, that the answer given by Christ contains no acknowledgment of *Caesar's* title to tribute, or of his authority as lawful. It is beyond doubt, that the question was captious, and that the design of the Scribes and Pharisees, in proposing it to Christ, was to have him ensnared in his words. This they thought themselves sure of, whether he should answer positively or negatively. For if positively, and so recognize and acknowledge *Caesar's* title, then they would have occasion to accuse him to the people, as an enemy to the laws, liberty and honor, of the *Jewish* nation. This is evident from ver. 26: "And they could not take hold of his words before the people." And then, if he should deny that it was lawful, they would have an opportunity or pretense of delating and delivering him to the *Roman* governor, as an enemy to *Caesar*. They seem, however, to have been confident, that he who taught the way of God in truth, without regard to any, would never inculcate it as a duty for them to give tribute to *Caesar*, subjection to whom, as their lawful governor, for conscience sake, was so contrary to the divine law given to the *Jews*, respecting their magistrates; and if so, they would not miss of sufficient accusation against him. But here infinite wisdom shone forth, in giving such an answer as declared their wisdom to be but folly, and at once disappointed all their malicious hopes; an answer which left *Caesar's* claim unresolved, as to any positive determination whether it belonged to him or not. The question is in direct terms. Our Lord does not directly answer to the question, in the terms proposed by the wicked spies. He neither expressly says it is lawful or unlawful to pay it, but gave his answer in such terms as they could not from it form an accusation against him, either to the people or to the governor. He, in general, teaches to give *Caesar* all things that, by the law of God, were due to him; at the same time enjoining them that, under pretense of giving to men their demands, they rob not God of what was his due, namely, a conscientious regard to all the laws he had given them, and universal obedience to all his commands, without regard to persons of any station. And it is certain, that *Caesar* was a proud, aspiring, idolatrous and bloody usurper (like the king of *Babylon*, Hab. ii, 5, for which causes the Lord denounces fearful wrath and judgments against him, Hab. ii, 7-14), having no other right to the most part of his dominions, than the Lord's providential disposal, which sometimes makes "the tabernacles of robbers prosper; into whose hand God bringeth abundantly;" Job xii, 6. "And for their sins gives *Jacob* to the spoil, and *Israel* to the robbers;" Isa. xiii, 24. "And giveth power to the beast, to continue forty and two months, and to have power over all nations;" Rev. xiii, 5, 7. So that, by looking into the divine law, which determines every one's due, according to their just character, and of which they could not be ignorant, they might see that he had a just title to all that was due to an usurper, idolater and murderer. That the *Jewish* coin did bear *Caesar's* image, could be no evidence of his being their lawful sovereign, seeing it is most common for the greatest usurpers and tyrants to stamp their image upon the coin of the nations they tyrannize over. And though it be granted that the *Jews* had, by this time, consented to *Caesar's* usurpation, yet that could not legitimate his title, nor warrant their subjection to him for conscience sake, seeing they could not consent to his authority, but in express contradiction to the many plain and positive scripture precepts, given by God unto them, as has been seen above. It is, therefore, violence done to the text (as also opposite to the sentiments of some eminent divines on the place), to say that it contains a command to pay tribute to *Caesar*; and it would appear from Luke xxiii, 2, that the *Jews* themselves did not understand it so. It may be further observed, that this is not the only instance where our Lord, in infinite wisdom, declined to give direct answers to the ensnaring questions of his malicious enemies. See John viii, 3-12; Matth. xxi, 23-28; John xviii, 19-21, where are questions of a similar nature, proposed with the same hellish intention, and all answered by him in like manner. In each of which, *Seceders* might, on as good ground as in the answer to the question anent tribute, say that Christ did shift and dissemble the truth. But the least insinuation of such a charge cannot be made from any of these answers, without the greatest blasphemy.

A *fourth* text used by them for maintaining their erroneous scheme, is Rom. xiii, 1-8. Without animadverting upon every part of their explication of this place of holy writ, it is sufficient to observe: 1. That the power here spoken of by the apostle, is not a *physical*, but a *moral* power; a power that is lawful and warranted, in regard of matter, person, title or investiture. A legitimacy in each of these must go to the making of a moral power; and an illegitimacy in any of these is an illegitimacy in the very being and constitution, and so a nullity to the power as moral, a making it of no authority. As the text speaks only of this moral power, so it excludes every unlawful power (see Mr. *Gee* on magistracy, on this text). 2. That the *being* of God, or the ordination God here spoke of, is not a being of God *providentially* only, but such a *being of* God as contains in it his institution and appointment, by the warrant of his law and precept; so that the magistrates to whom the apostle enjoins obedience, are such as are set up according to the preceptive ordination and will of God, as is evinced not only by the author referred to above, and other divines, but what sufficiently appears from the context, where the subjection enjoined, and resistance forbidden, with their respective reasons, are what can only be spoken with respect to powers ordained by the preceptive will of God. Again, by considering the office and duty of the powers, and the end of their ordination, as described, ver. 3, 4, which by no means agree to any but those moral powers ordained by the preceptive will of God, it appears a manifest abuse of this text, to apply it to every one advanced by providence to the place of supreme rule, not only without any regard, but in direct opposition to the preceptive will of God. It is most absurd and self-contradictory in professed testimony bearers for a covenanted reformation, to apply this text in a way of pleading the lawfulness of an Erastian, anti-christian constitution, that is destitute of all those qualifications already mentioned (and always included in the scriptural definition of a lawful magistrate), as necessary to constitute a moral power, viz., in regard of matter, person, title or investiture, &c. But of the power which they so zealously plead for, the matter is unlawful, being Erastian, partly civil, partly ecclesiastical, by the united constitution. The person invested with this supreme power, is one who is declared incapable, by the fundamental laws and covenanted constitution of the nations; the manner of investiture, and terms on which the crown is held, sinful—the constitution being in an immediate opposition to the unalterable constitution of the kingdom of the *Messias*, and founded on the destruction of the covenanted reformation. And it may be added, that it is unlawful, as to the exercise and application of it, which has been all along in opposition to all *true* religion, and a grievous oppression of the church, the kingdom of Christ, in the liberties thereof. And it must be so; for the tree must be made good, before the fruit can be such. By all which it appears, there is a nullity in the power as moral, being so very opposite to the revealed will of God. And from what is said, it is obvious that this scripture gives no countenance to their corrupt scheme, but furnishes with strong arguments against it.

A *fifth* scripture adduced is, Titus iii, 1: "Put them in mind to be subject to principalities and powers," &c. As *Seceders* apply this text to the same purpose, and explain it in the same manner, as they have done those others above mentioned, so what is already said is sufficient to discover the deceit of their use and explication thereof. The powers and magistrates the apostle requires subjection to, are only such as are so in a moral sense; none but such are accounted powers and magistrates in the sense of the text. The apostle must mean the same powers here he describes in Rom. xiii, 1-3, &c., otherwise he contradicts himself, which must not be admitted; and the powers he there speaks of, are moral powers, i.e., such as have not only proper abilities for government and rule, but also a right of constitution, impowering them to use their abilities for that purpose. How can one be expected or said to be the *minister* of God *for good*, or a *terror to evil doers, and a praise to them that do well*, if he is so disposed and inclined, as to love that which is evil, and hate that which is good, and so actually is a praise to evil doers, and a terror to such as do well? To suppose any such thing, is to overthrow the universally established connection between cause and effect, the means and the end. And so much (namely, that the powers there spoken of are moral powers), *Seceders* are forced to grant in their explication of Rom. xiii. Say they, "The text speaks only of powers in a moral sense." And this concession at once destroys their scheme, and confirms what the Presbytery plead for, namely, that none are lawful powers but such as are so according to the preceptive will of God in his word; which certainly, in the judgment of all *who would deal reverently with the oracles of God*, is, in this case, a rule far preferable "to the remainders of natural light, in the moral dictates of right reason," from which *Seceders* fetch the institution of this divine ordinance of magistracy, and on which they settle it, as on (what they call) "the natural and eternal law of God;" preferring that to the plain, perfect and complete, revelation of God's will in his word.

The *last* text used by them, is, 1 Pet. ii, 13 to 17, the import of which, they say, is, that all who have a constitution by consent of the civil society, are to be subjected to for the Lord's sake, as having an institution from him: and that, however seldom they were inclined or employed in the discharge of the duties proper to their office. It may suffice to observe, that while the apostle is here speaking, as in the above texts, of moral powers, as above described, it is evident, that by *every ordinance of man*, can only be meant the different kinds and forms of civil government, and governors set up by men, to each of which the apostle exhorts to a submission, providing, that in the setting up of these, they acted agreeably to the general laws and rules appointed by God in his word, both respecting the constitution of government, and the qualifications of governors. Then, as they bear the stamp of divine authority, they were to be submitted to for the Lord's sake. But what manifest abuse of scripture is it, to allege with them that the inspired apostle exhorts to submit to every monster of iniquity, if only set up by the civil society, though perhaps guilty of a number of crimes that by the law of God, and laws of men founded thereon, are punishable by a severe death? Sure, such can never have a title to that obedience which is due to the ordinance of God, who have not so much as a title to live upon the earth. Moreover, let it be considered, that in the above cited texts, the spirit of God enjoins either that obedience and subjection that is due to lawful magistrates, or that subjection only which is for a time, by an extraordinary and special command, such as Jer. xxix, 7, given to conquerors and usurpers, having no right but what is providential. If the first, then they cannot intend any but those moral powers who are said to be of God, in respect of his approbative and preceptive will. If the last, then these texts are not the rule of obedience to lawful rulers, who are set up qualified, and govern according to the law of God. But that these texts can only be understood of the first, is evident from this, that in them not only is the office, duty and end of the civil magistrate as particularly described, as the obedience and subjection commanded; but the one is made the foundation, ground, and reason of, and inseparably connected with the other. And therefore it was, that the renowned witnesses for Christ and his interest, contended so much for reformation in the civil magistracy and magistrate, in an agreeableness to the original institution of that ordinance, and endured so great opposition on that account.

To conclude this: as it is evident these texts give no countenance to the corrupt scheme of *Seceders*, but always suppose the power, to which subjection and obedience for conscience sake is enjoined to be lawful, in regard of matter, person, title, &c. So the Presbytery cannot but testify against them for perverting and wresting the scriptures of truth, to a favoring of their anarchical and anti-scriptural tenet, and for their so stiffly and tenaciously pleading for avowed apostasy and defection (which is the whole scope and amount of their declared scheme of politics), viz., that it is lawful for posterity to turn back to where their forefathers were, giving up with many precious truths, and further attainments in reformation, valuable and necessary, acquired at the expense of much zeal, faithfulness and treasure, and handed down to us, sealed by the spirit of God upon the souls of his people, as his work and cause; and on public scaffolds and high places of the field, with the dearest blood of multitudes of Christ's faithful witnesses, who loved not their lives unto the death. And this, in express contradiction to the land's solemn covenant engagements to the Lord, for maintaining and holding fast that whereunto we had attained. For notwithstanding all the regard and deference *Seceders* profess to the covenants and reformation principles, they are, all the while, directly pleading in defense of the same cause, advancing the same arguments to support it, and likewise giving the same corrupt and perverted explication of the above texts of scripture, that the merciless and bloody murderers and persecuters did, in the late tyrannous times, in their stated opposition to the cause and interest of glorious Christ, together with the indulged who took part with them, in opposing the kingdom and subjects of Zions exalted King. And as [pity it is] *Seceders* have pleaded the cause of malignants, and, rubbing the rust from their antiquated arguments, have presented them with a new lustre; so the Presbytery, in opposition thereto, are satisfied to plead the same cause, with the same arguments and to understand these scriptures in the same sense as was done by the witnesses for reformation, whom the Lord honored to seal his truths with their blood, as is sufficiently confirmed from the Cloud of Witnesses; where their concurring testimonies are harmoniously stated, upon their disowning the authority of the then anti-christian and Erastian government, even when acknowledged by the bulk and body of the nation, both civil and ecclesiastical. Whence also it is evident, that the persecution was not the cause of their casting off that authority; but that authority's assuming and usurping the royal prerogatives of Christ, the church's Head, was the cause of their disowning it; and then their refusing to acknowledge foresaid authority, was the cause of all their persecution.

3. The Presbytery testify against foresaid Associates, on account of their corruption in worship; particularly, in the duty of prayer, both as practiced by their ministers, and by them enjoined upon their people.

Wherein, in an inconsistency with a faithful testimony against the declared enemies of the church's head and king, they affect to express a superlative loyalty unto the prelatic possessors of power, not much differing from the forms imposed upon, and observed by the Erastian church. The Presbytery acknowledge it duty to pray for all men, in the various stations of life, as sinners lost, of the ruined family of Adam, standing absolutely in need of a Savior, that they may be saved and come to the knowledge of the truth; as is enjoined, *Tim.* ii, 1, 2. Which yet must not be understood in an unlimited sense, but with submission to the will of God, if they belong to the election of grace. Nay, they acknowledge it indispensable duty, as to pray, that the church may obtain such kings and queens, as shall he nursing fathers and mothers, according to the Lord's gracious promise; so, when such are granted to them, it is their duty to make prayers and supplications, in a particular manner, for them. But it is no less than an abuse of scripture, and flat contradiction to many promises and threatenings, to extend foresaid command to every person without distinction whom providence advances to the supreme rule over the people of God, in a way of acknowledging their authority as lawful, and of praying for success and prosperity to them (as Seceders do), to pray for success unto, and the continuance of wicked rulers, that are enemies to the Lord, and usurpers of his crown, and such whom the Lord in anger against a people for their sins, may send as a special punishment upon them, and from whom he has promised deliverance unto his people, as a peculiar blessing, is no less than the slighting of the promises, and deriding of threatenings, and in reality, is a taking part with God's enemies, against him and his cause. As it is impossible, sincerely to pray for the coming of Christ's kingdom, and advancement thereof, without also, as a necessary mean conducive thereto, to pray for the downfall and destruction of all his enemies, as such, whatever be their place and station (which is not at all inconsistent with praying for their salvation, as lost sinners); seeing Jesus Christ no less effectually destroys his enemies, when he makes them to bow in a way of willing subjection to the scepter of his law and grace, than when he breaks them in pieces with his iron rod of wrath; so, how self-contradictory is it in *Seceders*, to pray for the coming of Christ's mediatory kingdom; and, at the same time to pray for the success and preservation of one, in his kingly character, who themselves acknowledge, has, in that character, made grievous encroachments upon the royal prerogatives of the Lord Jesus Christ, is an usurper of his crown, and therefore, in that view, must be considered as an enemy to his kingdom?

That the above is no false charge against *Seceders*, is witnessed by a variety

of their causes of fasting, concluding with such prayers, which they have emitted, as well as by their daily practice: and particularly, *Antiburgher Seceders*, have
given a late recent proof of this; in what they call, A solemn warning by the *Associate Synod*, &c. Which unfaithful warning concludes with a self-contradictory
form of prayer, enjoined upon all under the inspection of said *Synod*. Among other
things, they "exhort all—the people under their inspection, to pour out earnest
and incessant supplications before the Lord, in a dependence upon the merit and
intercession of our great High-priest, that he may—bring about a revival of our
covenanted reformation,—removing all the mountains which stand in the way;
that he may abundantly bless our sovereign king *George*, and the apparent heir of
the crown,—blasting all the plots or efforts of whatever enemies, open or secret,—
against the Protestant succession to the throne of these kingdoms in the family of
Hanover; that he may be gracious to the high courts of parliament, in this and the
neighboring island,—leading them to proper measures for the honor of Christ;
that he may hasten the enlargement of the Mediator's kingdom," &c.

On all which, let it suffice to observe, 1. That as in no part of this prayer they
make any exceptions against, so they must be understood therein, approving of
the constitution of the king, the establishment, and limitation of the throne of
these kingdoms in the *Hanoverian* family, as presently by law established: and
also, approving of the *British* and *Irish*, parliaments, in their constitution as by
law established, though both of them grossly Erastian, and necessarily connected with maintaining *English* popish ceremonies, the whole *English* hierarchy, and
civil places and power of churchmen; in opposition to the word of God, reforming
laws, and covenanted constitutions of the nations. Hence, 2. This pattern of prayer
must be understood as containing earnest supplications to the Lord, that he may
continue and preserve an Erastian constitution, that he may perpetuate the limited succession to the throne in the family of *Hanover*; and that, in opposition to all
attempts whatever, toward any change, however much it might contribute to the
glory of God, good of the church, and revival of a covenanted reformation; and
also, seems to include a desire that, God may preserve and maintain a parliament
in the nations, one of the houses whereof, viz., the House of Peers, is composed
partly of *spiritual lords*, as essential members thereof,—an anti-christian designation, a title and office, not to be found in the book of divine revelation. So, 3. This
prayer seems to suppose a consistency between the preservation of all these, and
the revival of a covenanted reformation in these lands; and also that they, particularly a parliament, thus anti-christian in its constitution, are proper instruments
for promoting the honor and declarative glory of Christ; although the prelates,
constituent members therein, are a generation of men that were never yet known
to have a vote for Christ's kingdom and interest. And therefore, 4. This prayer consists of flat contradiction. (1.) In regard the revival of a covenanted reformation,
and the flourishing of Christ's mediatory kingdom, nationally, must be attended
with the overthrow of all constitutions, civil and ecclesiastical, that hinder and oppose the same; *Hag.* ii, 6, 7, and with the down bringing of all the enemies thereof,
from the height of their excellency. (2.) It is a contradiction for them to pray, that
the Lord would remove all the mountains that stand in the way of the revival of

our reformation; and yet, at the same time, pray for the preservation and continuance of the constitution, under which (as they themselves acknowledge, *Defense of their Princ., page* 51): "There is a mighty bar thrust into the way of our covenanted reformation, both in church and state; yea, a gravestone is laid, and established upon the same." (3.) It is a sinful and glaring contradiction for *Seceders* to rank an approbation of the *English* hierarchy among our public national sins and steps of defection (as they do, page 53 of their pamphlet); and yet themselves persist and continue in the same sin and guilt, homologating and approving the anti-christian constitution of the *British* and *Irish* parliaments, by praying (like their forefathers, in their fulsome address to *James* the Papist) for divine illumination and conduct to the Prelates in their civil places and power, as necessary members there, as they do in this prayer of theirs. Can such be supposed to be either truly sensible of sin, or humbled for it, who, notwithstanding all their confessions, still continue in the love and practice of it? But with such mock acknowledgements (of which a variety of other instances might be given) have they hitherto imposed on the generation. And so, 5. It is a prayer, that in several parts thereof, has no scripture warrant, no foundation in the promises of God. Particularly, on what scriptural warrant, what promise, can *Seceders* build their prayers for, or expectation of the Lord's answering them, by blessing an Erastian government to themselves or others, which being, in its constitution, contrary to the word of God,—is such, that under it (as they grant, *ibid*, page 46), a people cannot truly prosper in their civil concerns, nor be enriched with the blessings of the gospel? From what scriptural promise are they warranted to pray, that God may perpetuate the succession to the throne in any one family, and especially, when that succession is circumscribed and limited, in a way opposite to the laws of God, and mediatory kingdom of Christ? and therefore, a prayer that cannot be made in faith, and so cannot be acceptable to God in its complex form. No person can have faith in the merit and intercession of Christ, for obtaining anything in prayer, but what Christ has priorly merited, and does actually intercede for. But it would savor too much of blasphemy, to apply some of the particulars already noticed in this form of prayer, to the merit and intercession of our *great High-priest*. Sure it cannot be thought, that he makes intercession for the prosperity and success of his enemies, in their stated opposition to his kingdom and interest in this world; neither can it be consistent with fidelity to Christ, as a King, for his professed subjects to pray for it. What a fearful trifling with God in the duty of prayer, is it to pray that the Lord may bring down Popery and Prelacy; and next breath to pray that the Lord may continue, prosper, and preserve the Erastian head, and great bulwark of Prelacy?

4. Again, the Presbytery testify against the Associate party for their treachery in covenant. This is a sin that is in scripture, and even by the common voice of mankind, declared very heinous; but which, by what is already discovered anent said party, appears too, too justly chargeable upon them. It is notorious, and what themselves boast much of, that they professedly maintain the moral and perpetual obligation of the covenants, both the National Covenant of *Scotland*, and the Solemn League and Covenant of *Scotland, England*, and *Ireland*, entered into for reformation and defense of religion, and bringing the churches of God in the three

kingdoms to the nearest conjunction and uniformity in religion, according to the word of God. They also do in the most public manner profess, that they are the only true faithful witnesses for a covenanted reformation. But the consistency of such a profession with maintaining principles that are diametrically opposite to these covenants, and the cause of truth, sworn to in them (as has been made evident they do) is altogether unintelligible. Is it possible strenuously to maintain the lawfulness of a prelatical government abjured in the covenants, and yet at the same time sincerely and honestly, according to the profession made by the church, *Psal.* xliv, 17, 18, to contend for the moral obligation of the covenants, and the work of reformation sworn to in them? But further, the necessity of lifting up a testimony against *Seceders* for their treachery and unfaithfulness in the matter of the covenants, will appear by considering that they, after making a very solemn profession of renewing the National Covenant of *Scotland*, and the Solemn League and Covenant of the three lands, in place of practicing accordingly, have, in reality, made a new and very different bond or covenant, both in form and substance, which they have not only sworn themselves, but also imposed upon many honest people: and this as a renewing, nay, as the only right way of renewing said covenants according to the circumstances, of the times. That this bond entered into by *Seceders* (however good it may be, considered in an abstract sense) is not a renovation of the national covenants, as they assert it to be, but a treacherous and deceitful burying of these covenants, as to their sum and substance, is abundantly evident from their industrious keeping out, and omitting the most part of them out of their new and artificial bond. Particularly, although they pretend to a renovation both of the National and Solemn League and Covenant, yet they have almost entirely left out, and passed over the National Covenant of *Scotland*; and satisfying themselves with simply testifying against Popery, have omitted all the particular errors, and branches thereof expressly contained in the National Covenant. As to the Solemn League, of which they pretend their bond is also a renovation, there is very little of it to be found therein, as appears from a comparison of the one with the other. Thus they have left out that remarkable and necessary clause in the first Article, viz., "Against our common enemies:" and in place of endeavoring to bring the churches of God in the three kingdoms to the nearest conjunction and uniformity in religion, Confession of Faith, Form of Church Government, Directory for Worship and Catechizing, as in said article, there is an unintelligible clause or jumble of words brought in, viz., to promote and advance our covenanted conjunction and uniformity in religion, just as if that conjunction and uniformity had a present existence (in its native and original state and form) in the three lands; when, on the contrary, Presbytery is established in *Scotland*, yet not on the footing of the word of God and the covenants, and Episcopacy is established in *England* and *Ireland*, in contradiction to the word of God and the covenants. 2. They have kept out that necessary clause in the 2d article, viz., "Without respect of persons, endeavor the extirpation," &c, and instead thereof say, "Testify against Popery and Prelacy;" where appears not only a difference in expression, but a substantial difference. 3. They have altogether omitted and kept out the 3d and 4th articles. 4. They have kept out that material and necessary clause in the 5th article, viz., "That justice may be done on the willful opposers thereof," in manner expressed in the preceding article. 5. They have left out all the 6th article, excepting these words: "We shall not give ourselves up to a detestable neutrality and indifference in the cause of God." And 6. They have wholly omitted that material paragraph of the conclusion of the Solemn League. It is therefore evident, that the model of the covenants agreed to by *Seceders*, is different in substance, as well as form, from our ancient covenants; so that, under pretense of renovation, they have made a new bond.

But, again, that their pretended renovation is a real burying of the covenanted reformation, appears from their overlooking, casting by, and keeping out the National Covenant, as it was renewed in the year 1638, and the Solemn League and Covenant, as renewed in the year 1648, and going back to the years 1580 and 1581, as the pattern they propose to follow in carrying on of their covenanted testimony. And what can be the reason of this? Can it be, because Prelacy, and the civil places and power of churchmen, were, by the explication and application of the covenant, *anno* 1638, expressly and explicitly condemned, while they were formerly only implicitly, and by way of consequence? So they have at least, by this step back, both tacitly condemned our reformers, of giving themselves needless trouble in their explanation of the covenant, as condemning and abjuring Episcopacy; and also, do overlook, despise, and disgracefully bury the many advanced steps of reformation attained to in these covenanted lands between 1638 and 1649 (particularly the church of *Scotland's* testimony against Prelacy) in which time reformation arrived to a greater height of purity than ever was attained in any foregoing period of this church and nation. However, whatever their reasons were for so doing, that they have so done is clear, from their act *Edinburgh, February* 3d, 1743, where they conclude with a *nota bene*, lest it should not otherwise have been observed that they do so, and thereby declare their sin as *Sodom*, as if the publishing of it would make an atonement for it. "N.B. Only the National Covenant, as it was entered into, *annis* 1580, 1581 (without the bond wherein it was renewed *anno* 1638) and the Solemn League and Covenant (without the solemn acknowledgment of sins, and engagement to duties, *anno* 1648), are hereby prefixed unto the following act, agreeably unto the design of said act": and for this they pretend the example of our reformers, *anno* 1638, who renewed the National Covenant by a new bond, in place of that new bond wherewith it was renewed and sworn, 1590, which they omitted—wherein their deceit and unfaithfulness is very obvious from the following observations: 1. Hereby they have cast a most injurious calumny and reproach upon our honored reformers, and in their pretending to imitate their practice, in renovation of the covenants, are guilty of a most dreadful and deceitful imposition on the generation; for though our reformers did renew the covenants with a new bond, and perhaps very seldom swear them without some additions, yet they never went back from any part of reformation, espoused, and sworn to in the renovations that were before them, under a pretense, that such points of reformation formerly attained, were unsuitable, or not adapted to their circumstances, as *Seceders* have done. On the contrary, our reformers, in all the different renovations of the covenants, not only included all that was formerly attained to, binding themselves in strict adherence to all the articles priorly in the oath and covenant of God (at the same time solemnly acknowledging all former breaches thereof; and obliging themselves, in the strength of grace to the performance of the contrary, and consequential duties), but also, still went forward in explaining and more explicitly applying the covenants against the sins of the day, and more expressly binding themselves to the opposite duties, as is clear from the bond wherewith our reformers renewed the covenants 1638, and the solemn acknowledgment of sins, and engagement to duties, 1648; both which the *Seceders* have barefacedly cast by and exploded in their alleged renovation of the covenants; whereby, as it is manifest that our reformers always went forward to further degrees of reformation, so it is no less manifest, that foresaid party acting contrary to them, have gone backward. But 2d. They have not only rejected the renovations of the covenants by our ancestors 1638 and 1640; but even when they pretended to follow the renovation of the covenant, 1580 and 1581, they have kept out and perverted almost the whole of the national covenants, as was already observed; particularly in their new bond, they have cast away the civil part of the covenants altogether. For what reason they do so, is indeed hard to say. True, they allege it would be a blending of civil and religious matters together; and that it is not proper (or competent for them, as a church judicatory) to meddle in these matters that are of a civil nature. But seeing infinite wisdom has not judged it a (sinful) blending of civil and religious concerns together, to deliver the duties both civil and religious in one and the same moral law unto mankind; it is difficult to conceive, how the people of God their binding themselves in a covenant of duties to the conscientious performance of all the duties God required of them in his word, whether civil or religious, according to their respective or immediate objects, can be reputed a blending of them together; or that this has the remotest tendency to destroy that distinction which God in his revealed will has stated between what is immediately civil in its nature, and what is properly religious. This, therefore, is a mere groundless pretense and evasion; and if it has any force at all, as a reason, it strikes against the reformers who compiled these covenants. They are the proper objects at whom through the sides of others it thrusts; for they, at the framing of sundry of their covenants, and afterward at the renovation of their covenant, did it both without the ecclesiastical authority, and also without, and contrary unto, yea, at the hazard of suffering the greatest severities from the civil authority on that account. And yet the ecclesiastical judicatories of the church of *Scotland* afterward found it competent for them, as such, to approve of these covenants, both as to the matter and form of them, without branding and exploding them as a blending of matters civil and religious together, as *Seceders* have done. Again, as the covenants require no other than a lawful magistrate; and seeing *Seceders* acknowledge the present as lawful, and that it is their duty to be subject to, and support them as such, it is impossible to conceive any reason, why they have not honored the present rulers with a place in their new and artificial bond: unless perhaps this, that they were aware that would have been so glaring a contradiction to these covenants they were pretending to renew, as would doubtless have startled and driven away from them a good many honest people, whom they have allured and led aside by their good words and fair-set speeches; and yet it is pretty obvious they have included the present rulers in their bond, and taken them in an oblique and clandestine way, by swearing to the relative duties contained in the fifth commandment, seeing they acknowledge them as their civil parents. Again, as their bond is supposed to reduplicate upon the national covenants, and so to bind to every article in them, by native consequence, they swear to a prelatical government: for seeing they have made no exception in their bond, it must be applied to no other, but the government, which presently exists; and this, in flat contradiction to the covenants, by which such a government is abjured. So that their new bond is no less opposite to the national covenants, and is much mere deceitful, than if they had plainly and explicitly sworn allegiance to the present government therein; only the generality of their implicit followers do not so readily observe it. Upon the whole, how strange is it, that they should have the assurance to father their deceitful apostasy, and wretched burying of the covenants upon our reformers, so injuriously to their character, and at the hazard of imposing a heinous and base cheat upon the world, while, notwithstanding all their vain pretensions, it is undeniably evident to those who will impartially, and without prejudice, examine the method and order whereby our ancestors renewed our covenants, that in this they have been so far from following their example, that they have directly contradicted the same, and, in reality, buried much of the covenants and work of reformation sworn to in them. For though a people may very lawfully, by a new bond, enlarge and add to their former obligations that they brought themselves under; yet they can never, without involving themselves in the guilt of perjury, relax or cancel former obligations by any future bond. Accordingly, our worthy ancestors, by all the new bonds they annexed to former obligations, were so far from attempting to loose themselves from any covenanted duty that either they or their fathers were priorly bound unto, that they thereby still brought themselves under straighter bonds to perform all their former and new obligations of duty to God. But, as has been discovered, *Seceders*, by their artificial bond, have cast out the very substance and spirit of the covenants, by their rumping and hewing them at pleasure, to reduce them to the sinful circumstances of the time: and this, in opposition to their own public profession, that these covenants are moral in their nature and obligation upon these nations to the latest posterity. How surprising it is then, that after such a profession, they dare cast out of their bond the greatest parts of the covenants! This is not only to break these obligations, but it is to make a public declaration, that different times and circumstances do free men from their obligation to keep their most solemn vows to the Most High. To this, as very applicable, may be subjoined the words of Mr. *Case*, in a sermon relative to the covenants: "Others have taken it (viz., the covenant) with their own evasions, limitations and reservations: such a Jesuitical spirit has got in among us, by which means it comes to pass, that by that time that men have pared off and left out, and put what interpretation they frame to themselves, there is little left worth the name of a covenant." And, indeed, so many are the self-inconsistencies and gross contradictions attending this new bond, that it would have been much more for the honor both of the covenants, and of *Seceders* themselves, rather never to have attempted such a work, than to have done it in a way of tearing to pieces our solemn national vows. Wherefore the Presbytery cannot but, in testifying against them for their unfaithfulness, obtest all the lovers of truth, to beware of joining in this course of treachery, and apostasy from God and his covenanted cause.

5. The presbytery testify against foresaid party, for their unfaithfulness and partiality in point of testimony-bearing to a covenanted, work of reformation; while yet they not only profess to be witnesses, but the only true and faithful contenders for the said work and cause. The justness of this charge manifestly appears from the scope of their Act and Testimony, which seems to be principally leveled against the corruptions of the present church judicatories, and not equally against the corruptions of both church and state, in agreeableness to the faithful testimonies of the Lord's people in former times, and in a consistency with the reformation that was jointly carried on in both church and state, and solemnly sworn and engaged to in the covenants. They appear never to have fully adopted the testimony of the Church of *Scotland* in her purest times, when the profession of the true religion was by law made a necessary qualification of every one that should be admitted to places of civil trust and power in the nation. Nor are the faithful testimonies of the valiant sufferers and contenders, even unto death, for the precious truths of God in the late persecuting period, as stated against both church and state, fully stated, and judicially approven by them; much less have they fully adopted the testimony, as stated against the revolution constitution, both civil and ecclesiastical, which they did not in their testimony condemn as sinful; but, on the contrary, acknowledged the civil constitution lawful, notwith-standing of their complaining of some defects and omissions therein. Of which error in the foundation, it may be said, in respect of all the mal-administrations since, it was *fons et origo mali*. And seeing, in and by the revolution constitution, the nation was involved in the guilt of apostasy and treachery, in subverting and overturning the good and laudable laws for true religion and right liberty, a faint declaring against some omissions cannot be accounted sufficient; especially when what is thus partly complained of, is at the same time complexly extolled, as a great and glorious deliverance to the church and nation. Their testimony further appears to be partial and unfaithful, considering that their secession was not from the constitution of the Revolution Church, but in a partial and limited way, from a prevailing corrupt party in the judicatories of the church: upon which footing it was, that some of greatest note among them made their accession after their first secession, expressly declaring so much; whereby they have injured the true state of the testimony which the Lord honored his covenanted Church of *Scotland* to bear; which is stated against all lukewarm and *Laodicean* professors, as well as open en-emies, and against all Erastian usurpation, and sectarian invasion on the cause of Christ. Moreover, their unfaithfulness in point of testimony, convincingly appears from their bitter contentions, and almost endless disputes among themselves, after their breach, upon the religious clause of some burgess oaths, anent the true state of their own testimony, whether lifted up against the revolution constitution of the church, and settlement of religion, or not. Had necessary and real faithfulness been studied, in stating their testimony clearly and plainly, against all the defec-tion, and apostasy of the day from a covenanted reformation, there had been no occasion for such a dispute among them. And now, when the one party have more openly avowed their unfaithfulness, in receding from almost everything that had the least appearance of faithfulness to the cause and covenant of God, in their former testimony, and professedly adopted the revolution settlement, as theirs, ac-

knowledging the constitutions, both civil and ecclesiastical, as lawful, in an open contradiction to any testimony for reformation work: the other party, *to wit, Antiburghers*, have now indeed professedly cast off the revolution constitution of the church (at the same time continuing to make their partial Act and Testimony the basis of their distinguished profession); but yet, in an inconsistency therewith, and in contradiction to the covenanted testimony of the church of *Scotland*, continue to adopt the constitution of the State, as being, however defective, yet agreeable to the precept and so lawful. Hence, they are still most partial in their testimony, of which they have given a fresh and notable proof, in forementioned warning published by them: wherein though there are a variety of evils condescended upon, as just grounds of the Lord's controversy with the nations, yet there is not that faithfulness used therein, in a particular charging home of the several sins mentioned, upon every one in their different ranks, as, in agreeableness to the word of God, is requisite to work a conviction in every one, that they may turn from their sins, and as might correspond to the title given that performance. Thus, passing other instances that might also have been observed, they justly remark, *page* 31st, "The glorious sovereignty of our Lord Jesus Christ, as the alone King and Head of his church, is sadly encroached upon and opposed by the royal supremacy, in causes ecclesiastical. The king is acknowledged as supreme head, or governor on earth, of the churches of *England* and *Ireland*. The civil sovereign is thus declared to be the head or fountain of church power, from whence all authority and ministrations in these churches do spring, is vested with all powers of government and discipline, and constituted the sole judge of controversies within the same." "The established Church of *Scotland* have also, by some particular managements, subjected and subordinated their ecclesiastical meetings to the civil power." But while they acknowledge this to be the sin of the church, and an high provocation against the Lord; yet, as to the particular sin of the civil power, in assuming and usurping this Erastian supremacy unto itself, they are quite silent. They have not the faithfulness to say, in their warning, to the robber of Christ, in this matter, as once the prophet of the Lord said to the king of *Israel*, in another case, *Thou art the man*. On the contrary (which cannot but have a tendency to ward off any conviction of his sin that this warning, should it come into his hands, might be expected to work), they are guilty of the basest flattery, used by court parasites, stiling him, "the best of kings, of the mildest administration," as in *page* 13th; and acknowledge it, as a particular effect of the Lord's goodness, that we are privileged with such an one. But is he indeed deserving of such a character? better than which could not be given to the most faithful ruler, devoting all his power, as in duty bound, to the support and advancement of the kingdom and interest of Jesus Christ, that over reigned. Does he really merit such an encomium, who sacrilegiously usurps and wears the crown, that alone can flourish on the head of *Zion's* king? And is this such a blessing to the church, that an enemy to her Lord and Head rules over her? Oh! may not the Lord say? "I hearkened and heard, but they spake not aright."

6. The Presbytery testify against said Seceding party, because of the sinfulness of their terms of ministerial and Christian communion, as being partly destructive of that liberty wherewith Christ has made his people free. By which they have

both imposed upon themselves, and shut the door of access unto the privileges of the church, upon all such, as, in a consistency with their adherence to truth and duty, cannot accept of their unwarrantable restrictions. Of this, they gave early discoveries, as appears from the known instance of that notable, backslider, Mr. *Andrew Clarkson*, whom they obliged, before license, to make a public and solemn renunciation of his former principles and profession, respecting the covenanted reformation. [4] As also, their rejecting all accessions from his *Laodicean* brethren, wherein was contained an explicit adherence to the same, until they did drop their former testimony. This blind zeal in *Seceders*, against a testimony for truth in its purity, did gradually increase, until it hurried them on to a more particular and formal stating of their terms of communion, whereby were totally excluded all the free and faithful of the land from their communion, who could not approve of, nor swear the bond, whereby they pretended to renew the covenants: as in their act at *Edinburgh*, 1744; wherein they did resolve and determine, "That the renovation of the National Covenant of *Scotland*, and the Solemn League and Covenant of the three nations, in the manner now agreed upon, and proposed by the Presbytery, shall be the terms of ministerial communion with this Presbytery, and likewise of Christian communion, in admission of people to sealing ordinances; secluding therefrom all opposers, contemners, and slighters of the said renovation of our solemn covenants." By this act, *Seceders* have obliged their adherents to consent to their infamous burial of our national covenants with the Lord, and reformation therein sworn to, particularly as they were renewed, both 1638 and 1648. And that they might further evince their resolution to bear down the foresaid work, they afterward proceeded to subjoin unto their *formula* of questions to be put to candidates before license, and to probationers before ordination, the following questions, viz., "Are you satisfied with, and do you propose to adhere unto, and maintain the principles about the present civil government, which are declared and maintained in the *Associate Presbytery's* answers to Mr. *Nairn*, with their defense thereunto subjoined?" Whereby, in opposition to the professed endeavors for the revival of a covenanted reformation in the lands, they expressly bind down all their intrants into the office of the ministry, to an explicit acknowledgement of their anti-government scheme of principles anent the ordinance of magistracy; and thereby to an acknowledging of the lawfulness of a government, which themselves confess has not only departed from, and neglected their duty of espousing and supporting the covenanted principles of this church, but also opposed, contradicted and overthrown the glorious reformation once established in these nations. A government, under which, as they profess, the nations cannot be enriched by the blessings of the gospel; and that, because it does not, in all the appurtenances

---

[4] Mr. *Andrew Clarkson* originally belonged to the community of Old Dissenters under the pastoral inspection of the Rev. Mr. *John McMillan* senior; was educated and lived in communion with them, till upwards of the age of thirty years; during which time he wrote and published a book, entitled, *Plain Reasons, &c.*, setting forth the grounds why Presbyterian Dissenters refused to hold communion with the revolution, church and state; but, having no prospect of obtaining license and ordination among them, in regard they had then no ordained minister belonging to them but old Mr. *McMillan* alone, it appeared that, from a passionate desire after these privileges, he left his old friends, and made his application to the Associate Presbytery, who treated him as above narrated.

of its constitution and administration, run in agreeableness to the word of God. By all which it appears that although they refuse formally to swear any oaths of allegiance to the powers in being; yet they do materially, and with great solemnity, engage themselves to be true and faithful to a government, under which, and while it stands, they are certain, if their concessions hold true, that they shall never see the nations flourish, either in their temporal or spiritual interests. It is only needful further to observe, that *Seceders* in the terms of their communion, by debarring from the table of the Lord, all who impugn the lawfulness of a prelatic, Erastian government (as is notourly known they do), make subjection and loyalty to such an authority, a necessary, and, to them, commendatory qualification of worthy receivers of the Lord's supper, although none of those qualifications—required by God in his word. While (as has been already observed) they, with the most violent passion, refuse to admit the professing and practicing the true religion, a necessary qualification of lawful civil rulers over a people possessed of and professing the true religion, which is in effect to deny the necessity of religion altogether as to civil rulers, than which nothing can be more absurd.

Lastly, not to multiply more particulars, the Presbytery testify against the scandalous abuse, and sinful prostitution of church discipline, and tyranny in government, whereby the forementioned party have remarkably signalized themselves; and which, in a most precipitant and arbitrary manner, they have pretended to execute against such as have discovered the smallest degree of faithfulness, in endeavoring to maintain the principles of our reformation, in agreeableness to the true state of the covenanted testimony of the Church of *Scotland*; which has not only appeared in the case of *David Leslie*, and some others, on account of a paper of grievances given in to said Associates; against whom they proceeded to the sentence of excommunication, without using those formalities and means of conviction required and warranted by the church's Head, even in the case of just offenses done by any of the professed members of his mystical body; or so much as allowing that common justice to the sentenced party, that might be expected from any judicatory, bearing the name of Presbyterian. (Though the Presbytery are not hereby to be understood as approving every expression contained in foresaid paper.) But particularly, they have given notable proof of their fixed resolution, to bear down all just appearances in favor of *Zion's* King and cause, in the case of Mr. *Nairn*, once of their number, because of his espousing the principles of this Presbytery, especially, respecting God's ordinance of magistracy, against whom they proceeded to the highest censures of the church, upon the footing of a pretended libel; in which libel, they did not so much as pretend any immorality in practice, or yet error in principle, as the ground of their arbitrary procedure, further than his espousing the received principles of this church in her best times, and what stood in necessary connection with such a profession: although, in adorable providence, he has since been left to fall into the practice of such immorality, as has justly rendered him the object of church censure by this Presbytery. As also in the case of Messrs. *Alexander Marshall*, and *John Cuthbertson*, with some others, elders and private Christians, against whom they proceeded in a most unaccountable, anti-scriptural, and unprecedented manner, and upon no better foundation, than that noticed in the case above, pretended to depose and cast such out of the communion of their church, as never had subjected to their authority, nor formerly stood in any established connection with them.

And further, besides these instances condescended upon, they habitually aggravate their abuse of the ordinances of Christ's house, in pretending to debar and excommunicate from the holy sacrament of the supper, many of the friends and followers of the Lamb, only because they cannot conscientiously, and in a consistency with their fidelity to their Head and Savior, acknowledge the authority of the usurpers of his crown as lawful. From all which, and every other instance of their continued prostitution of the discipline instituted by Christ in his church, and of that authority, which he, as a Son over his own house, has given unto faithful gospel ministers, to the contempt and scorn of an ungodly generation; the Presbytery cannot but testify against them, as guilty of exercising a tyrannical power over the heritage of the Lord; and to whom may too justly be applied, the word of the Lord, spoken by his prophet, *Isa.* lxvi, 5: "Your brethren that bated you, that cast you out for my name's sake, said, Let the Lord be glorified: but he shall appear to your joy, and they shall be ashamed." Wherefore, and for all the foresaid grounds, the Presbytery find and declare, that the pretended *Associate Presbytery*, now called *Synod*, whether before or since, in their separate capacity, claiming a parity of power, neither were, nor are lawful and rightly constituted courts of the Lord Jesus Christ, according to his word, and to the testimony of the true Presbyterian Covenanted Church of Christ in *Scotland*: and therefore ought not, nay cannot, in a consistency with bearing a faithful testimony for the covenanted truths, and cause of our glorious Redeemer, be countenanced or submitted to in their authority by his people.

Again, the Presbytery find themselves in duty obliged to testify against these brethren who some time ago have broken off from their communion, for their unwarrantable separation, and continued opposition to the truth and testimony, in the hands of this Presbytery, even to the extent of presuming, in a judicial capacity, to threaten church censure against the Presbytery, without alleging so much as any other reason for this strange procedure, than their refusing to approve as truth, a point of doctrine, that stands condemned by the standards of the Reformed Church of *Scotland*, founded on the authority of divine revelation. But, as the Presbytery have formerly published a vindication of the truth maintained by them, and of their conduct, respecting the subject matter of difference with their *quondam* brethren, they refer to said vindication, for a more particular discovery of the error of their principle, and extravagance of their conduct in this matter. And particularly, they testify against the more avowed apostasy of some of these brethren, who are not ashamed to declare their backslidings in the streets, and publish them upon the house tops; as especially appears from a sermon entitled, *Bigotry Disclaimed*—together with the vindication of said sermon; wherein is vented such a loose and latitudinarian scheme of principles, on the point of church communion, as had a native tendency to destroy the scriptural boundaries thereof, adopted by this church in her most advanced purity; and which is also inconsistent with the ordination vows, whereby the author was solemnly engaged. This, with other differences, best known to themselves, occasioned a rupture in that pretended Presbytery, which for some years subsisted: but this breach being some considerable time ago again cemented, they constituted themselves in their former capacity, upon terms (as appears from a printed account of their agreement and constitution, which they have never yet disclaimed as unjust) not very honorable nor consistent with their former principles and professed zeal for maintaining the same. Which agreement was made up, without any evidence of the above author's retracting his lax principles, contained in the foresaid sermon. Whatever was the cause, whether from the influence of others (as was said by the publisher of their agreement), or from a consciousness of dropping part of formerly received principles, is not certain; but one of these brethren, for a time, gave up with further practical communion with the other, namely, Mr. *Hugh Innes*, late of the *Calton, Glasgow*; while yet it was observed, that both used a freedom, not formerly common to them, anent the present authority, in their public immediate addresses to the object of worship; which, together with their apparent resiling from part of their former testimony occasioned stumbling to some of their people, and terminated in the separation of others. Foresaid latitudinarianism and falling away, is also sadly verified, in the conduct of another principal member of their pretended Presbytery, who has professedly deserted all testimony bearing for the reformation principles of the Covenanted Church of *Scotland*. [5]

At last, after their declared interviews for that purpose, these brethren have patched up a mank agreement, which they have published, in a paper entitled *Abstract of the covenanted principles of the Church of Scotland, &c.*, with a prefixed advertisement in some copies, asserting the removal of their differences, which arose from a sermon on *Psal.* cxxii, 3, published at *Glasgow*,—by a disapprobation of what is implied in some expressions hereof, viz., "That all the members of Christ's mystical body may, and ought to unite in visible church communion."

Here is, indeed, a smooth closing of the wound that should have been more thoroughly searched, that, by probing into the practical application of said sermon, the corrupt matter of communion with the Revolution Church, in the gospel and sealing ordinance thereof, might have been found out; but not one word of this in all that abstract, which contains their grounds of union, and terms of communion. Nothing of the above author's recanting his former latitudinarian practices of hearing, and thereby practically encouraging, that vagrant Episcopalian, *Whitefield*; his communicating, which natively implies union, with the Revolution Church, in one of the seals of the covenant; nor his public praying for an Erastian government, in a way, and for a reason, that must needs be understood as an homologation of their authority. On which accounts, the Presbytery testify against said union, as being inconsistent with faithfulness in the cause of Christ; and against said abstract, as, however containing a variety of particulars very just and good, yet bearing no positive adherence to, nor particular mention of, faithful wrestlings and testimonies of the martyrs and witnesses for *Scotland's* covenanted cause. As also, they testify against the notorious disingenuity of their probationer,

---

[5] Mr. *John Cameron*, then a probationer and clerk to their Presbytery.

who, after a professed dissatisfaction on sundry occasions, with the declining steps of said brethren, particularly with the declaimer against bigotry, has overlooked more weighty matters, and embraced a probability of enjoying the long grasped for privilege of ordination, though it should be observed at a greater expense than that of disappointing the expectation of a few dissatisfied persons, who depended upon his honesty, after they had broken up communion with those he continues still to profess his subjection unto.

And further, the Presbytery testify against the adherents of foresaid brethren, in strengthening their hands in their course of separation from the Presbytery, rejecting both their judicial and ministerial authority, and the ordinances of the gospel dispensed by them. And more especially, the Presbytery condemn the conduct of such of them as, professedly dissatisfied with the above said left-hand extremes, and other defections of foresaid brethren, have therefore broken off from their communion; yet, instead of returning to their duty in a way of subjecting themselves to the courts of Christ, and ordinances instituted by him in his church, have turned back again to their own right-hand extremes of error, which once they professedly gave up, but now persist in, an obstinate impugning the validity of their ministerial authority and protestative mission, undervalue the pure ordinances of the gospel dispensed by them, and live as if there were no church of Christ in the land, where they might receive the seals of the covenant, either to themselves or their children; and therefore, in the righteous judgment of God, have been left to adopt such a dangerous and erroneous system of principles, as is a disgrace to the profession of the covenanted cause. [6]

[6] These people, referred to above, very unjustly designate themselves such *who adhere to the testimony for the kingly prerogative of Christ*. They did at first, before their agreement with the Presbytery, and ever since their elopement, do still profess to appear for what they call *An Active Testimony*, conform to the rude draft of a paper commonly known by the name of the *Queensferry Paper* or *Covenant* (see *Cloud of Witnesses*, Appendix, page 270). After their *activity* had carried them the length of avouching the most inconsistent anti-predestinarian, Arminian schemes of universal redemption, and not only to a total separation from the Presbytery, and rejection of their judicial authority, but even to an open denial of the protestative mission of the ministers therein, and of all others; the most part of them were, in God's holy and righteous justice, left to receive and submit to the pretended authority and ministrations of *William Dunnet*, a deceiver, destitute of all mission and authority, whom they were afterward obliged to abandon In 1771, they published a pamphlet entitled, *A short Abstract of their Principles and Designs*. In this they cunningly evade the acknowledgment of our Confession of Faith and Catechisms, decline to own the doctrine of the holy Trinity in *unity*, and do professedly adopt and avow the hypothesis of the famous modern Socinian, Dr. *Taylor, of Norwich*, anent the person of Christ. According to which he is no more than "a glorious being, truly created by God before the world." This pre-existent creature they call a *superangelic* spirit; which spirit, coming in time to be united to a human body, makes according to them, the person of Christ. A person neither truly God nor truly man, but a sort of being different from both. The absurdity and blasphemy of this hypothesis needs no elucidation. Thus they idolatrously worship *another* god than the Scripture reveals, and blasphemously substitute and trust in *another* savior than the gospel offers unto sinners. In the same pamphlet they declare and publish their resolution to take some of their number under formal trials, whom, upon being approved, they might appoint and send forth to preach the gospel and administer the ordinances of it. And all which they have accordingly

ADVERTISEMENT.

The following supplement, having been a competent length of time before the church in *overture*, was adopted in Logan county, Ohio, May, 1850. And, although without the formality of a judicial sanction, we trust it will not be found destitute of divine authority. The design of it is to show the application of the principles of our Testimony to society, as organized in the United States. For although conventional regulations, civil and ecclesiastical, in this land, are very different from the condition of society in Great Britain, where our Testimony was first emitted, yet the corruptions of human nature, embodied in the combinations of society, are not less visible in this than in other lands, nor less hostile to the supreme authority of the Lord and his Anointed. "The beast and the false prophet" continue to be the objects of popular devotion: Rev. xix, 20.

Cincinnati, Nov. 12th, 1850.

---

done, to the great dishonor of God, reproach of religion, and the profession of it.

And now, from the above principles and practices, the reader may justly conclude how unworthily these Christians (if they may be called such) profess to stand up for the royal prerogatives of Christ. What an arrogant and presumptuous invasion upon, and usurpation of, the powers and prerogatives of this glorious King, for any mortal to assume "to appoint and call men," not to the *work* (which yet is all that the Church of Christ, according to the will of God, and her privileges from Christ her head, ever claimed), but to the very *power* and *office* of the holy ministry, "and to *install* them in it." Besides, that their doctrine as to Christ's person, which denies his divine nature and sonship, saps the very foundations of *that* and all his other offices. We would, therefore, yet beseech them, by the mercies of God, "to repent them of all their wickedness, and to pray God, if perhaps the thoughts of their heart may be forgiven them."

SUPPLEMENT TO PART III.

Containing an application of the principles of our Covenanted Testimony to the existing condition of society in these United States.

The controversy which arose between the Associate and Reformed churches, on the doctrine of civil magistracy, was the occasion of greater divergency between them, on collateral subjects. From false principles, consistent reasoning must produce erroneous conclusions. Assuming that the Son of God, as Mediator, has nothing to do with the concerns of God's moral government beyond the precincts of the visible church, it would follow, that church members, as citizens of the "kingdoms of this world," neither owe him allegiance nor are bound to thank him for "common benefits." The assumption is, however, obviously erroneous, because, as Mediator, he is "head over all things to the church," Eph. i, 22, consequently, all people, nations and languages, are bound to obey and serve him, in this office capacity, and to thank him for his mercies.

While this controversy was keenly managed by the respective parties in the British isles, the Lord Christ interposed between the disputants, as it were, to decide the chief point in debate. By the rise of the British colonies west of the Atlantic, against the parent country, and their successful struggle to gain a national independence, a clear commentary was furnished on the long-contested principle, that, in some cases, it is lawful to resist existing civil powers. Seceders, forgetting, for the time, their favorite theory, joined their fellow colonists in casting off the yoke of British rule. Those who vehemently opposed Reformed Presbyterians, for disowning the British government, joined cheerfully in its overthrow. How fickle and inconsistent is man! During the revolutionary struggle might be witnessed the singular spectacle—humbling to the pride of human reason, revolting to the sensibilities of the exercised Christian—brethren of the same communion, on opposite sides of the Atlantic, pleading with the God of justice to give success to the respective armies! East of the ocean the petition would be, "Lord, prosper the British arms;" on the west, "Lord, favor the patriots of these oppressed colonies!" Such are the consequences natively resulting from a theory alike unscriptural and absurd—a principle deep-laid in that system of opposition to the Lord and his Anointed, emphatically styled "The Antichrist."

Great national revolutions are special trials of the faith and patience of the saints. No firmness of character will be proof against popular opinion and example at such a time, without special aid from on high. Reformed Presbyterians in the colonies rejoiced in the success of the revolution, issuing in the independence of the United States. Their expectation of immediate advantage to the reformation cause was too sanguine. A new frame of civil polity was to be devised by the colonies, now that they were independent of the British crown. This state of things called forth the exercise of human intellect, in more than ordinary measure, to meet the emergency. Frames of national policy are apt to warp the judgment of good men. Even Christian ministers are prone to substitute the maxims of human prudence for the precepts of inspiration. Many divines conceived the idea of conforming the visible church to the model of the American republic. The plan was projected and advocated, of bringing all evangelical denominations into one confederated unity, while the integral parts should continue independent of each other. This plan would have defeated its own object, the unity of the visible church, and subverted that form of government established by Zion's King. Upon trial by some of the New England Independents and Presbyterians, the plan has proved utterly abortive.

Prior to the Revolutionary war, a Presbytery had been constituted in America, upon the footing of the covenanted reformation. The exciting scenes and active sympathies, attendant on the Revolutionary war, added to a hereditary love of liberty, carried many covenanters away from their distinctive principles. The Reformed Presbytery was dissolved, and three ministers who belonged to it, joining some ministers of the Associate Church, formed that society, since known by the name of the Associate Reformed Church. The union was completed in the year 1782, after having been five years in agitation.

These ministers professed, as the basis of union, the Westminster standards; but the abstract of principles, which they adopted as the more immediate bond of coalescence, discovered, to discerning spectators, that the individuals forming the combination, were by no means unanimous in their views of the doctrines taught in those standards. Indeed, there were certain sections of the Confession *reserved* for future discussion, which, in process of time, were wholly rejected. This attack upon a document, venerable not so much for its age as its scriptural character, gave rise to zealous opposition by some in the body, and ultimately resulted in a rupture. Two ministers dissented from the majority, left their communion, and proceeded to erect a new organization, styled "The Reformed Dissenting Presbytery." This was in the year 1801. At this date, there were four denominations, in the United States, claiming to be the legitimate successors of the British reformers, viz., the Associate, Reformed, Associate Reformed, and Reformed Dissenting Presbyterians. Three of these professedly appear under the banner of a standing judicial testimony, which they severally emitted to the public. The Associate Reformed Church, by judicial declaration and uniform practice, is opposed to this method of testimony-bearing.

The Reformed Presbytery, which had been dissolved by the defection of the ministry, during the Revolutionary war, was reorganized toward the close of the eighteenth century. The troubles in Ireland, when the inhabitants united for the purpose of gaining independence of the British crown, were the occasion of bringing strength to the church in America. Reformed Presbyterians, feeling sensibly with others the arm of British tyranny, joined interests hastily with Papists and others, in one sworn association, for the purpose of overturning the existing government by force of arms. The enterprise, as might have been expected, was unsuccessful; Isa. viii, 11, 12; Obadiah 7; 2 Cor. vi, 17. Many fled to the asylum which God had provided, shortly before, in America. Among the refugees were some of the Covenanters, by which the church was strengthened in her ministry and membership.

Early in the nineteenth century, measures were taken by the Reformed Presbytery, in the United States, for re-exhibiting the principles of a covenanted reformation, in a judicial way. Accordingly, in the year 1806, the Presbytery published, as adopted, a work entitled "Reformation Principles Exhibited" — a book which has ever since been popularly called the American Testimony. The familiar designation, *Testimony*, the general complexion of the book, the orthodox aspect of terms, and even most of the leading sentiments of the work, gave it currency, and rendered it generally acceptable to pious and intelligent Covenanters. And however it seemed to the unsuspecting to sustain, it eventually and effectually supplanted the Scottish Testimony. The men who had the principal hand in giving shape and direction to the principles and practice of Covenanters in the United States, at that time, were located in some of the most populous and commercial cities on the Atlantic coast, where temptations to conform to this world were many and pressing. A disposition to temporize was manifested in these localities, soon after their principles had been judicially exhibited. The last war between the United States and England, subjected Covenanters to new trials in America. As aliens, they were deemed unsafe residents at the seaboard, and were ordered, by the government, to retire a certain distance to the interior (much like the course pursued by Claudius Caesar toward the Jews, Acts xviii, 2). To meet the exigency, a deputation of the church was appointed to repair to Washington, in 1812, and offer a pledge that they would defend the integrity of the country against all enemies. This measure was, however, never carried out.

The church increased in numbers and influence, and began to be noticed with respect and professions of esteem among surrounding denominations. Some of her members had ventured to act in the capacity of citizens of the United States, by serving on juries. This was of course managed for a time clandestinely. At length, waxing confident by success, they began to act more openly. This gave rise to a petition addressed to the supreme judicatory of the church. The petitioners were answered by instructing them to apply for direction to the inferior judicatories — thus shunning the duty of applying their own acknowledged principles. This was in the year 1823. This course did not satisfy the petitioners, and application was again made to Synod in 1825, to explain the import of their former Act. The reply was—"This Synod never understood any act of theirs, relative to their members sitting on juries, or contravening the old common law of the church on that subject;" a response obviously as equivocal as the preceding. As early as 1823, a motion was made in the Synod to open a correspondence with the judicatories of other denominations. This motion was resisted, and for the time proved abortive. At next meeting of Synod, however, the measure was brought before that body, by a proposal from the General Assembly to correspond by delegation. This proposal found many, and some of them able, advocates in the Reformed. P. Synod. The measure was, however, again defeated; but immediately after the failure, a number of ministers forsook the Reformation ranks and consorted with the General Assembly. In the year 1828, the Synod gave its sanction and lent its patronage to the Colonization Society, which was continued till the year 1836, when its patronage was transferred to the cause of Abolition. The spirit of declension became manifest at the session of Synod in 1831, when some of the most prominent and practical principles of the Reformed Church were openly thrown into debate, in the pages of a monthly periodical, under the head of "Free Discussion." Through the pernicious influence of that perfidious journal, sustained by the patronage of ministers of eminent standing in the church, a large proportion—neatly one-half—of the ministry were prepared, by the next meeting of Synod in 1833, to renounce the peculiar principles and long known usages of the Reformed Covenanted Church. Organizing themselves as a separate body, yet claiming their former ecclesiastical name, they deliberately incorporated with the government of the United States, and some of the senior ministers, more fully to testify their loyalty, in their old age, took the oath of naturalization!—thus breaking down the carved work which they had for many years assiduously labored to erect.

It was hoped that the severe trial to which the professing witnesses of Christ were subjected at that time, would have taught them a lesson not soon to be forgotten. It was thought by many that the church was now purged from the leaven which had almost leavened the whole lump. The Synod met in 1834, when a perverse spirit was evident in the midst of its members. The Colonization and Abolition Societies, with other associations—the exfoliations of Antichrist—had evidently gained an ascendency in the affections of many of the members. The altercation and bitterness with which the claims of these societies were discussed, evidenced to such as were free from their infection, that some of those present viewed these popular movements as transcending in importance, the covenanted testimony of the church. As the practice of occasional hearing was on the increase in some sections of the church, Synod was memorialized on that subject, but refused to declare the law of the church. The old spirit of conformity to the world was still more manifest in 1836, when Synod was importuned by her children, from the eastern and western extremes of the church, by petition, memorial, protest and appeal—growing out of the practice then generally prevalent of incorporating with the voluntary associations of the age. The response of the supreme judicatory was in this case as ambiguous as on any former occasion. The backsliding course of the factious majority was but feebly counteracted by dissent from only two members of Synod; a respectable minority having been outwitted by the carnal wisdom of those who were prompt in applying the technicalities of law. Hope was, however, cherished, that this check so publicly given, together with the practical workings of the system of moral amalgamation, would induce even reckless innovators to pause—to consider their ways and their doings. This hope, however rational and sanguine, was totally disappointed in 1838, when the table of the supreme judicatory might be said to be crowded with petitions, letters, remonstrances, memorials, protests and appeals. The just grievances of the children of witnessing and martyred fathers, were treated with contempt—"laid on the table," "returned," with the cry "let them be kicked under the table," &c. And when some attempted to urge their right to be heard, they were called to order, treated with personal insult, or subjected to open violence. A few of these, having thus experienced the tyranny and abuse of the ruling faction, declined the authority and communion of Synod, and established a separate fellowship.

When the Synod again met in 1840, the same measures which had been carried by mob violence at the preceding meeting, were pressed as before; but with less tumult—leaders having learned caution from the consequences following their former outrageous conduct. Matters had now come to a crisis, when a reclaiming minority were reduced to this dilemma—either to acquiesce in the almost total subversion of the covenanted constitution of the church; or, by separating from an irreclaimable majority, attempt, by an independent organization, to make up the breach. It is easy to see which alternative was duty, not only from the nature of the case, but from the well defined footsteps of the flock. Reformation has been effected in the church of God in all ages, by the protestation and separation of a virtuous Minority. At this juncture a paper was laid upon the table of Synod, of which the following is a true copy:

"PREAMBLE AND RESOLUTIONS.

"Whereas, It is the province and indispensable duty of this Synod, when society is in a state of agitation as at present, to know the signs of the times and what Israel ought to do: and whereas it is also the duty of this Synod, to testify in behalf of truth, to condemn sin and testify against those who commit it; to acquaint our people with their danger, and search into the causes of God's controversy with them and with us: and whereas it is the duty of Synod further, to point out to the people of God the course to be pursued, that divine judgments may be averted or removed—therefore,

"1. *Resolved*, That uniting with, or inducing to fellowship, by the members of the Reformed Presbyterian Church, in the voluntary and irresponsible associations of the day—composed of persons of all religious professions and of no profession—be condemned, as unwarranted by the word of God, the subordinate Standards of the church, and the practice of our covenant fathers.

"2. That an inquiry be instituted, in order to ascertain the grounds of God's controversy with us, in the sins of omission and commission, wherewith we are chargeable in our ecclesiastical relations.

"3. That the sins thus ascertained, be confessed, mourned over and forsaken, and our engagement to the contrary duties renewed; that the Lord may return, be entreated of his people and leave a blessing behind him."

This paper was instantly "laid on the table;" and when, at a subsequent session of the court, it was regularly called up for action, it was again and finally "laid on the table!" Ever since that transaction, this paper has been diligently misrepresented, as consisting only of *one* resolution, and that the *first*, contrary to its own evidence.

After the final adjournment of Synod, those individuals who, as a minority, had opposed the innovations and backslidings of their brethren, embraced an opportunity for consultation. It appeared that without preconcert, they were unanimous that all legal means having failed to reclaim their backsliding brethren, who constituted a large majority of Synod; both duty and necessity required them to assume a position independent *of* former organizations, that they might, untrammeled, carry out practically their testimony. Accordingly two ministers and three ruling elders proceeded to constitute a Presbytery on constitutional ground, declaring in the deed of constitution, adherence to all reformation attainments. This transaction took place in the city of Alleghany, June 24th, 1840. The declining majority continued their course of backsliding, following those who had relinquished their fellowship with slanderous imputations and pretended censure, as is usual in such cases. Since that time, there are no evidences given by them either of repentance or reformation.

The Synod of Scotland has for many years been in a; course of declension, in many respects very similar to that of America. As early as the year 1815, some ministers of that body began to betray a disposition to accommodate their profession to the taste of the world. The judicial testimony emitted by their fathers was represented as too elaborate and learned to be read and understood by the common reader, and too severe in its strictures upon the principles and practice of other Christian denominations. The abstract of terms of communion was viewed as too strict and uncharitable, especially the Auchensaugh Covenant became particularly obnoxious. By a persevering importunity for a series of years this degenerating party prevailed so far in the Synod as to have the Auchensaugh Deed expunged from the symbols of their profession. This was accomplished in 1822; and, taken in connection with other movements indicating a prevailing spirit of worldly conformity, this outrage upon the constitution of the Reformed Presbyterian Church, gave rise to a secession from the body, by the oldest minister in the connection, and a considerable number of others, elders and members. At the above date, the Rev. James Reed declined the fellowship of the Scottish Synod; and he maintained the integrity of the covenanted standards in a separate communion till his death: declaring at his latter end, that "he could not have laid his head upon a dying pillow in peace, if he had not acted as he did in that matter."

Deaf to the remonstrances of this aged and faithful minister, his former brethren pursued their perverse and downward course, until their new position became apparent by the adoption of a Testimony and Terms of Communion adapted to their taste. Their Testimony was adopted in 1837. This document ostensibly consists of two parts, historical and doctrinal; but really only of the latter as *authoritative*. This will appear from the preface to the history, as also that it is without the *formal* sanction of the Synod, which appears prefixed to the doctrinal part of the book. A considerable time before they ventured to obtrude this new Testimony on the church; they had prepared the way for its introduction, by supplanting the authoritative "Rules of Society," framed and adopted by their fathers. This was done by issuing what they called a "Guide to Social Worship," which the Scottish Synod sent forth under an ambiguous *recommendation*, and the spurious production was republished by order of Synod, in America, 1836, with the like equivocal expression of approbation.

What has been just related of the Ref. Pres. Church in Scotland, will apply substantially to that section of the same body in Ireland. On the doctrine of the magistrate's power *circa sacra*, however, there was a controversy of several years' continuance and managed with much asperity, in which Rev. Messrs. John Paul, D.D., and Thomas Houston were the most distinguished disputants. Their contendings issued in breach of organic fellowship in 1840. Indeed the sister-hood which had subsisted for many years among the Synods east and west of the Atlantic ocean, was violated in 1833; when the rupture took place in the Synod of America, by the elopement of the declining party, who are since known by alliance with the civil institutions of the United States. Among these five Synods, the principle called *elective affinity* has been strikingly exemplified; while what the Scripture denominates *schism*, has been as visibly rampant as perhaps at any period under the Christian dispensation.

This brief historical sketch may serve to show the outlines of the courses respectively pursued by the several parties in the British Isles and America, who have made professions of attachment to that work in the kingdom of Scotland especially, which has been called the Second Reformation. But the duty of fidelity to Zion's King, and even the duty of charity to these backsliding brethren; together with the informing of the present and succeeding generations, require, that we notice more formally some of the more prominent measures of these ecclesiastical bodies and so manifest more fully our relation to them. It is not to be expected however, that we are about to condescend upon *all* the erroneous sentiments or steps of defection, supplied by the history of these communities. To direct the honest inquiries of the Lord's people, and assist them in that process of reasoning by which facts are compared with acknowledged Standards, supreme and subordinate, that their moral character may be tested, is all that is proposed in the following sections.

SECTION I. The Secession from the Revolution Church of Scotland in that country assumed a position in relation to the civil institutions of Great Britain, which their posterity continue too occupy until the present time in the United States without material alteration.

1. They cooperate practically with all classes in the civil community, in maintaining national rebellion against the Lord and his Anointed. They give their suf-

frages toward the elevation of vile persons to the highest places of civil dignity in the American confederacy—knowing the candidates to be strangers or enemies to Immanuel. And although they have recently lifted a testimony against that system of robbery called slavery, which is so far right; yet this fact only goes to render their professed loyalty to an unscriptural frame of civil government, as manifestly inconsistent as it is impious.

2. The have all along in the United States renounced the civil part of the British Covenants, declaring that they "neither have nor ever had anything to do with them." Truth is not local, nor does the obligation of the second table of the moral law, on which that part of our covenants is plainly founded, depend on the permanency of our residence in a particular portion of the world. "The earth is the Lord's and the fullness thereof." It follows, that however solemnly or frequently they profess to renew their fathers' covenants; the whole transaction displays their unfaithfulness to the Lord, who is a party in the covenants; and is calculated to mislead the unwary.

3. Their unsteadfastness is further evidenced, by conforming to other ecclesiastical communities in the loose practice of occasional or indiscriminate hearing; and even in some instances of ministerial intercommunion—the law of their church on that matter having become obsolete. Against these courses, in some of which that body has obstinately persevered for more than a hundred years, we deem it incumbent on us to continue an uncompromising testimony. Many comments the Moral Governor of the nations has furnished in his providence within the last century, making still more intelligible the righteous claims of his word: but Seceders seem to have their moral vision obscured by a vail of hereditary prejudice. We trust the Lord is on his way to destroy the face of the covering cast over all people, and the vail that is spread over all nations; Is. xxv, 7.

SEC. II. Our testimony against the unfaithfulness of the Associate Reformed Church, continues also without material change since the rise of that body. The following among others may here be noticed, as constituting just grounds of opposition in a way of testimony-bearing, by all who would be found faithful to the Lord, and their covenant engagements.

1. Their very origin was unwarranted by scripture. All the scriptural attainments to which they profess to adhere, were already incorporated in the standards of the organic bodies, from whose fellowship they seceded. They did therefore make a breach without a definite object, and multiply divisions in the visible body of Christ without necessity. Thus they did violence to the royal law of love; for while under a profession of charity they invited to their new fellowship their former brethren; the nature of the case evinces a disposition to unmitigated tyranny. This state of things we think has not been generally understood. We shall here endeavor to render it intelligible. The fact of organizing that church (the Associate Reformed) said to both Covenanters and Seceders "It is your duty to dissolve your respective organizations, and join us." This is undeniable. The Covenanter or Seceder replies by asking—"What iniquity have you or your fathers found in us,

that you forsook our communion?" &c. "Not any," replies the Associate Reformed Church; "only some trifling opinions peculiar to you severally which we deem unworthy of contending about. Only join our church, and we will never quarrel with you, relative to your singularities." "Ah," replies the other party, "the matters about which we differ, are trifling in your account; how then could they be of such magnitude as to warrant your breaking fellowship with us? What you call *trifles, peculiarities*, &c, we cannot but still judge important principles, sealed by the precious blood of martyrs: must we deny these or bury them in silence, to gain membership in your new church? Is this the nature and amount of your professed charity? This is not that heaven-born principle 'that rejoiceth not in iniquity, but rejoiceth in the truth.' You break fellowship for what you esteem mere trifles—you propose to us a new term of communion, with which it is morally impossible that we should comply, without doing violence to our consciences. Is this charity or tyranny?"

2. Although covenanting was declared by this body at their origin, to be an "important duty," they never recognized the solemn deeds of their fathers as binding on them; nor have they ever attempted the acknowledged duty in a way supposed to be competent to themselves. Nay, the obligation of the British covenants has been denied both openly and frequently from the pulpit and the press; and even attempts have been made, not seldom, by profane ridicule, to bring them into contempt. The very duty of public, social covenanting, either in a National or ecclesiastical capacity, has been often opposed in the polemic writings of the ministers of this body, however often inculcated and exemplified in the word of God. The moral nature of the duty taken in connection with prophetic declarations, to be fulfilled only under the Christian dispensation, demonstrates the permanency of this divine ordinance until the end of the world.

3. This church set out with unsound views of church fellowship, as has been already in part made appear. But when their position came to be more pointedly defined, they made the novel distinction between *fixed* and *occasional* communion. The practical tendency of this unscriptural experiment was necessarily to *catholic* communion, which theory was soon advocated by some of the most prominent of the ministry; and accordingly eventuated in the merging of a large number of her ministry and membership, in the communion of the General Assembly.

4. On the doctrine of the divine ordinance of civil government, this church has all along been unsound; as is fully evidenced in the practice of her members, which has been similar to that of Seceders. Our testimony against the latter is, in this particular, equally directed against the former.

5. This church has appeared as the advocate of a boundless toleration, conforming her views and policy in a most servile manner to the infidel model presented in the civil constitutions of republican America. It would seem, indeed, that this body aimed at conforming their ecclesiastical polity to that standard, from the fact that the very symbol of their profession as a corporate body, is designated the "Constitution of the Associate Reformed Church"—a designation which might

be considered as militating against the supremacy of the Holy Scriptures. In this Constitution a sphere is assigned to conscience, which is incompatible with due subjection to the Supreme Lawgiver. As well might the *will*, or any other faculty of the soul of man, be invested with this impious supremacy, and immunity from control, by any authority instituted on earth by the only Lord of conscience. Jehovah will rule the *consciences* of his creatures, as well as their *judgments* and *wills*, by his holy law, in the civil commonwealth, in the church and in the family.

6. The unfaithfulness of this body appears further, in shunning to declare the *divine right* and unalterableness of Presbyterial Church Government, she testifies not against Prelacy or Independency. If this church is Presbyterial in practice, it is on no better footing than that of the Revolution Church of Scotland.

7. The purity of divine worship is not guarded by the terms of fellowship in this church. It is true, "No Hymns merely of human composure, are allowed in her churches." But what mean these guarded terms and phrases, "merely;" "churches?" The best interpretation of these cunningly contrived expressions is supplied by the practice of those ministers of the body, who scruple not to offer unto God "hymns merely of human composure" when occupying pulpits of other denominations, or sojourning for a night in families where these hymns are statedly used. It is known that this part of the order of public worship has been submitted in some instances, to the voice of the congregation by their pastor; thus manifesting in the same act, latitudinarianism in regard both to the government and worship of the house of God.

Lastly, to specify no further—Laxity of discipline is observable in this church. She has always admitted to her fellowship, and to a participation in her special privileges (the seals of the covenants), persons who openly deny the divine warrant for a fast in connection with the celebration of the Lord's Supper; yea, who ridicule that part of the solemnity as *superstitious!* The same privileges are granted in this church to such as habitually neglect the worship of God in the family. Nor does this church inculcate or enjoin, as a part of Christian practice, fellowship meetings for prayer and conference. We must, as witnesses for the cause of Christ, solemnly protest against these sentiments and correspondent practices, as inconsistent with the scripture and the reformation attainments of our covenant fathers.

SEC. III. The Reformed Dissenting Church embraced more of the peculiar principles of the covenanted reformation than either of the two preceding. On the doctrines of magistracy and toleration, abstractly considered, they have manifested commendable fidelity. Nevertheless, in the practical application of these doctrines and in other respects, we are constrained to continue a testimony against them.

1. What has been remarked of the origin of the Associate Reformed body, is partly true also of the party which dissented from them: their organization was uncalled for, there being no scriptural attainment embraced by them, which was not already exhibited under a judicial banner. Those who erected the Reformed Dissenting Presbytery may have been harshly treated by ministers of the Reformed

Presbytery, when attempting negotiations for union, as public fame has often rumored: yet supposing this to have been the case, multiplying separate fellowships was not a happy expedient for effecting union in the truth.

2. This body of Christians have been all along unfaithful in applying their own avowed principles relative to magistracy. Their innovation in this respect would seem to have been a carnal expedient to reach a two-fold object: the one, to retaliate on the Reformed Church for supposed indignities offered; the other, to render themselves more popular in the eyes of other communities. They admit that a constitution of civil government may be so immoral, that it cannot be considered as God's ordinance; that in such a case "no Christian can, without sinning against God, accept any office supreme or subordinate, where an oath to support such a constitution is made essential to his office." These admissions are equally just and important; yet these concessions are wholly neutralized in practice by these people, for they claim it as their privilege to choose others to fill those offices, which they say, they themselves cannot fill "without sinning against God." We must continue our earnest testimony against this attempt to separate in law, between the representative and his constituents, involving as it does, if consistently carried out, the total overthrow of the covenants of works and grace, and ultimately of God's moral government by his annotated Son! The effort made to sustain their practice in this matter, from the examples of the Marquis of Argyle and Lord Warriston, is very disingenuous; simply because the church of Scotland had not at the date referred to, reached the measure of her attainments on that head. Indeed, the whole drift of their argument goes to justify the position, that in some cases, it is expedient to do evil that good may come.

3. On the doctrine of faith this church has, we think, darkened counsel, by words without knowledge. Their distinctions and caveats relative to *assurance*, are calculated rather to bewilder than enlighten the mind of the general reader. "Receiving and resting on Christ as offered in the gospel," amounts to "appropriation, certainty, assurance," &c. There is evidence of a tendency to "vain jangling" here, against which, even suppose there be no error couched in the terms, we ought to testify.

4. This church evinces a disposition to intercommunion, in the practice both of ministers and members, wholly inconsistent with steadfastness, and at war with her own declared views of toleration. Occupying pulpits in common with more corrupt communities, doing this in connection with the celebration of the Lord's Supper, and attendance and co-operation with others in conventional proceedings among those who style themselves "Reformed Churches," are practices among these people, on which we feel constrained to animadvert with decided disapprobation. As also their violation of the form of Presbyterian church government by one minister with ruling elders presuming to set apart candidates to the office of the holy ministry.

SEC. IV. To speak thus publicly against those who may be the precious sons of Zion, is a painful duty. That charity, however, which rejoiceth in the truth, requires of

Christ's witnesses that they censure and rebuke, in a way competent to them, those of the household of faith whom they see and know to be in a course of error or of sin; *Isa.* **lviii, 1;** *Tit.* **i, 13.**

Many of those with whom we were wont to take pleasure in displaying a banner jointly, and in a judicial capacity, are now, alas! arrayed against us. To the real friend of Jesus, and the truth as it is in Jesus, there cannot be a more lamentable spectacle than the *professed witnesses* of the Lamb disposed in rank under hostile colors as the company—not of two, but of many armies, ready to engage in mutual destruction! And indeed those who bite and devour one another, are in danger of being consumed one of another. The Lord is righteous in all that is come upon us; for we have sinned against him—both we and our fathers. We know not how to avert more wrath from the Lord, reclaim backsliders, confirm the wavering, direct sincere inquirers, apprise the unsuspecting of their danger, and exonerate our own consciences, otherwise than by giving open, candid and honest testimony for Christ and truth, against those, even once brethren by covenant bonds, who have dishonored him, and caused the way of truth to be evil spoken of.

Against those who separated from us in Philadelphia, 1833, erecting a rival judicatory, and dishonestly claiming the name Reformed Presbyterian Church, we bear our feeble testimony for the following among other reasons:

1. They did then openly enter on a course subversive of our whole covenanted system of doctrine and order, by withdrawing their dissent from the civil institutions of the United States, and incorporating with the National Society—knowing the same to be, by the terms of the national compact, opposed in many respects, both to godliness and honesty.

2. This party had, in a clandestine way, exerted their influence to seduce and draw away disciples after them for a series of years. This is evident from the petitions addressed to Synod on the jury law, issuing from those who are known to have been in correspondence with some of the leaders in that defection.

3. This party are chargeable with mutilating the Judicial Testimony emitted in Scotland, 1761; and also with changing the terms of communion, and obtruding a mutilated formula upon an unsuspecting people, contrary to due order.

History and *argument* are excluded from the terms of Church Fellowship, on the very face of "Reformation Principles Exhibited;" and the Auchensaugh Covenant expunged from the formula of terms of communion, without submitting them in overture to the people for inspection. We say these steps of defection and apostasy are chargeable to the account of those who made the breach in 1833: *First,* Because the senior and leading ministers in that separation were the men who framed the American Testimony and Terms of Communion; and so had many years before laid the platform and projected the course on which they violently entered at that date. *Second,* These separatists, in the edition of these symbols of their profession lately published, have consistently left out of the volume, the Historical

Part, and also remodeled the formula of Terms of Communion.

4. This body continues to wax worse and worse, against all remonstrance from their former connections and others, as also in the face of providential rebukes;—losing, because forfeiting, the confidence of conscientious and honorable men, exemplified in the frequent meetings, and to them, disastrous results, of the Convention of, so called, Reformed Churches.

SEC. V. With the foregoing party may be classed those different and conflicting fellowships in Scotland and Ireland, whose recent Terms of Communion and Judicial Testimony, substantially identify with those mentioned in the preceding section.

1. Public fame charges the Eastern Synod of Ireland, and the Synod of Scotland, with connivance at the members and officers under their inspection, in co-operating with the immoral and anti-christian government of Great Britain. They are therefore guilty of giving their power and strength to that powerful and blood-thirsty horn of the beast. We are inclined to give more credit to public fame in this than we would in many other cases, because:

2. These Synods have opened a door in their new Testimony for such sinful confederacies. "What!" will the simple and uninitiated reader of the Testimony ask, "does not that Testimony declare, often and often, that the British constitution is anti-christian?" We answer, the *book* declares so; but we caution the reader to be on his guard, lest he judge and take for granted, without a careful examination, that the book and the Testimony are the same thing. Let the honest inquirer consult the *preface* to the *Historical* part of the book, and then the preface to the Doctrinal part: the latter, he will find, on due examination, to constitute the Testimony. True, in page 8 of the preface to the volume, it is said, "the Testimony, as now published, consists of two parts, the one *Historical* and the other *Doctrinal*." This sounds orthodox; but, in the same page, when these two parts come to be defined, it is said, "when the church requires of those admitted into her fellowship, an acknowledgement of a work like the present, the approbation expressed has a reference to the *principles* embodied in it, and *the proper application* of them," &c. "So they wrap it up"—better than our fathers succeeded in a similar enterprise in America. The truth is what they call the *historical* part is largely *argumentative*; and both these parts are carefully and covertly excluded from the *terms of fellowship*! We shall have occasion to recur to this subject, as there are many others likeminded with these innovators.

3. These people are also deeply involved in the popular, so called, benevolent associations of the world, Sunday Schools, Bible Societies, Temperance Reforms, Missionary Enterprise, &c, evidencing a wide departure from our covenanted uniformity, based upon our covenanted Testimony.

SEC. VI. Those who in 1838, on account of sensible tyranny, growing out of defection on the part of the majority, declined the authority of Synod, have shared all along in our sympathies; and it has been our desire that they and we could see eye to

eye in the doctrines and order of the house of God.

Although this party promised fair for a time, and apparently contended for "all the attainments of a covenanted reformation," in process of time it became apparent that they possessed not intelligence sufficient to manage a consistent testimony for that cause. They seem to have been under the influence of temporary impulse, arising from the experience of *mal-administration*; rather than to have discovered any *constitutional* defection in the body from which they separated. This is apparent indeed if we have access to any credible source of information relative to the principles they profess, and their Christian practice. More particularly,

1. Although that paper which they designate "Safety League," has the sound of orthodoxy; yet, as originated, and since interpreted by them, there is a lamentable falling off from the attainments and footsteps of the flock. *First*, so far as we can ascertain, that instrument had clandestine origin being framed and subscribed by those *who were yet in fellowship with the Synod!* This might be earnest, but, we think, not honorable contending for the truth. *Second*, when this paper comes to be interpreted by its framers and signers, it seems to cover only the American Testimony and Terms, as remodeled by breach of presbyterial order. At other times, it will conveniently extend to the Scottish Testimony, 1761, and the Auchensaugh Deed, 1712! From which we infer that these people have no settled standards.

2. We testify against these people for unwarrantable separation from us. One of their elders co-operated in organizing the Reformed Presbytery in 1840; this in official, and, as then distinctly understood, representative capacity. Yet, some time afterward, he and his brethren withdrew from said Presbytery, without assigning justifiable reasons.

3. Efforts are known to have been made, by some then in their fellowship, to have social corresponding meetings established among them, but without success; in opposition to the well-defined example of our witnessing fathers, whose example they affect to imitate.

Lastly, these quondam brethren are not, to this day, distinguishable, in the symbols of their profession, from any party who have more evidently and practically abandoned the distinctive principles and order of a covenanted ancestry. There is no constitutional barrier in the way of their coalescence with any party, whom interest or caprice may select.

SEC. VII. Against that party usually, but improperly, styled the Old Lights, are we obliged to testify more pointedly than against any other party now claiming to be Reformed Presbyterians. *First*, **because we believe there are among them still, real Covenanters; and, in proportion to the whole body, a greater number of such than in any other fellowship. These we would undeceive, if the Lord will; for we earnestly desire renewed fellowship with all such on original ground.** *Second*, **because the leaders among these make the fairest show in the flesh, and, calculating on spiritual sloth and the force of confirmed habit, hope to lead honest people insensibly after them**

back into Egypt. *Third,* **because they are more numerous, and, from habit, more exemplary than other parties; and therefore more likely to influence honest Christians unwittingly to dishonor Christ, and gainsay his precious truth.**

1. These former brethren acted, in 1833, very similar to the policy of the Revolution Church of Scotland in 1689. Instead of repairing the breaches made, and going on to fortify our New Testament Jerusalem, against the assaults of enemies in future, they rested in their present position, providing only for a new edition of Reformation Principles Exhibited, with a continuance of the history to that date. It was urged, at the time, that the argumentative part of our Testimony should be hastened to completion, but without effect. As the apostate Assembly of Scotland, 1689, admitted unsound ministers, curates, &c., to seats in court; so, with the like politic design, members were admitted to seats in Synod, 1833, who claimed "a right to withdraw to another party, if they should see cause" — yea, one of these was called to the moderator's chair!

2. At next meeting, 1834, when the continuation of the historical part of the Testimony was read, and referred to a committee for publication in the forthcoming edition of Reformation Principles Exhibited, it was directed that the terms of communion should be inserted, supplying the deficiency in the first term, in these words: "and the alone infallible rule of faith and manners." In the new edition these important words were omitted, as before! Several ministers seemed to be influenced in social relations, at that time, more by public opinion, than by the infallible rule. No further progress was made with the argumentative part of the Testimony, and a petition from Greenfield, to have Synod's mind relative to occasional hearing, was returned. Against these steps of unfaithfulness we lift our protest.

3. Against the tyranny manifested at the next meeting, there were some to stand up at the time; but the spirit of the world prevailed in all the important transactions. We testify against those who refused to permit petitions, memorials, and other papers addressed to that court, to be read. Especially do we protest against that satanical spirit evidenced in misrepresenting certain respectful and argumentative papers, as being "abusive," "insulting," &c.: also the unrighteous attempt, by some guilty members of that court, to stop the mouth of petitioners; and we condemn the reason assigned for so doing, viz., "They had no right to petition, because they were under suspension"! This reason is worthy of double condemnation, as coming from the mouth of him who, in this instance, acted the ecclesiastical tyrant, and who would come down from Zion's walls to the plains of Ono, mingle in political strife, that he might open his mouth for the dumb; and because a brother in covenant bonds would demur, censure him, and then make the fact of censure a reason why he should not be heard when petitioning for relief from such tyranny! "Revolters are profound to make slaughter."

4. As papers were numerous on the table of Synod in 1838, so they furnished occasion for displays of character and conduct, humiliating to all lovers of Zion, who witnessed the transactions of that meeting of the supreme judicatory.

This was the first time, so far as we know, when that body was called upon formally to review and rectify, in a way competent to them, some parts, both of the constitutional law and administration of the Reformed Presbyterian Synod and Church in America. For a series of years, and chiefly through the influence of leaders in that faction which separated from the body in 1833, high-handed measures of tyranny had transpired: and some of the subjects of that tyranny were yet writhing under a sense of accumulated wrongs; others had, by death, been released from this species of persecution. Some thought it dutiful to call Synod's attention to these matters, and a *petition* was laid before them, from Rev. Robert Lusk, requesting that certain cases of discipline, which the petitioner specified, be reviewed; and especially asking, that "the term *testimony* be restored to its former ecclesiastical use." As this was, in our deliberate opinion, the most important measure brought under the cognizance of the church representative in America, during the current of the nineteenth century, it was thought the court would take the matter under deliberate consideration. Whether through ignorance of the matter proposed, or that sectional interests engrossed the attention of parties, or that the prevailing majority desired to be untrammeled in their future course, the petition was smuggled through and shuffled by, under the cognomen of a "letter," which a member of Synod answered on behalf of the court, as though it were a matter of the smallest importance imaginable! We solemnly testify against this manner of disposing of a weighty matter at that time, whether through inattention or design. We protest also against the violent conduct of those ministers, and others on the same occasion, who made the place of solemn worship and judicial deliberation, a scene of confusion, by vociferations, gesticulations and physical force, in violation of God's law, ordination vows, and the first principle of Presbyterian church government.

5. Here we can advert only to a tithe of the fruits of darkness, which had been increasing in quantity and bitterness, since the meeting of Synod in New York, 1838. To carry out measures of worldly policy, in 1840, diligent electioneering was carried on during the intermediate time, that the court might be what is technically called a *packed Synod.* That court was chiefly composed of such ministers and elders as were known to favor innovations; and some who were known to be disposed to resist defection, were excluded from seats in court. Against this dishonest, partial and unjust measure, we protest. And here we lift our testimony against this course, as having greatly retarded the Lord's work for many years before, and as having facilitated the introduction of error, disorder and open tyranny, in manifold instances, during the same period.

6. We testify against the tyranny exercised upon James McKinney, of Coldenham, who was not allowed to read his vindication and justification, when he asked permission to do so, from the published sentiments of some of those who condemned him!!! Also the cruelty practiced toward Miss King, an absent member, whose representation of her case to the Synod, could not so much as be heard. We bear testimony against those who in that Synod would interrupt, call to order—in violation of order—those members who were appearing in defense of injured

truth, and who were often silenced by tumult, or the call of order by an obsequious moderator. Especially do we testify against the dishonesty and unfaithfulness of that body, displayed by them in disposing of the paper inserted (see p. 132), calling Synod's attention to what we firmly believe to be the source of all the error, guilt and distractions incident or attending to that body for many years.

On the practice of confederating with the enemies of God, we testify against this party, not only for the *fact* of so confederating, but also, and chiefly, for resisting the evidence of God's word, often adduced in condemnation of the practice — refusing to hear the testimonies, experience, and reasoning of Christ's witnesses and martyr's when cited from the Cloud of Witnesses, Informatory Vindication, Gillespie on Confederacies, &c; and for obstinately going on in this trespass, in the face of manifold convictions from living witnesses and providential rebukes.

As it respects ecclesiastical relations, we testify against these former brethren for having wittingly, perseveringly, and presumptuously fostered *schism* in the visible church, manifestly for carnal ends, during many years. It is notorious that five Synods are in organic fellowship, while hardly two of them will hold ministerial or sacramental communion! What a picture does this state of things in the professing church of Christ present to the infidel; how hardening to the self-righteous and the openly profane! And although conventional regulations be lightly looked upon by many, not being based upon express words of scripture; yet when framed and engaged to, according to the general rules of scripture, much sin is the result of violating them, and trampling them under foot, as has often been done by this body of people. This has been the case in Presbyteries, subordinate Synods, and especially in the general Synod. Subordinate Synods have been dissolved by the action of the general Synod after they had ceased to be; and without consulting the Presbyteries, who alone were competent to decree or dissolve the delegation form of the general Synod, that court dissolved itself, after having many years trampled upon the law of Presbyteries fixing the ratio of delegation. Against such reckless, disorderly procedure we testify as being the cause or occasion of much sin against Zion's King, and much suffering to his precious people.

Finally—We solemnly enter our protestation against this church, as having taken the lead of most others in razing the very foundation stone of the covenanted structure. All the evils that have befallen the professed friends of a work of reformation on both sides of the Atlantic are traceable to a *setting aside* the *footsteps* of the flock from being terms of ecclesiastical communion. It is now more than ten years since this important matter was expressly submitted to the Old Light Synod's consideration, and during the subsequent period, in various forms, the same has been pressed, but without effect; except as manifesting more fully their obduracy. They refuse still to return, Ephraim-like, going on frowardly in the way of their own heart.

That uninspired history ought to be incorporated among the terms of communion in the Church of Christ, is a proposition which we firmly believe, on the evidence both of reason and Scripture, although denied, condemned, and rejected by all pretenders to reformation attainments. That *history* and *argument* are so re-jected by all parties affecting to be *reformed* churches, will appear from the follow-ing citations from their own authoritative judicial declarations: "Authentic history and sound argument are always to be highly valued; but they should not be incor-porated with the confession of the Church's faith." "The Declaratory part is, the Church's *standing Testimony.*"—Ref. Prin. Exhibited, preface—edition, 1835. Here history and argument are both excluded, not only from the Church's *testimony* but also from her confession! This is the declared sentiment of Old and New Light Covenants, together with the Safety League people—evidencing to all who are free from party influence, that however they differ in practice, on this all important point they perfectly harmonize in principle. East of the Atlantic, among the three Synods professing to follow the footsteps of the flock, the declared sentiment is the same, but then they differ from their brethren in practice—mingling with the heathen and learning their works without scruple. In this respect they are more consistent than the other parties, though more visibly corrupt.

The Reformed Dissenters "prefix a *Narrative* to their testimony," thus reject-ing *history* from *testimony.* Some advocates for union in conventions of reformed churches, have plead for a historical introduction to their proposed *testimony*; but they have carefully assured the public that this introduction shall constitute no *term* of union or communion. Thus, it is evident, that all the professed followers of the British Reformers around us, have cast off this reformation attainment from the standards of their professions severally. We condemn this church-rending and soul-ruining sentiment, and testify against all who maintain it, for the following reasons:

First, on their part it is inconsistent and self-contradictory. They all say they are following the footsteps and holding the attainments of the Scottish Reformers. But how do they discover these footsteps, or how ascertain these attainments? Are they recorded in the Bible? No. Are they to be found elsewhere but in *uninspired history*? Certainly no where else. Yet all these parties absurdly reject uninspired history from their bonds of fellowship! and still venture to tell the world, they are holding fast these attainments!! This is solemn trifling, profane mockery. *Second.* This position is unsound and false in the light of reason. All civilized nations, as well as the Jews, have it written in their laws, "That the testimony of two men is true." The witnesses do not need to be inspired to be credible. "We receive the witness of men," although a "false witness will utter lies." No society can exist without practical recognition of the credibility of human testimony; and this is especially true of the "Church of the living God, which is the pillar and ground of the truth;" for, *Third.* In the light of Scripture, her members cannot perform some of their most important duties, either to God or to one another if they irrationally and wickedly relinquish this principle. God's people are charged "not to forget his mighty works;" Psa. lxxviii. 7. Are these works all written in the Bible? They are required to confess their fathers' sins, as well as their own. Since the divine canon was closed, many sins have been, and now are chargeable against profess-ing Christians. Are these recorded in the Scriptures? And thus the reader may ask himself of sin and duty to any extent, in relation to God as a party.

And the same is true of the second table of the moral law. For example: in reference to "the first commandment with promise," should the Christian minor be asked as the Jew did his Lord, "Who is your father?" How shall he answer? Is he warranted to appeal to God to manifest his earthly sonship? No; but he is required by God's law to "honor his father;" and his obedience to this command is grounded on human testimony as to the object to whom this honor is due. Thus consistency, reason and scripture combine, to accuse and fasten guilt—the guilt of apostasy upon all who have renounced that fundamental principle of our glorious covenanted reformation—*that history and argument belong to the bond of ecclesiastical fellowship.* With any who hold the theory here condemned, however exemplary or even conscientious in morals and religion they may appear, we can have no ecclesiastical fellowship; for, however ardent their attachment or strong their expressions of affection to Confession, Catechisms, Covenants, &c.; they give no guarantee of competent intelligence or probable stability; as alas! we see in the present declining course of many in our day.

We would earnestly and affectionably beseech all well wishers to a covenanted work of reformation: that they would take into their serious consideration whether these things are, or are not connected inseparably with the wellfare of Zion. Especially would we expostulate with such as have any regard for the Judicial Testimony adopted at Ploughlandhead, Scotland, in 1761: that they conscientiously compare it with the book called Reformation Principles Exhibited, and also with the new Scottish Testimony, where it is practicable, and all these with the supreme standard, the holy scriptures. They will find on examination, that these are wholly irreconcilable in the very form of testimony-bearing. Particularly, let the reader notice that our fathers in 1761, considered *history* and *argument* as constituting their testimony: and did not look upon *doctrinal declaration* as formal testimony at all. Look at the very title page of their Testimony; where you read, "Act, Declaration and Testimony," plainly distinguishing between *declaration* and *Testimony*. Now, all innovators make doctrinal declaration their testimony, reversing our fathers' order; yea, we would add God's order, for he distinguishes between his law and testimony; Ps. lxxviii, 5-7; cv, 42-45. God's special providences toward his covenanted people constitute his testimony by way of eminence; Exod. xx, 1, &c., and their conduct under his providences constitute their testimony, which must consist of history; and by this and the blood of the Lamb, Christ's witnesses are destined to overcome all anti-christian combinations.

In attempting thus to follow the approved example of our covenant fathers, whose practice it was to testify not only against the corruptions of ecclesiastical, but also of civil constitutions, where their lot was cast, we deem it incumbent on us to continue our testimony first published in 1806, against the immoralities incorporated with the government of these United States.

Believing that a nation as such, is a proper subject of God's government, and that those nations favored with his law as revealed in the holy scriptures, are peculiarly required to regard the authority of the Lord and his Anointed, therein made fully known: it is with deep regret that we feel constrained to designate and testify against evils in the Constitution of this nation. Notwithstanding numerous excellencies embodied in this instrument, there are moral evils contained in it also, of such magnitude, that no Christian can consistently give allegiance to the system. There is not contained in it any acknowledgment of the Christian religion, or professed submission to the kingdom of Messiah. It gives support to the enemies of the Redeemer, and admits to its honors and emoluments Jews, Mohammedans, Deists and Atheists—it establishes that system of robbery by which men are held in slavery, despoiled of liberty, and property, and protection. It violates the principles of representation, by bestowing upon the domestic tyrant who holds hundreds of his fellow creatures in bondage, an influence in making laws for freemen proportioned to the number of his own slaves. This constitution is, in many instances, inconsistent, oppressive and impious.

Much guilt, and of long standing, is chargeable against this nation, for its cruel treatment of the colored race, in subjecting them ever since 1789 to hopeless bondage; its unjust transactions with the Indian race, and more recently waging an unjust war with a neighboring republic, as would appear, for the wicked purpose of extending the iniquitous system of slavery.

"Arise O God, judge the earth: for thou shalt inherit all nations."

PART IV.

A brief declaration or summary of the principles maintained by the
Presbytery, as to doctrine, worship, discipline, and government,
in agreeableness to the word of God, our Confession of Faith and
Catechisms, and whole covenanted testimony of the Church of
Scotland.—The contrary doctrines condemned.

Unto what has been more generally laid down in the preceding pages, with
respect to the principles and practice of this church and nation, both in former and
present times; the Presbytery proceed to subjoin a positive and explicit declaration
of their principles anent the truths of our holy religion, whether by the generality
agreed unto, or by some controverted.

I. OF GOD.—The Presbytery did, and hereby do acknowledge and declare,
that there is one infinite, eternal, self-existent, and independent Being; and that
this only true and living God, absolutely all-sufficient, having all being, perfection,
glory, and blessedness, in and of himself, subsists in three distinct, divine persons,
the Father, Son, and Holy Spirit (in one and the same undivided essence and god-
head), all equally the same in substance, power, and glory, although distinguished
by their personal properties; according to Deut. vi, 4; 1 Cor. viii, 6; 1 Tim. i, 17;
Acts xvii, 24, 25; 1 John v, 7; Matth. xxviii, 19; Confession of Faith, chap. 2; larger
catechism, quest. 7—11; shorter catechism, quest. 4—6.

II. OF THE HOLY SCRIPTURES.—Again, they confess and declare, that although the light of nature discovers unto us that there is a God, yet of itself it
is absolutely insufficient to teach us the saving knowledge of the invisible Being
and his will; and therefore God of his infinite condescension has given us a most
perfect revelation of himself and of his will in the scriptures of truth, contained in
the sacred books of the Old and New Testament; which scriptures the Presbytery
assert to be of divine authority, and not to be believed and received because of any
other testimony, than that of God their author, who is truth itself. Which word of
God is the alone perfect and complete rule, both of faith and practice, containing
a full and ample revelation of the whole counsel of God, both respecting his own
glory and the salvation of men; by which all spirits are to be tried, and to which all
doctrines and controversies in religion are to be brought, as to the supreme judge,
in whose sentence alone we are to acquiesce; according to Rom. i, 19, 20; 1 Cor. ii,
13, 14; Heb. i, 1; 2 Tim. iii, 16; 2 Pet. i, 19, 21; 2 Tim. iii, 15; Gal. i. 8, 9; Eph. ii, 20,

and our standards, Confess. chap. 1; larger Cat. quest. 2-5; shorter Cat. quest. 2, 3.

III. OF THE DECREES OF GOD.—Again, they assert and maintain, that Jehovah, according to his own most wise counsel, and for his own glory, has, by one immanent act of his will from eternity, purposed and decreed all events in time; and particularly, that by his absolute sovereignty, he has unchangeably determined the final state of all intelligent beings, visible and invisible. That God of his mere good pleasure, abstracting from all other causes whatever, for the praise of his glorious grace to be manifested in time, has from all eternity predestinated a certain definite number of mankind sinners, in and through Jesus Christ, to eternal life, together with all the means leading thereunto. And also, by the same sovereign will, has passed by, and left others in their sins, foreordaining them to bear the just punishment of their own iniquities; as is evident from Rom. ix, 11, 13, 15, 16, 18; Eph. i, 4, 6, 9, 11; Jude verse 4; and according to Confess, chap. 3; larger Cat. quest. 12, 13; shorter Catechism quest. 7.

IV. OF CREATION.—In like manner they acknowledge and declare, that as God, from the infinity of his being and goodness, has communicated a finite created existence to all other beings, framing them with natures wisely suited and adapted to the different ends of their creation; so by the same all-powerful word whereby they were at first created, he preserves and upholds all his creatures in their beings, and by the incessant care and invariable conduct of his divine providence, does constantly direct and overrule them and all their actions unto his own glory; according to divine revelation, Gen. i, throughout; Col i, 16; Rom. xi, 36; Psal, cxlv, 17, and xxxiii, 9; and cxix, 91; Heb. i, 2, 3; Confess, chap. 4, 5; larger Cat. quest. 14; short. Cat. quest. 8.

Likewise they profess and declare, that God, as the last and finishing part of his workmanship in this lower world, created man an intelligent being, endued with a living, reasonable and immortal soul, whose greatest glory consisted in his having the gracious image of his God and Creator drawn upon his soul, chiefly consisting in that knowledge, righteousness and inherent holiness wherewith he was created. And further, that God, in his favor and condescension to man, was pleased to enter into a covenant with him, as the public head and representative of all his posterity, wherein God promised unto him eternal life and blessedness with himself in glory, upon condition of personal, perfect and perpetual obedience; to the performance whereof, he furnished him with full power and ability, and threatened death upon the violation of his law and covenant, as is evident from the sacred text; Gen. i, 26, 27; Eccl. vii, 29; Gen. ii, 17; Rom. x, 5, and according to our Confess, chap. 4, § 2; chap, 7, § 1, 2; chap. 19, § 1; larger Cat. quest. 20; short. Cat. quest. 10, 12.

V. OF THE FALL OF MAN.—They again assert and maintain, that the first and common parents of mankind, being seduced by the subtilty of Satan, transgressed the covenant of innocency, in eating the forbidden fruit; whereby they lost the original rectitude of their nature, were cut off from all gracious intercourse with God, and became both legally and spiritually dead; and therefore they being the natural root of all mankind, and the covenant being made with *Adam*, not as a private, but a public person, all his descendants by ordinary generation, are born under the guilt of that first sin, destitute of original righteousness, and having their nature wholly depraved and corrupted; so that they are by nature children of wrath, subjected unto all the penal evils contained in the curse of a broken law, both in this life, and in that which is to come; Gen. iii, 6, 13; Eccl. vii. 20; Rom. v, from 12 to 20; Rom. iii, 10-19; Eph. ii, 3; Confess, chap. 6: larger Cat. quest. 21, 22, short. Cat. question 13 to 20.

In like manner they assert and declare, that all mankind, by their original apostasy from God, are not only become altogether filthy and abominable in the eyes of God's holiness; but also, are hereby utterly indisposed, disabled, and entirely opposite to all good, the understanding become darkness, and the will enmity and rebellion itself against God; so that man, by his fall, having lost all ability of will to what is spiritually good, cannot in his natural state, and by his own strength, convert himself (being dead in trespasses and sins), nor can he in less or more contribute to his own salvation, or in the least prepare himself thereunto; neither is there any natural, necessary or moral connection between the most diligent and serious use of the means, and obtaining salvation thereby. Although the Presbytery maintain, that as a God of grace has promised the converting influences of his Spirit to be showered down upon dead souls, in the use of means of his own appointment; they are therefore to be attended to with the utmost care and diligence; as appears from Rom. v, 6; John vi, 44, 65; Tit. iii, 3-5; Job xiv, 4; Confess. chap. 9, § 3; larger Cat. quest. 25.

VI. OF THE COVENANT OF GRACE.—Likewise they assert and declare, that Jehovah, in the person of the Father, having purposed to save a certain number of the ruined family of *Adam*, did from all eternity enter into a covenant transaction with Jesus Christ, his eternal and only begotten Son, who contracted as the second *Adam*, in the name of all his spiritual seed. In which covenant, the Father promising to confer eternal life upon a select number given unto Christ, upon condition of his fulfilling all righteousness for them; the Lord Jesus Christ did again stipulate and engage, as the condition of the covenant by him to be fulfilled, that in the fullness of time, assuming the human nature into a personal union with the divine, he would therein, and in the elect's name fulfill, not only the preceptive part of the law, but also bear the whole punishment contained in the threatening thereof: which covenant, that it might be absolutely free to sinners, and that the salvation therein provided for them, might not be of debt, but of grace, was unto Jesus Christ a covenant of redemption, nothing being therein promised to him, but upon his paying a full price, adequate to the most extensive demands of law and justice; according to Psal. lxxxix, 2, 3, 28, 34, 35; Tit. i, 2; Isa. liii, 10, 11; Matth. v, 17; Confess. chap. 7, § 3; Larg. Cat. quest. 30, 31; Short. Cat. quest. 20.

VII. OF THE MEDIATOR.—In like manner they profess, assert, and declare, that the Lord Jesus Christ, the second person in the glorious and adorable Trinity, being by the Father's appointment constituted mediator and surety of the new covenant, did, in the fullness of time, assume the human nature, consisting of a true body and reasonable soul, into a personal union with his divine; which two natures, in the one person of our Immanuel, God-man, remain distinct, without conversion, composition, or confusion. And being every way completely qualified and furnished for executing his mediatory offices of prophet, priest, and king, was called to the exercise thereof, by God the Father, who put all power and judgment into his hand, and gave him commandment to execute the same; Prov. viii, 23; Heb. ii, 14; 1 Tim. ii, 5; John vi, 27, and v, 27; Confess. chap. 8 throughout; Larg. Cat. quest. 21-23; short. Cat. quest, 21, 22.

Again, they acknowledge and declare, that the Lord Jesus Christ our RE-DEEMER, the only begotten Son of God, by eternal and ineffable generation, is most properly a divine person, true and very God, one in essence, equal and the same in power, eternity, glory, and all divine perfections with the Father and Holy Ghost: and that therefore it is most blasphemous to assert, that the terms, *necessary existence*, and *supreme deity*, and the title of *the only true God*, do not belong to the Son equally with the Father, as the same in substance, being expressly contrary to these texts of sacred writ which assert the opposite truth; John i, 1-4; Phil, ii, 6; John x, 30; 1 John v, 20, and to our standards, Confess. chap. 8, § 2; Larg. Cat. quest. 36; Short. Cat. 6.

They likewise further acknowledge, assert, and declare, that the Lord Jesus Christ, the eternal Son of God, and only Mediator between God and man, being designed from everlasting the REDEEMER of his people, and having all fullness, power, and authority lodged in him for the execution of his mediatory trust, has, ever since the fall of mankind, as the great and good shepherd of *Israel*, undertaken the care, government, protection, and instruction of the Church of God, in agree-ableness to the above said trust: which he did all along under the Old Testament, and still continues faithfully to discharge in all the parts thereof; so that whatever revelation God made unto his church since the fall, was by Jesus Christ as the great prophet and preacher of righteousness. Particularly, it was he that first appeared unto lapsed man, and as the great revealer of the council of peace, called upon him in the voice of mercy, saying, *"Adam*, where art thou?" It was he that, pleasing himself in the forethoughts of his future incarnation, and as a prelude thereto, condescended at different times to appear in a human form, and speak unto the fathers. By him, as the messenger of the covenant, were the lively oracles delivered to the Israelitish church; and by his Spirit in the prophets, successively raised up to instruct his church in the knowledge of the divine will, was signified and foretold the grace that should come, until the fullness of the time appointed in the council of Heaven, when it was promised he should come, and by his personal presence fill his house with glory. Then did God in these last days speak unto men by his Son, whom he has appointed heir of all things; who, not only by himself, but also, after his ascension, by his evangelists and apostles filled with the Spirit, has made known all things that he heard of his Father. And now, after the canon of scripture is completed, and no new revelation to be expected to the end of time, continues by his word and spirit to instruct sinners in the knowledge of all things necessary for their sanctification and salvation; according to Acts x, 38, and iii, 22; Luke iv,

18, 21; John i, 18; 1 Pet. i, 10-12; Heb. i, 1, 2; Eph. iv, 11-13; Confess. chap. 8, § 1; Larg. Cat. quest. 43; Short. Cat. quest. 24.

In like manner, they profess and declare, that the Lord Jesus Christ, being called of him that said unto him, "Thou art my Son, this day have I begotten thee," unto the honorable office of High Priest over the house of God, and confirmed therein by all the solemnities of the oath of God, he did most willingly undertake this work, saying, *Lo, I come to do thy will, O God!* And that he might finish and fulfill the same, in agreeableness to his eternal engagements to the Father, to the Old Testament types and sacrifices, promises and prophecies, wherein he was foresigned and revealed to be the seed of the woman, that should bruise the serpent's head, did, in the fullness of time, humble himself to be made of a woman, made under the law, in the form of a bond servant to Jehovah. In which character, he not only fulfilled the preceptive part of the law, but also, with the most unparalleled meekness, patience and resignation, submitted to the most grievous and dreadful sufferings, both in body and soul, even all that divine wrath, indignation and punishment, wrapped up in the terrible curse of a broken covenant of works. By which obedience of his unto the death, through the eternal Spirit offering himself without spot unto God, a proper, real and expiatory sacrifice for sin, he has fully satisfied divine justice, made reconciliation for the iniquities of his people, and purchased an eternal inheritance for them in the kingdom of glory. The saving benefits of which redemption, by the Spirit's effectual application thereof, he does, by his intercession at the Father's right hand, as an arisen, living, and now glorified Savior, constantly and certainly communicate unto all those whom the Father has given him. Further, the Presbytery declare, that however they acknowledge the standing of the world, as a theater to display the riches of divine grace, the preaching of the gospel indefinitely to mankind sinners, and all the common favors of life indifferently enjoyed by them, do all result, as native, necessary and determined consequences, from the interposition of Christ in behalf of his spiritual seed, and have their ultimate foundation in the infinite sufficiency, fullness and perfection, of the blood and sacrifice of Christ, God-man: yet they affirm, that, as a certain elect and select number were given unto Christ, to be redeemed from among men, so, for their sakes alone, he engaged his heart to approach unto God. For their sakes, he sanctified himself; in their name, i.e., in their law-room and stead, and for their good, as the surety of the better covenant, he became obedient unto death, and endured the whole of that punishment threatened by the law, and incurred by the transgression of it. He subjected himself to that very curse, bore that wrath and died that death, which they themselves should have undergone. And hereby, by his doing and dying, he made a proper, real, full and expiatory satisfaction to the justice of God for their sins. Wherefore it is impossible but that to all those for whom Christ has purchased this complete redemption, and for whose sins he has given this full satisfaction accepted of God, he will certainly and effectually apply and communicate the same in the saving benefits thereof; seeing that it is his will who has merited it, that all those who are the Father's choice by election, and his purchase by redemption, should be *ever with him where he is, that they may behold his glory*; and since, as he is thus willing, he is also able, to save them to the uttermost that come to God by him. So that all for whom Christ died, all that are redeemed by his blood, are, in consequence hereof; effectually called, justified, sanctified and glorified; according to Psal. xl, 7, 8; Heb. x, 5-11; Phil. ii, 8; Gal. iv, 4, 5; Heb. ix, 14, 28; Dan. ix, 24; Psal. lxxv, 3; Isa. xlix, 8; John vi, 37, 39, chap. x, 15, 16; Eph. i, 7; Rom. viii, 34, and ver. 29, 30; John xvii throughout; John xi, 52; Confess, chap. vii, § 4, 5, 8; Larg. Cat. quest. 44; Sh. Cat. quest. 25.

They also acknowledge, assert and declare, that the Lord Jesus Christ is, by the appointment of God the Father, set as King upon his holy hill of Zion; over which, as his special kingdom, he is invested with an absolute power and supremacy, as the sole and only head thereof, to appoint offices, officers, laws and ordinances. And that accordingly, by virtue of this solemn investiture, the same Lord Jesus Christ has, in all ages, called out of the world, and maintained therein, a church unto himself, which he visibly governs by a complete system of laws, officers and censures, instituted in his word, and has not left the affairs of his church, in which (as a Son over his own house) he peculiarly presides, to be regulated and modeled by the carnal policy and invention of men. Also, that, as King in *Zion*, he powerfully and irresistibly, in a day of efficacious grace, subdues the perverse hearts and wills of sinners unto his obedience, persuading and enabling as many as were appointed to obtain salvation through him, to believe in his name, in order thereunto. All whom he either preserves from, or supports under, the various temptations, trials and afflictions, they are liable to in this mortal life; till at last, completing a work of grace in their souls, he advances them to a state of perfection and glory.

Further, the Presbytery declare and maintain, that, in subserviency to this his special mediatory kingdom, the Lord Jesus Christ has a supreme and sovereign power given unto him, in heaven and in earth, and over the infernal powers of darkness—angels, authorities and powers being put in subjection to him; that he has the management of all the wheels of providence put into his hand, whereby he restrains, disappoints, and at last totally destroys, all the enemies of his interest and glory; and by which he orders and overrules all the events that fall out in time, for the accomplishment of the great and glorious ends of his incarnation, and lasting good of those that love him: according to Psal. ii, 6; Isa. ix, 6, 7; Isa. xxxiii, 22; Matth. xxi, 5; Isa. lv, 4, 5; Gen. xlix, 10; Heb. iii, 6; Psal. cx, 1, 2; Matth. xxviii, 18; John vii, 2; 1 Pet. iii, 22; Phil, ii, 9-11; Confess, chap, viii § 3; Larg. Cat. quest. 45; Sh. Cat. quest. 26.

They again declare and assert, that as the light of nature is absolutely insufficient to give a just discovery, either of the grievous malady of sin, or the blessed remedy provided for sinners, so none, however diligent they may be to frame their lives according to the dictates of nature's light, can possibly attain to salvation, while they remain without any objective revelation of Jesus Christ, as the great propitiation and peace-maker, who has abolished death, and brought life and immortality to light, by the gospel. And further, that there is no other name, doctrine or religion, whereby any can be saved, but in the name, doctrine and religion of the Lord Jesus Christ, of which he is the great author and institutor; in the profession and faith whereof, he leads his people through this world into the possession of endless felicity and glory in the world to come.

VIII. OF THE GOSPEL OFFER.—They further declare, that, as God the Father, out of his unbounded love, has, on the footing of the infinite sufficiency of the death and sacrifice of Christ, made a free and unhampered gift and grant of him, as an all-sufficient Savior, unto sinners of mankind lost, as such, in the word: so the ministers and embassadors of Christ (according as they are expressly authorized and commanded by him) are to publish this gospel, these glad tidings of great joy to all the world, wherever they may be called or cast, in the providence of God, and make a full, free and unhampered offer of Christ and his whole salvation to sinners, without distinction, assuring them of God's mercy and grace, through Christ, in whom he proclaims himself well pleased; of Christ's omnipotent power and ability to save to the uttermost all that come unto God by him; and that there are no impediments, bars or hinderances, *ab extra*, between Jesus Christ, as held forth in the offer of the gospel, and sinners lost, why they, even every one of them, may not receive and appropriate him, as the Lord their righteousness. And the above said frank and unhampered gift of Christ, and him crucified, by God the Father, as a full and all-sufficient Savior unto lost and ruined sinners, the Presbytery view as the great and prime foundation, both of the ministerial offer, and of, faith in the Lord Jesus, for life and salvation: as is clear from Rom. x, 14; 1 Cor. i, 21-25; Isa. lv, 1; Mark xvi, 15; John iii, 16; Confess, chap, vii, § 3; Larg. Cat. ques. 67; Sh. Cat. ques. 31, &c.

IX. OF JUSTIFICATION.—Again, they profess and declare, that the active and passive obedience, or the complete mediatory righteousness, of the Lord Jesus Christ, is the only meritorious cause of a sinner's justification, pardon of sin, and acceptance of his person and services with a holy God; and that true and saving faith, which is also the gift of God, is the alone instrumental cause of the sinner's justification in his sight; or that evangelical condition, or internal mean, in and by which the soul is interested in Christ, and the whole of his righteousness and salvation. Which righteousness, received and rested on by faith, is the only foundation of a sinner's title to eternal life and glory; as appears evident from Rom. iii, 22-29; Rom. v, 17-20; Jer. xxiii, 6; Gal. ii, 16; Acts x, 43; Col. i, 27; Acts viii, 37; Rom. x, 9; Mark v, 36; Eph. ii, 8; Confess, chap. 11, 14; Larg. Cat. ques. 70, 73; Sh. Cat. ques. 3.

They likewise profess and maintain, that believers, by the righteousness of Christ being justified from all things, from which they could not be justified by the law of Moses, are by Jesus Christ perfectly delivered from the law, as a covenant of works, both as commanding and condemning; so as that thereby they are neither justified nor condemned, it being dead to them, and they to it, by the body of Christ, to whom they are married. However, notwithstanding of this freedom, they are still servants unto God; still under the moral law, as a rule of life in the hand of their glorious Mediator and new covenant Head, directing them how they are to walk, so as to please God; the obligation whereof, as such, remains perpetual and indissoluble; and that this privilege is peculiar to believers only, all others being still under the old covenant obligation, both as to the debt of obedience and punishment; according to Rom. vi, 14, and vii, 4, 6; Gal. iv, 4, 5, and ii, 16; Rom.

viii, 1; Gal. iii, 10; Confess, chap, xix, § 5, 6; Larg. Cat. ques. 97; Sh. Cat. ques. 43, 44.

X. OF GOOD WORKS.—Again, they assert and declare, that as no works are truly and spiritually good, but those that are performed by a person united to the Lord Jesus Christ by faith, and under the influence of his Holy Spirit; and consequently, that none of the actions of the unregenerate, however in themselves materially agreeable unto the letter of the law, are either pleasing or acceptable to God; nor can they dispose or prepare their souls for receiving his grace, though their omission and neglect of these is still more displeasing unto God, and destructive unto themselves. So likewise they declare, that even the best works of obedience performed by the regenerate, can neither merit the pardon of any one sin, nor procure them the smallest measure or God's grace or favor, because of the manifold sins and imperfections they are still attended with, and because of the infinite distance between God and them, with respect to whom, when they have done all that they can, they are but unprofitable servants. Neither is their ability to do them at all of themselves, but wholly from the Spirit dwelling in them. And further, that the spring and principle motive of true love to God, and acceptable obedience to him, is not self-interest or love to our own felicity, nor yet a slavish fear of punishment; but the glorious perfections and transcendent excellencies of the Deity, manifested in the face of Jesus Christ, who is the brightness of the Father's glory, and express image of his person, are the prime and chief motives both of love, fear and obedience unto God; all who really love God loving him principally for himself. As also, that all acceptable service to God, performed by believers, is principally influenced by the authority of a God of grace, stamped upon his word, springs from faith in Jesus Christ, as an animating and active principle in their souls, and is ultimately directed to the glory of God in Christ, as the great end thereof. Hence, therefore, although God has graciously connected his own glory and his people's felicity inseparably together, that yet no actions, however good in themselves or beneficial to others, which arise only from a principle of self-interest, love to one's own bliss, or fear of hell, are evidential of saving grace in the soul, or any more than what one in a state of nature may perform; according to Gen. iv, 5; Heb. xi, 4, 6; Matth. vi, 2, 5, 16; Hag. ii, 14; Amos, v, 21, 22; Tit. i, 15, and iii, 5; Rom. iii, 20, and iv, 2, 4, 6; Job xxii, 2, 3; Eph. i, 6; 1 Pet. ii, 5; Exod. xxviii, 38; Confess, chap. 16 throughout; Larg. Cat. ques. 73, 101; Sh. Cat. ques. 44.

XI. OF ASSURANCE OF GRACE.—In like manner they declare and assert, that although there may be much darkness, and manifold doubts and fears, seated in the same soul where true and saving faith is: and although true believers may wait long before they know themselves to be believers, and be assured that they are really in a state of grace; and even, after they have arrived at a subjective assurance of their salvation, may have it much shaken, clouded and intermitted; that yet there is no doubting, no darkness, in the saving acts of a true and lively faith: but in all the appropriating acts of saving faith, there is an objective assurance, an assured confidence and trust in Jesus Christ, and the promise of life in which he is revealed to the soul; according to Isa. 1, 10; Mark ix, 24; 1 John v, 13; Psal. lxxvii, 1 to 11; Psal. lxxxviii, throughout; Gal. ii, 20; Mark xi, 24; Confess, chap. 18 throughout; Larg. Cat. ques. 72, 80, 81; Short. Cat. question 86.

XII. OF THE PERSEVERANCE OF THE SAINTS.—They further assert and declare, that whosoever, of any of the children of men, in all ages, have attained salvation, did believe in, and receive the Lord Jesus Christ, the promised Messiah, and only Savior from sin, to whom all the prophets bear witness, in whom all the promises and lines of salvation do center; and particularly, that however much the faith of the disciples and apostles of our Lord and Savior Jesus Christ in him, as their only Redeemer, might be at any time overclouded, yet it was never totally subverted; and that the noble grace of faith in the souls of believers cannot be totally lost; but that such is the immutability of God's decrees, and his unchangeable love; such the efficacy of their Redeemer's merit, and constant abiding of the spirit of holiness in them; and such the nature of the new covenant, that, notwithstanding of various temptations and afflictions, the prevailing of remaining corruption in them, they must all and every one of them, certainly and infallibly persevere in a state of grace unto the end, and be at last saved with an everlasting salvation; as appears from Heb. xi, 13; John iv, 42; Phil. i, 6; John x, 28, 29; 1 Pet. ii, 9; Jer. xxxiv, 4; Confess, chap. 8, § 1, chap. 14, § 2, and chap. 17 throughout.

XIII. OF LIBERTY OF CONSCIENCE.—They further assert and declare, that the noble faculty of conscience, God's deputy in the soul of man, over which he alone is absolute Lord and Sovereign, is not subjected unto the authority of man; neither are any human commands further binding upon the consciences of men, than they are agreeable unto, and founded upon the revealed will of God, whether in matters of faith or practice. And although the Lord Jesus Christ has purchased a glorious liberty unto believers from sin, and all the bitter fruits thereof, and of access to a throne of grace with boldness; and has procured unto his church freedom from the yoke of the ceremonial law, with a more abundant communication of gospel influences: yet, inasmuch as conscience is the rule ruled, not the rule, ruling, none can, without manifest sin, upon pretense of conscience or Christian liberty, cherish any forbidden lust in their souls, nor are left at freedom to reject any of the divine ordinances instituted in the word, to change or corrupt their scriptural institution, by immixing human inventions therewith, or in the least deviating from the punity thereof. And that therefore, all who vent or maintain tenets or opinions, contrary to the established principles of Christianity, whether in the matter of doctrine, divine worship, or practice in life, which are contrary to, and inconsistent with the analogy of faith, and power of true godliness, or destructive to that pure peace and good order established by Christ in his church, are accountable unto the church; and upon conviction, ought to be proceeded against, by inflicting ecclesiastical censures or civil pains, in a way agreeable unto the divine determination in the word concerning such offenses.

And further, they declare, that it is most wicked, and what manifestly strikes against the sovereign authority of God, for any power on earth to pretend to tolerate, and, by sanction of civil law, to give license to men to publish and propagate with impunity, whatever errors, heresies, and damnable doctrines, Satan, and their own corrupt and blinded understandings, may prompt them to believe and embrace; toleration being destructive of all true religion, and of that liberty wherewith Christ has made his people free; and the great end thereof, which is, "That being delivered out of the hands of our enemies, we may serve the Lord—in holiness and righteousness, all the days of our lives." Agreeable to James iv, 12; Rom. xiv, 4; Acts iv, 19, and v, 29; 1 Cor. vii, 23; Matth. xxiii, 9; 2 John 10, 11; 2 Cor. i, 24; Matth. xv, 9; Col. ii, 20, 22, 23; Gal. ii, 4, 5, and v, 1, 13; Isa. viii, 20; Acts xvii, 11; Hosea v, 11; 1 Cor. v, 1,5, 11, 13; Tit. i. 10, 11, 13, and iii, 20; Matth. xviii, 15-17; Deut. xiii, 6-12; Ezek. vii, 23, 25, 26; Zech. xiii, 2, 3; Rev. ii, 2, 14, 15, 20; Confess, chap. 20; Larg. Cat. quest. 100, 103; Sh. Cat. quest. 49, 50.

XIV. OF TESTIMONY-BEARING.—Again, they declare and assert, that all true believers, members of the church invisible, are by the indissoluble bond of the Spirit, and true faith in Christ, their Head, savingly united unto, and have communion with him in grace and in glory, in this life and the life to come. In all their afflictions he is afflicted, and shares with them in their sufferings and trials, is with them in and through death, exalteth them at last over all their enemies, receiving them into glory and blessedness with himself, that they may behold and share in his glory with him through eternity: and that all of them being knit and joined together in holy love and affection, do participate mutually of each others gifts and graces; and are indispensably bound to exercise themselves in the practice of all commanded duties, for preserving the love of God, and life of grace, in their own, and one another's souls. And further, they declare that the visible church, and the members thereof, are externally in covenant with Christ their Head, have one and the same Lord, profess the same faith in doctrine and worship, receive the same seals of God's covenant, baptism, and the Lord's Supper: and are thereby bound to hold fast the Head, to be subject to his authority, keep the faith they have received, and maintain an holy communion and fellowship in the worship of God; closely abiding by the standard of Christ, their captain and leader, and lifting up the banner of divine truth, in opposition unto, and holy contempt of all their enemies of every kind. And further, they affirm, that as the visible church in general, is bound to be faithful to Christ, their Head and Lord, and to preserve inviolate, the whole of that sacred *depositum* of truth wherewith she is intrusted by him, not quitting with, nor willfully apostatizing from the same, in profession or practise: so no particular subject of this spiritual kingdom of Christ can recede from any part of divine truth, which they have received, and whereof they have made profession, without lese-majesty unto the Son of God, and violation of their obligations they have come under, at receiving the seals of the covenant, with whatever other lawful vows they have made unto the Most High; according to 1 John i, 2, 3; Eph. iii, 16-19; John i, 16; Heb. x, 24, 25; Acts ii, 42, 46; Eph. iv, 4-6; Phil. iii, 16; Rev. ii, 25, and iii, 3; Confess, chap. 2, 6; Larg. Cat. quest. 63; Short. Cat. quest. 50.

XV. OF CHURCH GOVERNMENT.—They likewise affirm and declare, that the Lord Jesus Christ, our exalted Immanuel, the sole and supreme Head, Lawgiver and King of his church, which is his spiritual and absolutely free and independent kingdom, has herein warranted, instituted and appointed certain office-bearers (who derive their mission and authority from him alone) to regulate, administer, judge and determine in all the affairs of his house, to whom alone the keys of the kingdom of heaven are by him committed. Particularly, they are intrusted with the key of doctrine, to discover the mind of God, and preach Christ crucified unto sinners; the key of government for preserving that beauty of order, purity and power in the house of God, which he has enjoined should take place therein; the key of discipline, to inflict ecclesiastical censures upon such as turn aside after their *crooked ways*, or continue obstinate in their offenses; the key of ordination and mediate mission, in ordinary circumstances of the church, solemnly to set apart and send forth church officers unto that sacred function and official trust in the house of God, on the regular trial of the suitableness of their gifts and qualifications for that spiritual service and ministration; according to 1 Cor. xii, 28; Eph. iv, 11; Matth. xviii, 19; John xx, 23; Matth. xviii, 18; Acts xv, throughout, and xvi, 4; Matth. xxviii, 19, 20; Mark xvi, 15; Acts vi, 6; 1 Tim. iv, 14, and iii, 10; Confess, chap 30, § 2, 3 and 31; § 3. Form of church government, books of discipline, and the several laudable acts and constitutions of this church; particularly, *Act* of *Assem.* at *Edinburgh, August* 4th, 1649, *Sess.* 4, entitled, *Directory for electing of ministers.*

They likewise assert and maintain, that the Lord Jesus Christ, the church's glorious Head, hath appointed a certain form of government therein, distinct from civil government, and not at all subordinate to civil rulers. And that the only ecclesiastical government warranted by Christ is his word, and to continue in his church unalterable, is Presbyterial church government, exclusive of all superior dignity above a teaching presbyter, and consisting in her judicative capacity of kirk-sessions, in subordination to presbyteries; of presbyteries, in subordination to provincial synods; of provincial synods, in subordination to national; and national to ecumenical assemblies, or general councils.

And further, they assert, that the office-bearers of the Lord's house, are, according to the command, and in the name and authority of the Lord Jesus Christ, the only Lawgiver and King of his church, and by virtue of the church's intrinsic power derived from Christ, to assemble, constitute and adjourn these several courts of his house, nominate the fixed or occasional times of their subsequent meetings, as the church's condition or exigencies require; although they grant that the Christian magistrate may, in extraordinary cases, or otherwise, call together a synod of ministers, and ether fit persons, for consultation and advice in religious matters: but in which they have no power to judge or determine in matters of faith; but only discretively to examine, whether the synod's determinations and decisions be consonant and agreeable to scripture, and accordingly to acquiesce therein; Isa. ix, 6, 7; Ezek. xliii, 10, 11; Acts xv, 2, 4, 6; 1 Tim. v, 17; Heb. xiii, 17; 2 Chron. xix, 8-11; Acts xvii, 11; Confess, chap. 30, § 1 and chap. 31, § 1, 2, and conform to act of assembly, anno 1647; § 2,3; 2d book of discipline, and propositions for church government.

They likewise assert and maintain, that the office-bearers in the church of Christ, according to their different places and stations therein, must give evidence of their being possessed in some suitable measure of the qualifications which God in his word requires to be in any that are to be placed in such stations or offices, particularly that of devotedness to the cause and honor of Christ. And they further assert, that ministers of the gospel, and other church officers, must enter into the exercise of their office, at the door of Christ's appointment, by the call and choice of the Christian people, who are capable with judgment to give their consent; 1 Tim. iii, from verse 2 to 12; Tit. i, 5, 6, 7; Acts vi, 2 to 6; Chap, xiv, 23; John x, 4, 5, and agreeable to the laudable acts and ordinances of this church and state, in favor of reformation principles, books of discipline, &c.

XVI. OF CIVIL GOVERNMENT.—In like manner they assert and maintain, that God Almighty, the Sovereign Lord of all things, and special protector and preserver of his professed subjects in this lower world, hath for his own glory and the public good, authorized and instituted in his word the office and ordinance of civil government and governors, for the preservation of external peace and concord, administration of justice, defense and encouragement of such as are, and do good, and punishment of evil doers, who transgress either table of the law. For all which ends, subordinate unto that of his own glory, God, the alone supreme fountain of all power, has instituted and appointed this ordinance. And further they maintain, that a due measure of those qualifications which God, the great lawgiver requires in his word, together with what other stipulations according to the same unerring rule, a Christian people, who are blessed with the light of divine revelation, have made the fundamental conditions of civil government among them, are essentially necessary to the constitution and investiture of lawful authority over such a people. No other but such a constitution and investiture, can either be approven of by God, or answer the ends, ultimate or subordinate, of this ordinance, unto the honor of the great institutor, as appears from Prov. viii, 15, 16; Psa. cxlvii, 19, 20, and cxlix, G, 7, 8, 9; Isa. xlix, 23; Rom. xiii, 1, 2, 3, 4; Deut. xvii, 14, 15; 2 Sam. xxiii, 2, 3, 4; Exod. xviii, 21. Confess, chap. 23, § 1. Seasonable warning by the general assembly, July 27, 1649. Act 15, Sess. 2, Parl. 1, 1640.

They further assert and maintain, that the constituting of the relation betwixt rulers and ruled, is voluntary and mutual; and that the lawful constitution of civil magistrates, is, by the mutual election of the people (in whom is the radical right, or intermediate voice of God, of choosing and appointing such as are to sway the scepter of government over them) and consent of those who are elected and chosen for the exercise of that office, with certain stipulations according to scripture and right reason, obliging each other unto the duty of their different stations and relations. And further they affirm that when magistrates are so constituted, Christians are bound by the law of God to pray for the divine blessing upon their persons and government, reverence and highly esteem them, yield a conscientious subjection and obedience to their lawful commands, defend and support them in the due exercise of their power; which power magistrates are especially to exert for the outward defense of the church of God, against all her external enemies, restraining or otherwise punishing, as the case may require, all open blasphemers, idolaters, false-worshipers, heretics, with all avowed contemners of the worship and discipline of the house of God; and by his civil sanction to corroborate all the laws and ordinances of Christ's house, providing and enjoining that every thing in the house of the God of heaven, be done according to the law of the God of heaven; Deut. xvii, 14; 2 Kings xi, 17; 1 Sam. xi, 15; 1 Tim. ii, 1,2; 1 Peter ii, 17; Rom xiii, 2 to 8; 2 Kings xviii, 4, and xxiii, 1 to 26; 2 Chron. xxix, and xxx, chapters throughout; Ezra vii, 23. Confess. chap. 23, § 3, coronation oath of Scotland, sworn and subscribed by Charles II. at Scone, January 1st, 1651, and oath of fidelity by the people.

XVII. OF CORRUPTIONS IN THE TWO PRECEDING ORDINANCES.—But, with respect to these two great ordinances of divine institution, the magistracy and ministry, with the qualifications of the persons and duty of the people, as before asserted, the Presbytery reject, like as they did, and hereby do reject and condemn the following contrary errors, tenets and opinions, whether of older or later date, vented either by open enemies or professed friends to the reformation cause. And,

1. They reject and condemn that loose latitudinarian tenet and opinion of opening the door of communion with the church in her judicative capacity, or sealing ordinances, unto the grossly ignorant, loose, careless, profane and scandalous: and to the anti-christian deist, blasphemous heretic, or any who maintain doctrines, principles and opinions contrary to, and eversive of the cardinal and fundamental doctrines of Christianity, or such principles and practices as oppose, obscure or darken the church's beauty and purity, and spoil her of her power, and particularly that of the church of *Scotland*, in her attainments in reformation; this being evidently destructive and ruinous to truth and holiness, the only foundation and basis of external union and concord in the church, and consequently of all durable, harmonious and comfortable communion among the ministers and members of Christ's mystical body: See Eph. v, 11; Isa. viii, 20; Amos iii, 3; 1 Cor. vi, 10; Heb. xii, 14; Rev. xxii, 14, 15; 2 Cor. vi, 17, 18; and conform to the acts and practice of this church, in her best and purest times, in excluding from her communion, and refusing to unite with any chargeable as above.

Again, they hereby reject that false and ungodly principle and opinion, That a God of infinite wisdom has left his professing people destitute of any declaration of his will (which they are absolutely bound to regard) concerning both the institution, administration and qualifications of such persons as should administer these two distinct ordinances, government, civil and ecclesiastical; or that these two different species of government have not their foundation and institution, as the ordinances of God, in his revealed will; but that either (with the corrupt revolution church) he hath left the government of his house a matter of indifference, and the pattern thereof to be moulded by the discretion of the wise men of this world, and according to the corrupt will and fluctuating inclination of the people; or, with their public resolution-brethren, the *Seceders*, exchanging the clear scriptural and covenanted basis of civil government, with the obscure foundation of the law and light of nature, or the more dissolute basis of mere election and acknowledgment of whomsoever the *primores regni*, though never so wicked and licentious, choose and set up as magistrates. Which notion contains an injurious and impious impeachment of divine revelation, as a rule imperfect and insufficient to guide Christians into the knowledge of the will of God, and their duty, as the peculiar and professed subjects of the King of kings, and supreme lawgiver, concerning all his ordinances; and is contrary to 2 Tim. iii, 16; Rom, ii, 14; Ezek. xliii, 11; and xliv, 5; Lev. xviii, 2, 3, 4, 5; Matt, xxviii, 20. Confess, chap. 23, § 3.

They in like manner reject and condemn the ecclesiastical headship of the church, blasphemously arrogated by that man of sin, and son of perdition the Pope of *Rome*; with all that superiority of dignity and office in the house of God, claimed by anti-christian Prelates, together with the whole of their hierarchical order, and the civil places and power of churchmen, by both usurped; which is a most wicked attempt to overturn God the Father's deed, constituting his Son Christ, sole King and Head of his church, an exauctorating of Jesus Christ from his throne, and headship in his church, an elevation of his ministers, contrary to his will, and the nature and ends of their office; and an anti-scriptural and confused blending together of different and distinct ordinances. Psa. ii, 6; Isa. ix, 6, and xxii, 24; Col. i, 18; Mark x, 42, 43; Luke xxii, 25, 26; I Pet. v, 3; 2 Chron. xix, 12; 1 Cor. vii, 2. Confess. chap. 25, § 6, and contrary to our solemn covenants, and many acts and ordinances of both church and state, in times of reformation.

They likewise reject and condemn that gross Erastian principle, That the civil magistrate is supreme head over all persons, and in all causes, ecclesiastical as well as civil, whether in more ancient and later times of tyranny and persecution, openly and blasphemously usurped, or at and since the Revolution, more craftily yet too manifestly claimed; as appears from the 37th article of the church of *England*, and king's declaration prefixed to the said articles: and is further evident from the many encroachments made upon the royal dignity and headship of Christ, by the usurpers of his throne, practically vesting themselves with power and authority to convene and adjourn at their pleasure, and give laws and ordinances to the church, which is a daring attack on the prerogative, sovereignty, wisdom and power of her absolute King and Lord, on whom, as a nail fastened in a sure place, his Father has hung all the glory of his house, and vested him with the sole supremacy over the same, being filled abundantly with the spirit of wisdom and understanding, with the spirit of counsel and of might, to direct and preside in the management of all her concerns, and to preserve from and overcome all her enemies; Isa. xxii, 24, and xi, 2, 3, and ix, 6; Col. i, 18; Eph. i, 22; 2 Chr. xxvi, 18; Heb. v, 4; Confess. chap. 25, § 6.

They also reject and condemn that Erastian tenet and opinion, that the whole or any part of the power, mission, qualifications, or administration of ecclesiastical officers, or ministers of the church of Christ, depends upon the authority and dictation of the civil magistrate, because it is manifestly destructive of the church's power and authority, under Christ her Head, and derived from him, and likewise of the ministerial freedom and faithfulness of Christ's embassadors: and particularly they reject and condemn, as gross Erastianism (whether practiced before or since the Revolution, and especially since the incorporating union with *England* on terms diametrically opposite to our covenant union), the civil magistrate's limiting the mission of office-bearers in the church, according to his will; prescribing certain qualifications, and restricting to certain limitations; such as the test, indulgences, allegiance, assurance, and abjuration oaths, act restoring patronages, and the act anent *Porteous*, together with the threatened deprivation of office and benefice, upon non-compliance; 1 Cor. xii, 28; Matt, xviii, 17, 18; John xx, 23.

They further reject and condemn that Erastian opinion, that the external government of Christ's house is left unto the precarious determination of sinful men, or hath either its immediate or mediate dependence upon the will and pleasure of the civil magistrate, according to the import of the claim of right, the anti-scriptural basis of the revolution settlement. This being evidently an impious reflection on the perfect wisdom of the church's Head, subversive of the beauty of his house, and fertile of disorder therein, laying the kingdom of Christ obnoxious to spiritual tyranny and oppression, when strangers, enemies, or such as have no call or warrant to build the house of the Lord, put to their hand to model the form of her government as best suits their perverse inclinations and secular views, in express contradiction to the will and law of the God of heaven, Exod xxv, 40, and xxvi, 30; Ezek. xliii, 11; 1 Chron. xv, 12, 13; Neh. ii, 20, with many other texts above cited.

Again they reject and condemn that latitudinarian tenet, That the Lord Jesus Christ, the alone Head of the church, hath left his house void of any particular form of government, of divine institution exclusive of all other, under the New Testament dispensation: which, is a manifest reflection upon his fidelity to him who appointed him, and most absurd to suppose of him who is true and faithful, as a Son over his own house, and contrary to Isa. ix, 6, 7; 1 Tim. v, 17; Heb. iii, 2, 3, 5; 1 Cor. xii, 28; Rom. xii 6, 7, 8; Acts xx, 17, 28; Matt, xxviii, 20. Confess. chap. 30, § 1, and to the propositions for church government.

They further reject and condemn that sectarian principle and tenet, whether in former or latter times maintained, that a kirk session, or particular congregational eldership, is vested with equal ecclesiastical power and authority, with any superior judicatory, and is neither subordinate nor accountable to them (in the Lord) in their determinations. They likewise reject as sectarian, That the community of the faithful or professing Christians, in a private station hath any scriptural warrant for public teaching, or judicative determination in the church; both which opinions are not only expressly contrary to scripture, Acts xv, throughout, and xvi, 4; I Cor. v, 4; 1 Tim: v, 17; Heb. v, 4, and xiii, 17, &c, but also have been found hitherto most hurtful and dangerous to the church of God, depriving her ministers and members of just and necessary recourse to superior judgment and decision in matters difficult, discrediting and prostituting the sacred office of the ministry, and tending to overthrow a standing ministry in the church of Christ, and subvert that comely and beautiful order he hath prescribed therein.

In like manner they reject and condemn that gross invasion and encroachment upon the church's liberties, by the intrusion of popish patronages, whether imposed as a law by civil, or executed by ecclesiastical powers. Of the latter of these, the ministers and judicatories of the now corrupt, harlot Church of *Scotland*, cannot but be more egregiously guilty. The nature of their sacred function and trust obliges them to preserve inviolate the church's freedom and liberties: but in place of this, their hands are *chief in the trespass*, in an authoritative and active enforcement of this wicked act—an act evidently destructive of the very nature and essence of that mutual relation between pastor and people, and which has the native and necessary tendency to schism in the church, spiritual leanness, and starving of the flock, by thrusting in idle, idol shepherds upon them, such as serve not our Lord Jesus Christ, but their own bellies; feed themselves, but not the flock; and seek not them, but theirs, contrary to John x, 2, 9; Heb. v, 4; 1 Tim. iii, 3; 1 Cor. xii, 14, with many more; and to acts of both church and state, in times of reformation in these covenanted lands.

But, on the other hand, that the Presbytery, when thus condescending on particulars, pass not over in sinful silence, what stands opposite to the word of God and their declared principles, as above concerning civil authority, the administrators thereof, and subjection of the people thereto: they reject, likeas they hereby reject and condemn that anti-scriptural principle and opinion, that the divine scriptural ordinance of magistracy has not its foundation in the moral preceptive law of God (wherein alone his will is revealed and declared unto his people, concerning the nature, use, and ends of all his ordinances), but in the subjective light of nature (even as corrupted), so confused and dark in its discoveries, so gross and selfish in its principles, motives, and ends, that neither the true nature of this, nor any other of the ordinances of Jehovah, as revealed in his word, can hereby be known, or the true use and ends thereof sufficiently discovered or obtained.

They likewise testify against, and reject that equally absurd opinion, as a stream flowing from the foresaid corrupt fountain, that the office, authority, and constitution of lawful magistrates, does not solely belong to professing Christians, in a Christian reformed land, but that the election and choice of any one whosoever, made by the civil body (whether Pagan, Papist, Atheist, Deist, or other enemy to God, to man, and to true religion), makes up the whole of what is essential to the constitution of a lawful magistrate according to God's ordinance. A tenet contrary to the light and dictates both of reason and scripture.

And they hereby also disclaim that corrupt notion, that all providential magistrates, who are, and while they are acknowledged by any civil society especially in an apostate backsliding land and people from the scriptural standard (in respect of the origin of their office), are also preceptive; and that the office and authority of all so constituted and acknowledged, in itself considered, does equally arise from, and agree unto the preceptive will of God, contrary to scriptural precepts, Deut. xvii, 18; what falls under scriptural reproof, Hos. viii, 4; and what greatly depreciates the valiant contendings of our honored ancestors for civil reformation, and tends to invalidate their deeds of constitution thereanent.

Again the Presbytery testifies against, and condemns that principle, that the Christian people of God ought to give explicit acknowledgment of, implicit subjection and obedience to, whatever civil authority (though most wicked and unlawful) the Lord in his holy providence, may, for the trial and punishment of his church, permit a backsliding people to constitute and set up, without regard to the precept of his word. And they hereby reject whatever in opposition to the covenanted principles of the Church of *Scotland*, does justly, and in its own nature imply a voluntary and real acknowledgment of the lawfulness of the title and authority of an anti-scriptural, anti-covenanted, and Erastian government, constituted upon the ruins of our scriptural covenanted reformation. Particularly, they testify against praying for success and prosperity to such, in their stated opposition to the Lord and his Anointed, or in any form implying a homologation of their title as lawful, swearing oaths of fidelity and allegiance to such, accepting any office from such, and executing these in their name and authority under them, military associations with such, by a voluntary enlisting under their banner, and fighting for their support and establishment. And that in regard these are actions, as they express a proper and explicit owning of the lawfulness of that authority, which they immediately respect, so they are such as cannot be obtained without the actual consent of the party performing, and must therefore imply a deliberate approbation of foresaid iniquitous authority.

Further, they testify against a direct and active, free and voluntary paying of tribute and other dues, unto such, and that for conscience sake, as unto the ordinance of God, according to his precept; and particularly, when these dues are required as a tessera of loyalty to such; or when required, as an evidence of a person's active contributing to the accomplishment of some wicked action, expressly declared to be the immediate end of the imposition. Thus the case was in the time of persecution, when the declared end of the additional cess, was the immediate suppression of the pure preaching of the gospel in the fields. As also, not only against professed witnesses for reformation principles, their prosecuting of their witnessing brethren at law before the courts of anti-scriptural, unqualified judges; but generally, against all law processes, in a way of direct counteracting any part of reformation attainments, or express homologating the authority of an unlawful judge. And, in fine, against all voluntary subjection, for conscience sake, unto such powers as are not the ordinance of God, according to his revealed preceptive will, as contrary to scripture; 2 Sam. ii, 10; 2 Kings xi, 4, 17; 2 Chron. xix, 2; Isa. viii, 12 and lxv, 11; Rom. xiii, 1 to 8; 1 Cor. vi, 1 to 8, contrary to the acts of this church approving, and ordinances of the state, establishing the civil authority upon its scriptural foundation, and thereby discovering the proper object of a Christian people's voluntary and conscientious subjection; and particularly, to the act of classes. While in the meantime, it must be acknowledged, that the state and condition of Presbyterian Covenanters in these lands, continuing, as a community, to witness and contend for reformation of both church and state, that obtained, and was established, between 1638 and 1650, cannot be regarded as that of a free people enjoying their ancient privileges and liberties, but as that of an oppressed people, brought under the power of a conqueror, and no better than captives in their own land. As this was evidently the state of the suffering remnant under the persecuting period, when, by the force of the sword, they were robbed of their former liberties, and reduced to the most deplorable condition. So, however the Revolution did alter some circumstances in the condition of Covenanters; yet, in regard it was established upon, and did homologate the overthrow of the reformation, to which that people do still adhere, it could make no substantial change in their condition, from what it formerly was. And moreover, as it is necessarily requisite to the constituting of the relation between magistrate and people, that there be a mutual and voluntary consent; and as the community of presbyterian Covenanters did never, at or since the Revolution, give such consent; but, on the contrary, have, in the most public manner, protested against the constitution and installment of rulers in agreeableness thereto, as being contrary to the word of God, covenanted constitution, and fundamental laws of the nations; as is evident from their printed testimonies and declarations. It follows, that their state is that of an oppressed people, in passive subjection to a conquering power, whose duty is, to wait with patience upon *Israel's* God for his return to revive his work, and recall the bondage of his *Zion*. And while they are to take care to do nothing that justly implies their consent to the continued opposition made unto the covenanted reformation, yet they ought to observe a proper difference between such actions and things as are necessary, and in themselves just and lawful, by a moral obliga-tion, and those that are not so. As also, between that which cannot be had, nor the value or equivalent of it, unless the person actually give it; and that which may be obtained, whether he actually contribute to it or not. [7] Most applicable to this our present condition, are the words of the *Levites*, expressing the distressed state of

---

[7] It has been complained by some, that the sense of both the members of this partic-ular paragraph is obscure, and not so intelligible as it should be to many readers; but this complaint seems rather to arise from the want of proper attention and consideration, than from any other cause. As to the first branch of the sentence, Among—"Such actions and things as are necessary, and in themselves just and lawful by a moral obligation"—may be reckoned the payment of county tolls on highways and bridges, for the benefit of an easy and commodious passage—keeping watch in cities which have no settled or regular guard, to prevent public damage by fire or otherwise. In like manner, the payment of cus-tom in public markets or fairs, or of town dues, all of which, being intended for the benefit of public corporations, are given or paid as the price of liberty and privilege of trade and commerce. And to this may be added, such necessary instances of *self-defense* as a person may be obliged to, when maliciously and villanously attacked in his character or goods, by persons perhaps designedly taking advantage of his Christian temper, or profession. Or when perhaps a person may be maliciously charged with, and prosecuted for crimes not only peculiarly dishonorable to religion, but even capital, as has been the case with some individuals. In all such cases, self-defense at law becomes necessary before the ordinary courts and judges of any nation, or place of the world whatever, when such defenses are admitted without the formal and explicit acknowledgment of the lawfulness of unjust or usurped authority (when such happens to be in place, as in the instance of Paul's appeal to Caesar, Acts xxv), or acting any otherwise contrary to justice and charity. And with regard to the other branch of the sentence where it is observed—"That a difference ought to made between those things that cannot be had, nor yet the value and equivalent of them, unless the person actually give it," &c.: This is sufficiently explained in a paragraph, page 163, near the foot. Prayers for God's blessing on any government—enlisting and bearing arms in their service—accepting offices and places of power from them—swearing oaths of fidelity to them, &c.—are such things as can by no means be got, nor yet the equivalent of them, unless the party actually consents and grants them. These, therefore, and, such like, are the only instances of action which, the Presbytery judge, do, in their own nature, contain and express a proper and explicit acknowledgment of the lawfulness of that authority which they immediately respect.

Israel, which they had brought themselves into by their sins, as recorded by Neh. ix, 36, 37: "Behold we are servants this day; and for the land thou gavest unto our fathers, to eat the fruit thereof, and the good thereof, behold we are servants in it: and it yieldeth much increase unto the kings which thou hast set over us, because of our sins; also they have dominion over our bodies, and over our cattle, at their pleasure, and we are in great distress."

Likewise the Presbytery testify against all ministerial or church communion with such, who, though they may occupy the place of office-bearers in the church of Christ, yet are destitute of those qualifications indispensably required by the church's Head, or enter not into their office by the door he has appointed in his word, own another head than Christ, or apostatize and fall from the truth and cause of Christ, formerly espoused and sworn to by them in a church capacity; against all active owning and countenancing of such, by attending upon any of their corrupt official ministrations, or receiving any ordinances from such, to whom the Lord has denied his blessing. Against all voluntary contracting with prelates, curates, or such officers of human invention in the church, for paying tithes or other dues unto them, as unto lawful, scriptural parish ministers. For besides that there is nothing due unto them, their office having no divine authority; so there being under the New Testament a change of the priesthood, there is also a change of the law, respecting tithes; according to 2 Cor. vi, 17; Rev. ii, 20, &c.

By all which it appears, from what is above asserted and declared concerning these two divine distinct ordinances, the ministry and magistracy, that the principles maintained thereanent by the Presbytery, are nothing else than an endeavor, as a judicatory of the Lord Jesus Christ, constituted in his name, to hold fast the church of *Scotland's* testimony, agreeable to the scriptures of truth, for confession and covenants, fundamental acts and constitutions both of church and state and this, according to the command of the church's sole King and Head; Rev. ii, 25, and iii, 11. And what is testified against, is, in the nature of it, an homologation of the church's faithful opposition to backsliders, in their course of defection, from the national, attainments in religion and reformation, resisting even unto blood, striving against sin.

XVIII. OF OATHS AND VOWS.—The Presbytery further assert and declare, that oaths and vows are a part of religious worship, warranted in the word of God, and under the New Testament dispensation, and may be lawfully taken and entered into by the Lord's people. That such oaths and vows only are warrantable, as are lawful both for the matter and the manner of them; and those that are so, when once engaged in, must not be violated on any consideration, and that, because of the authority of the awful name of God interposed in them. And further, they declare, that the right of administering oaths is competent only to those vested with such authority as is agreeable to the word of truth. As also, that it is the incumbent duty of Christians, by solemn oath to bind themselves to maintain and defend the persons of righteous rulers, in the lawful exercise of their authority; and to such only, it is lawful to swear oaths of allegiance and fidelity. And hereby, they disapprove the principle of refusing allegiance to lawful authority. At the same time, the Presbytery testify against, as above, all the oaths of allegiance in being, to an Erastian Prelatical government. And further, they reject and detest that sinful, idolatrous and superstitious form of swearing, in laying the hand upon, and kissing the gospels, practiced by the Prelatical churches of *England* and *Ireland*, and even introduced into *Scotland*, as a gross profanation of that holy ordinance, and contrary to the scripture examples thereof. Hereby they also testify against all sinful swearing, whereby the name of God, his titles, perfections, or graces of his Holy Spirit, are profaned in ordinary discourse. As also, the unnecessary oaths of customhouse, trade, &c., as a reiterated and fearful profanation of the name of God. And moreover, they testify against, and condemn that ungodly and superstitious oath, practiced by that unhallowed club, called *Free Masons*: according to Deut. x, 20; Exod. xx, 7; Neh. xiii, 25; Ezra x, 5; Deut. vi, 13; Matth. iv, 35, 36; Ezek. xvii, 16, 17, 18, 19; Rev. x, 5, 6; Jer. iv, 2. and v, 2; Confess. chap. 22.

Again, they testify and declare, that the work of solemn covenanting with a God in Christ, is a duty warranted in the scriptures of the Old and New Testament, and by the examples of the godly, agreeable thereto; and that not only to individuals in particular, but to churches and nations in general. Which covenants once entered into, and being for the matter of them lawful, are most sacred, and therefore inviolably binding; and what cannot be broken or transgressed, without manifest guilt, and incurring the dreadful resentment of a holy and jealous God, who has severely threatened to punish covenant-breakers. And hence they assert, that the National Covenant of *Scotland*, and the Solemn League and Covenant entered into by the three nations, for reformation and defense of religion, and for the maintainance and preservation of the truths and ordinances of God in purity, and sworn by our honored ancestors, not only for themselves, but including also their posterity, are of divine authority, as having their foundation upon the word of God; therefore moral, and so perpetually binding upon the nations, and every individual of them, to the latest posterity. Wherefore, the Presbytery testify against the principle of refusing the lawfulness of national covenanting, particularly, under the New Testament dispensation, and all principles and practices that strike against the moral obligation of these covenants; see Deut. vi, 13, Isa. ix, 18, and xliv, 5; Jer. 1, 5; Deut. xxix, 12 to 16, 24, 25; Lev. xxvi, 25, 26; Josh, ix, 14, 15, 18, 19; 2 Sam. xxi, 1; Ezek. xvi, 59, and xvii, 15, 16, 18, 19; Hos. x, 4; Gal. iii, 15; 2 Cor. viii, 5. See also acts and ordinances both of church and state in times of reformation, respecting the taking, and binding obligation, of the covenants.

Again, the Presbytery hereby testify and declare their approbation of, and adherence unto, all the different steps of reformation, that ever, in any period, were attained unto in this church and land: particularly, besides what has been mentioned above, they declare their adherence to the Westminster Confession of Faith, as it was approven by act of the General Assembly of the Church of *Scotland, anno* 1647: Catechisms, larger and shorter; Form of church government, Directory for worship, and Books of Discipline, as agreeable to, and extracted from the sacred oracles.

And with respect to the fourth article of the 23d chapter of our Confession, the

Presbytery hereby declare, that they reject that corrupt sense and gloss which has been imposed upon it, whether by open enemies, or false friends to our covenanted reformation in former or latter times, viz., That a reformed Christian people, having generally received, and publicly professing the true religion; and more especially, having expressly and solemnly bound themselves by public national vows to the Most High, for the preservation of it, may warrantably set over them an infidel, or one of a religion differing from the true religion, and thereupon acknowledge and submit themselves unto him, as their lawful civil ruler for conscience sake. And moreover, they declare that they understand said articles, as principally relating to the condition of a people emerging out of the darkness and superstition of Paganism or Popery, &c., before that religion has obtained the sanction of civil authority; when, although the major part or bulk of a people should embrace the true religion, yet that does not dissolve or loose the relation subsisting between them and their civil rulers, prior to their conversion, agreeable to, and founded upon the just and reasonable laws of the realm. In this case only, it is granted, that an infidel, or one of a different religion, may have authority just and legal over a people partly converted to the knowledge and gospel of Christ. Thus it was with the primitive Christians, and thus it was particularly with our ancestors in *Scotland*, at the beginning of the reformation; and this perfectly well agrees to the apostolic precept and determination in a case similar to the above; 1 Cor. vii, 12, 13 and 39, and 2 Cor. vi, 14.

As also, they further declare their approbation of, and adherence to all the faithful testimonies, declarations and protestations, emitted by the witnesses for the work of reformation, whether before or under the late times of tyranny and persecution, in prisons, scaffolds, or in the fields, by land or sea; or by such, as since that time have succeeded. them in the self same testimony, as they are founded upon, and agreeable to the word of truth, and as a just and proper vindication of foresaid covenanted cause. And particularly with the above proviso and limitation, they declare their adherence to the *Rutherglen, Sanquhar* and *Lanerk* declarations, *annis* 1679, 1680, 1682; as also to the declarations published at *Sanquhar*, 1683, 1684, 1692, and 1695, 1703, 1707; to the *informatory vindication*, and *cloud of witnesses*; to the *covenants national* and *solemn league*, sworn at *Auchensaugh*, near *Douglas*, in the year 1712, at *Crawfurd-john* 1745; with the additional acknowledgments of sins, and engagements to duties at these times; to the declarations published at *Sanquhar*, 1718, and at *Montherrick*, 1740, 1741. And in like manner, they testify their adherence to the *Act* formerly emitted by this Presbytery, in condemnation of the universal scheme. And they do hereby testify against, and disapprove all partiality and unfaithfulness, whether in respect of right or left hand extremes, in any testimonies, published in a way of professed adherence to reformation principles; particularly, they reject the testimony published by those designated the *Associate Presbytery*, as no adequate testimony for truth, because of the partiality and unfaithfulness, both to God and the generation, discovered therein; being, instead of a faithful vindication, no better than a burial of some of the most important attainments in reformation of this church and land. And they likewise reject, detest and abhor that spurious brat, stuffed with gross error, blasphemy and nonsense, most falsely and unjustly designated, "A testimony for the word of Christ's patience," by that sacrilegious usurper of the ministry, *William Dunnet*, who, being once plunged into the depths of enthusiasm, such is his madness, that under pretense of an immediate mission from heaven, he not only daringly usurps the whole of the ministerial function, but also wickedly claims an Erastian exercise of the office of the civil magistrate, in a stupid unaccountable declaration of war, offensive and defensive, against all mankind, himself, and his blind-folded confederates only excepted; having probably had these anti-scriptural notions instilled into him by the industry of some unstable heads, who, after they had made a professed subjection to this Presbytery, in the Lord, did, with some others of the same stamp, in a most unwarrantable and schismatical manner, break off from their communion, without so much as discovering any shadow of reason, in justification of their rash, ungrounded and precipitate separation.

Upon the whole, the Presbytery, protesting that they have been influenced to this necessary work of displaying a judicial banner for the covenanted cause and interest of our exalted Redeemer, purely out of a regard to the glory of God, a desire that Christ's kingdom may be advanced, and his buried truths revived, as also a concern for the welfare and happiness of the present and succeeding generations, do earnestly, in the bowels of our Lord Jesus Christ, beseech and obtest all and every one, into whose hands this testimony may come, that, without considering the insignificancy of the instruments, and laying aside prejudice and carnal selfish considerations, they receive the truth as it is in Jesus, not only in the notion, but in the love and power of it; that they take with the many just and highly aggravated grounds of the Lord's controversy, and causes of his wrath against us, not only on account of private and personal wickedness come to a very great height, but particularly on account of the general opposition to the public concerns of his glory, in what respects the doctrine, worship, government and discipline of his house. Alas! our public abominations are both obstinately persisted in and publicly justified. That they lay to heart the great and terrible wickedness of the day and generation, with deep humiliation before the Lord, while he waits to, be gracious, and is calling all ranks to humble themselves, and saying, "Rend your heart and not your garments, and turn unto the Lord your God, for he is gracious and merciful;" Joel ii, 13. That, in the way of flying under the covert of the atoning blood of the Son of God, by faith in his name, for the remission of sins, and endeavoring after personal reformation, as to all the impiety and irreligion, all the detestable indifferency, lukewarmness and hypocrisy, in the matters of God, which universally prevail; they also study and set about public reformation, every one in their several stations, according to our solemn national engagements, concurring to restore the Lord's ruined and buried work, and rebuild his house, which is now lying as a desolate heap, covered over with the rubbish of manifold errors, corruptions and human inventions. If we still hold fast our abominations, and will not, by repentance and reformation, return and give glory to the Lord our God before he cause darkness, then, when he returns for the salvation of *Zion*, "He will come treading down the people in his anger, and making them drunk in his fury, and bringing down their strength to the earth;" Isa. lxiii, 6. "But is there no hope in *Is-*

rael concerning this thing? Is there no balm in *Gilead*? Is there not a physician there?" Is there not virtue in Christ's blood for the most desperate cases, that churches, as well as particular persons, can be in? Is there not ground to hope, that the Lord will not altogether forsake these sinful lands, which were given to him of old for an inheritance, and wherein he has so long maintained his possession, but that he will yet build up our *Zion*, and appear in his glory therein, will plead his own cause, revive his own work, a covenanted work of reformation, and remove all the contempt and ignominy which it presently lies under? Sure the continuance of his gracious calls and invitations to return to him, gives ground to hope, that our "*Israel* hath not been forsaken, nor *Judah* of his God, of the Lord of Hosts, though their land was filled with sin against the holy One of *Israel*;" Jer. li, 5. And though, while so much of error, prejudice and carnal interest, lie as impassable mountains in the way, there is little appearance of the nations taking this course yet the Lord seems still to bespeak us in that endearing language, Jer. iii, 12, "Go and proclaim these words towards the north, and say, Return thou backsliding *Israel*, saith the Lord, and I will not cause mine anger to fall upon you; for I am merciful, saith the Lord, and I will not keep anger forever." Though we have nationally torn our marriage contract with heaven, and taken away our names, yet the Lord has not. *Turn, O backsliding children, saith the Lord, for I am married unto you.* Let all, then, *repent, and turn themselves from all their transgressions, so iniquity shall not be their ruin*; but if not, then let all the impenitent despisers of the repeated calls of mercy know, that abused patience will at length turn into fury, and the Lord Jehovah, who has already furbished his sword, and prepared the instruments of death, will speedily give that dreadful commission to the executioners of his wrath: "Put ye in the sickle, for the harvest is ripe; come, get you down, for the press is full, the fats overflow, for their wickedness is great:" Joel iii, 13. "But because God will do this to *Israel*, let us prepare to meet our God." Further, the Presbytery invite and entreat all who tender the glory of God, the removal of the causes of his wrath and indignation, and who desire the continuance of his tabernacle and gracious presence among us, to come and join in a harmonious, zealous and faithful testimony for the precious truths and interest of *Zion's* glorious King, and against every course that has a tendency to heighten, and at last to lay on the copestone of our defections. Consider it is the Lord's call and command to every one, even in their most private station, *Contend earnestly for the faith once delivered to the saints*. It is the burden he, at this day, lays on his church and people: *Hold fast what thou hast till I come, that no man take thy crown*; hold fast by our former attainments in reformation. And finally, the Presbytery exhort all with whom they are more particularly connected, *To stand fast in one spirit, with one mind, striving together for the faith of the gospel, and in nothing terrified by your adversaries*. Let the flame of fervent and true love to God, his truths, and to one another, prevent and extinguish the wild fire of unnecessary and hurtful mutual animosities; and *endeavoring to keep the unity of the spirit in the bond of peace*, study oneness in promoting the Lord's opposed work, and in walking in the good old way, without turning aside to the right hand or to the left, because of the lion that is therein, and without laying other foundations than what were laid. Let none of Christ's true and faithful witnesses suffer their hearts to sink into despondency; the cause is the Lord's, and assuredly he will thoroughly plead that cause which is his own. It will outlive all its enemies, and yet have a glorious resurrection; and this will be the crown and comfort of all such as continue, amidst all trials and sufferings, contending for him, in the blessed expectation of the conqueror's everlasting reward. Therefore, *lift up the hands that hang down, and strengthen the feeble knees*; greater afflictions have been accomplished in those that are gone before, and are now inheriting the promises, than any wherewith the Lord is presently trying his church. And as the God of all grace, after they had suffered awhile, made them perfect, and put them in possession of that eternal glory to which they were called by Jesus Christ, so shall he establish, strengthen and keep his people still from falling, and, after all their sorrows and sufferings, present them faultless before the presence of his glory, with exceeding joy. "Return, we beseech thee, O God of Hosts; look down from heaven, and behold and visit this vine; and the vineyard which thy right hand hath planted, and the branch that thou madest strong for thyself, it is burnt with fire, it is cut down, they perish at the rebuke of thy countenance. Let thy hand be upon the man of thy right hand, upon the Son of man whom thou madest strong for thyself, so will not we go back from thee; quicken us, and we will call upon thy name; turn us again, O Lord of Hosts, cause thy face to shine, and we shall be saved: Let God arise, let *Zion's* immortal and omnipotent King Jesus reign, and let all his enemies be scattered; but let them that love him be as the sun, when he goeth forth in his might."

Extracted by JO. THORBURN, Pr. Clk.

ADDENDA.

In addition to what is said (from page 65 to 67 preceding, respecting the establishment of Popery in Canada), the Presbytery deeply lament, that, in the present edition of their Testimony, they are furnished with fresh matter to animadvert upon the continued tendency of the British administration in favor of the religion of Antichrist.

Not long after the civil establishment of Popery in Canada, new privileges, civil and religious, were bestowed upon the professors of that religion at home, both in England and Ireland, by which Catholics have received toleration, under the sanction of law, openly to profess and practice their idolatry, to open seminaries of learning for the public instruction of youth in their own religion, and to purchase and transfer estates to their Popish relations, in direct opposition to the established laws of the land, framed by our Protestant ancestors, under the sense of felt necessity, whereby Catholics were laid under disabilities, as to the enjoyment of those privileges, which they saw to be inconsistent with the peace of the state and safety of the Protestant religion, on account of the barbarous massacres committed by Catholics upon Protestants, and the numerous hostile attempts made to overturn, by violence, the Protestant religion within these lands, as proceeding from the sanguinary spirit of Popery. The modern plea set up in favor of those privileges being conferred upon Popery, that the Catholics of this day have candidly renounced the whole of their old principles which they held, as inimical to a Protestant country, never can be admitted, while they still retain the most dangerous of all their principles, viz., implicit faith in the doctrines of supreme councils, and the dispensing authority of the Pope. Against this sinful indulgence granted to Popery, the Presbytery testified at the time, in a separate piece, entitled, A Testimony and Warning against the Blasphemies and Idolatries of Popery, &c., to which they still refer the reader. An attempt also was made to extend a similar indulgence to Catholics in Scotland, but which was happily frustrated through the zealous exertions of the people, who, pleading the established laws of the land, boldly reclaimed against the measure, which produced the desired effect of compelling the government to desist. But alas! no sooner, was the popular zeal cooled, than government sowed tares by enlarging the privileges of Catholics with regard to civil property. The deplorable fact now is, that Popery, basking in the sunshine of legislative power, advanced to the legal possession of new privileges, and shielded by a formal toleration in the neighboring kingdoms, may be considered as enjoying the actual protection of government in Scotland. In Ireland, privileges of a still more exalted nature are bestowed upon Popery, while the Catholic is so far enfranchised, that, in conjunction with the Protestant, he may give his voice for members to serve in the legislature of the country. What greatly adds to the evil is, the lamentable alteration of public opinion, so lately displayed against the measures of government in former indulgences bestowed upon the Catholic interest; but which has now changed into an entire approbation thereof, both by the great body of the people and the minority in the two houses of Parliament; and the only complaint against government on that score is, that, stopping short of meeting just claims of Catholics, they have not ingrafted them into all the privileges of British subjects, and for ever done away the odious distinction between Protestant and Catholic, as to privilege.

When we open our eyes to the measures of the present day, we behold still more abominations. The government so far from remembering whence they are fallen, repenting and doing their first works, have started again in the cause of Antichrist, by leaguing themselves in a military expedition with a group of Popish despots on the continent, who have long given their power to the beast; of this expedition one object evidently appears to be the re-establishment and support of Popery in France, where under the administration of the omnipotent, and avenging holy providence of God, in the pouring out of the vials of his wrath upon the beast, that false religion has received a sore and bleeding wound, and where the people, long crushed under the tyranny of a despotic throne, and usurpation of an imposing priesthood, have risen to extricate themselves from the accumulated oppression, and by their astonishing efforts have shaken off the Papal yoke, by renouncing their accustomed allegiance to the head of the Antichristian states at Rome, have withdrawn their wonted supplies from his treasures, and completely overthrown the temporal power of his religion in their own country, which had for many ages kept them in fetters. If any doubt should be entertained with regard to the support afforded to the sinking cause of Popery in France by this expedition, the declaration published by the brother of the late King of France, stiling himself Louis XVIII, at the head of the emigrants in arms, exhibits the fact in the clearest point of view, while he plainly and unequivocally says, in that declaration, that their designs are the erection of the throne and altar, by which are meant the civil government and the Catholic religion, as they existed in France prior to the revolution. Britain, not satisfied with sending forth numerous hosts to the field abroad, and lavishing her treasures to supply the exhausted finances of the coalesced powers, has opened her arms at home to receive flying emigrants, caressed by her, as if they had been sufferers in the cause of genuine Christianity. By the voice of Episcopal dignitaries the Popish clergy have been extolled, as men of the most eminent piety, while places have been furnished by government, to accommodate them in their mass service; and a branch of the bloody house of Bourbon, whom divine vengeance has reduced to the abject state of a wandering exile, is admitted among us, with all marks of honor, and, with his train, provided for, as if he were a zealous supporter of the Protestant cause, seeking an asylum from the rage of Papal persecution in this reformed land. It cannot escape the notice of the attentive observer, how closely the crown of Britain has become allied to this false religion, in consequence of the conquest of the island of Corsica, and the accession of the crown of that island to the crown of Britain. According to the new constitution of Corsica, the king of Great Britain, as represented by his viceroy, makes an essential branch of the parliament, all the acts whereof must be assented to by him, in order, to give them the force of law. Now, it is to be remarked, that in this constitution Popery is expressly declared to be the only established religion in the island; it is therefore agreed to be divided into districts, to be filled up with ministers of the Catholic religion, endowed with legal maintenance. So the king of Britain, as wearing the Corsican crown, engages to unite this constitutional establishment of the Catholic religion, the king of Great Britain, as the king of Corsica, gives his firm assent. Moreover, to provide for the more extensive propagation of Popery in Corsica, the legislature stipulate to consult with the See of Rome; here, also, he engages to join the wisdom of his counsels to those of the Pope, for the express purpose of giving a wider spread to Popery. If the prophet Jehu accused Jehoshaphat, though a good prince, when he was returning from a military expedition with Ahab, king of Israel, in such cutting language; 2 Chron. xix, 2, *Shouldst thou help the ungodly, and love them that hate the Lord? therefore, is wrath upon thee from the Lord*: in what words shall we pronounce upon this conduct of Britain, in mixing with her politics and wars, active measures to raise again the falling Dagon of Popery from the threshold, and to help forward the interests of a religion which the Lord has solemnly declared he will destroy with the judgments of his hand and the brightness of his coming. Besides the iniquity of the thing itself, in giving direct aid to this religion; our guilt derives great aggravations from a view of the present dispensations of Providence in visibly sending down terrible judgments (no matter through what rough hands) upon that anti-christian power, that has long, sat upon many waters; and the loud voice of Jehovah is uttering, on the awful crisis of its downfall, to all the fearers of his name to escape a share in its judgments, by flying away from all communion with its evils; Rev. xviii, 4, *Come out of her, my people, that ye be not partakers of her sins, and that ye receive not of her plagues.* But, blind to his avenging hand, and deaf to this summons, Great Britain, once without, is now again returning into a most unlawful communion to support this adjudged power, by which she constitutes herself a partner in its sins, and thereby exposes herself to a portion of its plagues. In vain will it be urged as a plea of justification, that the authors of the revolution in France, having overturned the constitution of their own country, and spread desolation through the wide extent of it, menaced other nations, and us also; and that, therefore, Britain, acting on the first principle of nature's law, self-preservation, joined the allied powers for her own defense. Though the Presbytery are by no means to be understood as giving their suffrage for the lawfulness and justice of the war on our side; yet, for the sake of argument, allowing the plea—what then? Will this sanctify the measures adopted by Britain, in recovering, supporting and propagating the cause of Popery, that the conquest of the enemy, and her own safety are the ends ultimately to be gained by them? The Christian maxim, that evil is not to be done that good may come, binds as strongly nations as individuals. Popery is not a local evil; it is still the mystery of iniquity, as much in France, and in Corsica, as it is in Great Britain; it is everywhere the forbidden fruit, not to be touched. If the security of a Protestant country is to be sought for, in dependence upon, or in any state of connection with the co-existence and maintenance of Antichrist, we have indeed a feeble pillar to rest upon, for, as sure as God himself has spoken it, the Papal kingdoms are the Babylon to fall and to rise no more again at all. Perhaps, our allies would not be pleased with another mode of conduct; and shall we run the hazard of displeasing the God of all our salvation, to gratify, in sin, the friends of the man of sin? If the crown of Corsica cannot be worn, but upon the condition of supporting Popery, and joining in councils with the Church of Rome, to advance her interest there, we are afraid the weight of it, like a millstone, will sink us deep in the gulf of God's wrath. But Popery was the former religion of that island, and the people wished no change. If the wretched inhabitants, loving darkness rather than the light, refused to be reclaimed, leave them to themselves, but why should we have fellowship with them in their unfruitful works of darkness. The Presbytery would not wish to be understood as if they meant that Protestants ought to raise a crusade, in order to exterminate Catholics in foreign lands, as Catholics have attempted to do against Protestants, for the weapons of our warfare, in propagating religion are not carnal. But it certainly is the incumbent duty of all Protestant nations to abstain from anything, that has a tendency to uphold and propagate their religion; and as no positive countenance should be given to it, so it is highly proper that Catholics should be kept in such a state of restraint, as they may not again have it in their power to repeat those bloody scenes, which Popery had acted upon us. With a view to deliver themselves from the guilt of participating in the evil, the Presbytery do lift up a judicial testimony against the present anti-christian courses of administration; as, also, against those state fasts, proceeding from an Erastian supremacy, which have been appointed to be observed by all persons, in order to engage by prayer the Almighty to crown their measures with success. Likewise, the Presbytery do testify against the national church, particularly her ministers, who from their station ought to act as spiritual watchmen, and give pointed warning of sin and danger on the present occasion; but, who, instead of faithfully discharging this duty, sanction all these measures of government, which cannot fail to produce a hardening effect upon the generation.

N.B. Since writing the above, by a reverse in the war, Britain has lost possession of Corsica, but while this does not acquit her of the guilt of her anti-christian administration there, neither will it supersede the necessity of our testimony against it.

* * * * *

ADVERTISEMENT.

The late Reformed Presbytery, June 2d, 1845, adopted the following doctrinal and practical declarations. They have therefore a judicial sanction; and having been in overture before the people prior to the action of Presbytery, we subjoin them as a suitable supplement. *Cincinnati, Nov. 12th*, 1850.

JUDICIAL DECLARATIONS.

1. Man is a free agent, unconscious of restraint in his volitions by the execution of the immutable decree of God; and it is not possible for him, in any instance, to avoid fulfilling that decree: yet the law of God—not his decree—is the rule of man's conduct, and the standard of final judgment.

2. It is the duty of a Christian to pray for the church of Christ—to inquire diligently into her scriptural character, and to seek covenant blessings in her communion.

3. If the majority should violate the terms upon which church members were united, it is lawful for the minority to testify against the defection, and to walk by the rule of their former attainments. And when any community assuming to be the Church of Christ, imposes sinful terms of communion—when the constitution is anti-scriptural—when the administration is corrupt, and attempts at its reformation have proved ineffectual—it is the duty of Christians to separate from it: "*Come out of her, my people,*" &c.; Rev. xviii, 4.

4. No member of the Reformed Presbyterian Church can, without contracting guilt, in the present state of society, take the oath of allegiance to the government of these United States, hold office, exercise the elective franchise, act as a juror, or hold communion in other ecclesiastical bodies, by what is commonly styled *occasional hearing*; Rev. xi, 1-3.

TERMS OF MINISTERIAL AND CHRISTIAN COMMUNION IN THE REFORMED PRESBYTERIAN CHURCH.

* * * * *

1. An acknowledgment of the Old and New Testament to be the Word of God, and the alone infallible rule of faith and practice.

2. An acknowledgement that the whole doctrine of the Westminster Confession of Faith, and the Catechisms, larger and shorter, are agreeable unto, and founded upon the Scriptures.

3. An acknowledgment that Presbyterian Church government is of divine right, and unalterable: and that the most perfect model as yet attained, is exhibited in the Form of Government and Directory for Worship, as adopted by the Church of Scotland, in the Second Reformation.

4. An acknowledgment that public, social covenanting, is an ordinance of God, and obligatory on churches and nations under the New Testament dispensation: and that the National Covenant of Scotland, and the Solemn League and Covenant of Scotland, England and Ireland, were an exemplification of this divine institution: and that these solemn deeds are of perpetual obligation upon the moral person, as continued by representation and accession: and in consistency with this, acknowledging the renovation of these covenants at Auchensaugh, 1712, to be agreeable to the Word of God.

5. An approbation of the faithful contendings of the martyrs of Jesus, against paganism, popery, prelacy, malignancy, and sectarianism; and against immoral constitutions of civil government—Erastian tolerations and persecutions which flow therefrom: the Judicial Act, Declaration and Testimony, emitted by the Reformed Presbytery in North Britain, 1761, together with the Historical and Declaratory Supplements adopted by the Reformed Church in North America, 1850—as containing an noble example for their posterity to follow, in contending for all divine truth, and in testifying against all corruptions embodied in the constitutions of either church or State.

6. Practically adorning the doctrine of God our Savior, by walking in all his commandments and ordinances blamelessly.

Lector House believes that a society develops through a two-fold approach of continuous learning and adaptation, which is derived from the study of classic literary works spread across the historic timeline of literature records. Therefore, we aim at reviving, repairing and redeveloping all those inaccessible or damaged but historically as well as culturally important literature across subjects so that the future generations may have an opportunity to study and learn from past works to embark upon a journey of creating a better future.

This book is a result of an effort made by Lector House towards making a contribution to the preservation and repair of original ancient works which might hold historical significance to the approach of continuous learning across subjects.

HAPPY READING & LEARNING!

LECTOR HOUSE LLP
E-MAIL: lectorpublishing@gmail.com